Inside

One Woman's Journey

Through the Inside Passage

Susan Marie Conrad

Epicenter Press

Inside
One Woman's Journey Through the Inside Passage

Published by Epicenter Press, a regional press publishing nonfiction books about the arts, history, environment, and diverse cultures and lifestyles of Alaska and the Pacific Northwest.
For more information, visit www.EpicenterPress.com.

Section maps reprinted by permission of Garmin LTD:
"Copyright 2015 Garmin Ltd or its Subsidiaries. All Rights Reserved"

Chart image of author and entire route
reprinted by permission of the artist,
Alan James Robinson, *www.TheMapGuy.com*

Library of Congress Control Number: 2015960539

ISBN: 978-1-935347-57-6
ISBN eBook: 978-1-935347-65-1
Editor: Janet Kimball
Cover and Text Design: Jeanie James, *www.Shorebird-Creative.com*
Administrative Assistant: Aubrey Anderson

10 9 8 7 6 5 4 3 2 1

For Jim Chester

*My forward bearing
and back azimuth.*

Table of Contents

Inside to Alaska

Map reproduced by permission of the artist,
Alan James Robinson, "The Map Guy."
www.TheMapGuy.com

Foreword

IN THE LATE SPRING OF 2010, Susan Conrad stood on the threshold of a great adventure. Before her stretched a landscape of incomparable beauty. Abundant with wildlife, congregations of sea birds, pods of whales, lone bears, forested islands, fjords of great majesty—all awash with ancient history. But beauty comes at a price. She faced danger from storms, riptides, huge tidal surges, ever-present bears, enormous ferries lumbering through the channels, and unforeseeable circumstances. There would be few people along the way. But behind her stood an icon of exploration, Jim Chester, noted caver, paddler and hiker, and dearest friend. He would be watching from the sidelines to guide, to inspire and pull her along through his tender yet demanding will. But ahead, she was alone, and most of all alone with herself, something most of us rarely experience any more in our hectic wired world.

Susan was embarking on her dream—to paddle the Inside Passage, a revered waterway along the Pacific Coast of Washington State, Canada and Alaska, winding through myriad islands and along fjords carved out by glaciers eons ago.

It is an area long inhabited by Native Peoples. The Passage is believed to have been a major pathway for peoples who came over the Bering Land Bridge from Asia on their way south to the Americas some 15,000 years ago. More recently, the Passage was visited by Western Explorers who hoped it would lead to the elusive Northwest Passage, the water route from Europe to China. In the nineteenth century, Russians colonized a few islands before selling out to the fledgling colonizing Americans, and the remains of their settlements can still be seen. Today, the Passage is home to more than forty groups of Native Peoples. The Passage is also a challenging, and oft sought destination for a handful of intrepid kayakers like Susan. But Susan—like her book—stands out. In vivid immediate detail, she has written a rapturous book that recounts her journey, bringing her odyssey and the majestic land she traveled through into sharp focus.

Susan threads her narrative with personal insights, a history of betrayal and sadness that led her to this challenge. One constant is the presence of Jim Chester, whose notes and encouragement help her in even the most dire of times. It is a great testament to her courage and determination that she found the strength to see the journey to the end.

I was lucky enough to meet Susan when she was planning her journey with Jim on Salt Spring Island in British Columbia. I was instantly captivated by her quiet charm, inspired by her and not a little jealous at what lay ahead for her. Years earlier, a much younger me stood in a similar place looking out onto the vast stretches of the Egyptian Western Desert, camels in hand, wondering what lay ahead. Such journeys are life changing. I went on to found and lead WINGS WorldQuest for fifteen years, where I had the honor of working with and helping the leading women explorers of today. Susan belongs in this pantheon.

Susan captures the splendor of the lands she traveled through. Her evocative and sometimes searing tale is immediate and revelatory. While it is the story of one woman, it is a book for the adventurer in all of us, men, women, young and old. In one sweeping tale, Susan takes us on a journey through a breathtaking land of challenge and reward.

—Milbry Polk
Founder, Wings WorldQuest
co-author of *Women of Discovery*
and *the Looting of the Iraq Museum, Baghdad:
The Lost Legacy of Ancient Mesopotamia*

Preface

Believe that you can do anything you set your mind to.
Your passion should be your path
and your path should be your passion.

—Rosita Arvigo

IT HAS BEEN SAID that a person doesn't take a trip, but rather a trip takes a person. The Inside Passage took me—in a kayak—from Anacortes, Washington, to Juneau, Alaska. The Inside Passage pulled me forward, into the now, as my past ebbed away and my future flooded in. In turn idyllic and epic, it took me through glacially carved landscapes and impenetrable forests, narrow channels and wide ocean passages, spellbinding seas and mixmaster waves. And it took me deep within myself, humbling me, reminding me that I had much to learn. I have still only begun to understand its impact.

In Spring 2010, with my world scaled down to an 18-foot sea kayak and a 1,200-mile ribbon of water known as the Inside Passage, I launched a journey of the sea and the soul that took me both north to Alaska and inward to the discovery of the depths of my own strength and courage. My journey took 66 days, during which time I lived in a wetsuit, paddled marathon distances for weeks on end, forged friendships with quirky people in the strangest of places, and pretended not to be intimidated by seven-hundred-pound grizzly bears and forty-ton whales. I lived my dream.

That dream entailed paddling through wild, steep country, subject to strong currents and wind, and extreme tidal differences. The realities of hypothermia, dwindling food supplies, nonexistent beaches, and alarmingly high walls of water rising over twenty feet were part and parcel of the journey. At times I floated in a magical world among whales and icebergs and immeasurable beauty; other times I paddled wildly with fear at my back.

I didn't set out to research, discover, or prove anything, although the logistical planning often took on Olympian proportions. And, of course, the concept of paddling *to* Alaska was astronomical in itself. I'd never been to Alaska, let alone *kayaked* to it. Although I was an experienced kayaker and had *some* knowledge of the Inside Passage, I expected lessons would be presented along the way and prepared myself for mental, emotional, and physical extremes.

The "IP," as those familiar with the waters of the Inside Passage refer to it, meanders along the western edge of North America. Touted as one of the most scenic and challenging paddling trips on the continent, its Holy Grail-ness seduced me. I'd first heard of the IP in 1992, when I met Jim Chester, a world-renowned adventurer whose own IP trip had blazed a trail for mine. He'd recently returned from his solo voyage, yet I thought nothing more of it, and certainly never intended to paddle the thing on my own. But life, I found, throws curveballs, and perspectives change.

In 2009, I watched my father, a once strong and comical man, deteriorate into a catatonic slump from advanced Alzheimer's, finally dying in an upstate New York nursing home. Other unfortunate life events avalanched around me, heavy doors slammed in my face, and I lost my sense of where I belonged in space. I longed for a drama-free chunk of time where things would not repeatedly blow up around me. Then a book about a woman who kayaked the Inside Passage crossed my path. While devouring the pages, I wondered if my own life wasn't on the cusp of something new and exciting, if certain opportunities had closed their doors so that life could simply make room for new doors to open. I finished the book, and in the privacy of my own company, defiantly proclaimed, "I'm paddling to Alaska!" Once I flung that door open, I began a new chapter—one that was dog-eared, highlighted, bookmarked, tattered and torn. After all, adventures are not tidy little things.

OVER TIME, JIM CHESTER'S own journey up the Inside Passage would prop open a few more doors—understated portals that stood patiently waiting for me to walk through them. Jim's desire to share his solo experience led him to hammer out his entire handwritten journal on a Smith-Corona typewriter. These words graced the top of the first page:

> *They can't understand. Can't comprehend. Can't relate. I existed on a different plane for a summer. Not necessarily better, nor worse, just different. My experience was personal. My very own. No one else's. It cannot be adequately related to another. Case in point—it cannot even be successfully transferred from my mind to this paper.*

When I first knew Jim, before I had experienced the Inside Passage myself, I thought that I understood. But it would take eighteen years for me to begin to comprehend what a journey of this nature meant and what could manifest along the way. As I began to chronicle my own experiences on "the Inside," I slowly began to relate to all that his trip encompassed and how his complex involvement with mine would change my perspective—not only on this adventure we circuitously shared, but on all of life.

This is a journey through the physical, emotional and spiritual landscapes of the Inside Passage, told largely through my own lens of experience, but also, in part, through Jim's. We supported each other through this cumulative adventure as it morphed into a story of two adventures. To fully engage in our stories, it's important that the reader knows who this man was, and understands how he influenced me and what he meant to me and my journey.

Jim was a tall man, with large, square shoulders, and a deep, learned voice. Handsome in a disheveled manner, his chestnut-brown hair dangled halfway down his back, restrained in a scraggly ponytail. A thick salt-and-cinnamon beard kept company with a bushy mustache. His skin, weathered from elements and age, stretched taut over a prominent Adam's apple. On his beak-like nose sat a pair of perpetually smudged glasses, and behind those lurked penetrating steely blue eyes that could pierce your soul.

A long-time member of the Explorers Club, Jim had the honor, on two occasions, of carrying the Explorers Club flag, once in 2007 and once in 2009. The flags were placed at the depths of the world's uncharted, deepest caves. Jim had dined on chocolate-covered tarantulas and alligator sushi, petted exotic reptiles, and rubbed shoulders with New York's finest glitterati in the heady atmosphere of the Waldorf Astoria where he stood groomed and polished, or at least as much as a country boy caver from Montana could be, waiting his turn at the podium—right behind fellow honoree Buzz Aldrin. The 106th Explorers Club Annual Dinner was a gala event where Jim would be presented with the Citation of Merit award, in recognition of his outstanding services to the Club, a professional society dedicated to scientific exploration of Earth, its oceans, and outer space.

In the eighteen years I knew Jim, I witnessed a marked adventurous streak coursing through his body. A voracious reader, he still had his childhood copy of *The Adventures of Tom Sawyer*, read over and over, until, in Jim's words, "its spine dropped off and the book's pages threatened to scatter like a flock of surprised birds." In the 43 years after Jim first opened that tome, he sea kayaked over two-thousand miles, dived thermal features in Yellowstone Lake, rappelled into a 240-foot well in a European medieval castle, and logged over 2,000 hours underground: long, sodden, and often miraculous hours that involved 475 descents and 210 caves. He loved to climb mountains, too. He dabbled in whitewater kayaking as a diversion from far-reaching hauls in his longer, lissome boat; and skied dry Montana powder when the water turned a bit hard during the winter months.

Undoubtedly, Tom Sawyer and his cronies were only one of many catalysts that hurled Jim into a life of exploration, risk and adventure—a life that he often shared with me. Together, we mucked about in caves, huffed up mountaintops, and careened down nerve-wracking rivers; but it was the sea kayaking, particularly paddling over longish periods of time, that enraptured me the most. It was like backpacking on the water, I thought, without the heavy weight on your shoulders and the blisters on your feet.

Without Jim, the Inside Passage would have just been something "out there" that I would not have experienced at the privileged level I did in 2010. His own Inside Passage journey was one of several catalysts for me to embark on my own adventure. From the conception of my plan to the very last paddle stroke, he became an integral player and wholeheartedly supported my desire to paddle the IP. I trusted Jim implicitly. He helped me find my true north—and my way back—and for that I am forever grateful. It's my hope that throughout these pages, you will hear Jim's voice and you will come to understand just how immensely he helped me with this journey, and through that you will also come to see, as I ultimately did, what a huge impact he had on my life.

TO WRITE THIS BOOK, I relied on my own memories—both written down and locked away in my mind—as well as on Jim's journal. The myriad of email posts he wrote while I was underway, the responses to those emails, and the thousands of photos I took also greatly assisted in this memoir.

This is not intended to be a guidebook, nor is it a how-to book. The Inside Passage is an enormous place, and this book only scratches its surface. The route I chose, and the manner in which I executed it, represent a single option and only one experience: mine. Craving challenge, stability and enlivened potential, I chose this complex coastline to reawaken my sense of adventure, to find answers to questions I had not yet asked—and to live wildly. To abandon myself to the possibility of it all and to be open to all that it could teach me, to feel free and run with the wind, the waves, the sea itself.

Adventure yanks at *all* our shirtsleeves. It is my hope that the pages of this book will kindle *your* sense of adventure—whether you set foot in a kayak or not—and that by sharing the magic of this beautiful coastline, it will impart a stronger connection to the natural environment and inspire you not only to explore it, but to cherish and protect it. May that insatiable curiosity to know what's around the next corner be your moxie, as it was ultimately mine.

One

Why, When and What If?

Too many of us are not living our dreams because we are living our fears.

—Les Brown

One Pea in a Fog

"IT'S NOT AN ADVENTURE until things start going wrong," Yvon Chouinard once said. *Okay, Yvon, I get it, but REALLY? Does it nearly have to kill me?* I was nearing the end of Grenville Channel, a 45-mile trough of water contained within steep walls rising more than two-thousand feet, its north end roughly 35 miles south of Prince Rupert, British Columbia. Pretty much in the middle of nowhere.

Places to land were scarce and my hopes to stop and camp were dashed on two occasions that day when grizzly bears—cubs in tow—stood defiantly along the shoreline. By the time I did find a marginal place to set up camp, I was a soggy, string-of-bad-luck, hypothermic bundle of exasperation. Had my adventure truly just begun? I didn't know, but what I did know was that any residual arrogance I may have had was now whupped out of me. I was paddling solo on the Inside Passage, and I was being handed a pivotal lesson—almost along with my ass.

"Give me a fucking break!" I screamed at the top of my lungs—at the wind, at the stinging rain, at everything and at nothing, thrusting my chest forward, my arms hyper-extended behind me, all ten fingers spread wide in outrage. I was 38 days into my expedition and had come to accept, even expect, being cold and wet. But this was different—and much more dire.

My primal screams filled the forest, only to be reabsorbed by the howling wind, sullen seas, and the sucking mud of this godforsaken bay I was stuck in. I was attempting to set up camp a hair's-width above the briny dung of what appeared to be a saltwater chicken coop, a goopy, flat area where the funky smell of seabird guano met my nostrils. Debris from last night's high tide hung like Christmas garlands from the fringes of the impenetrable forest behind me. My campsite would certainly be under water in the middle of that night and the reality of having to deal with that made me sick to my stomach. Remembering that my sleeping bag was damp and my tent waterlogged, frantically crammed in the back hatch earlier that morning, made my heart sink even further.

A vigorous rain pelted the right side of my face, which was swollen and disfigured from the previous day's blood-sucking black fly attack. Moments before, I'd shivered violently in sopping wet clothes, and struggled with a nylon tarp as the wind belligerently whipped it out of my hands. My fingers, barely able to tie the knots to secure the corners, became less and less dexterous. Gale force winds had descended upon Grenville Channel and were only slightly diffused by the landmass I was hiding behind.

Earlier that day, I'd briefly fallen asleep in my drifting kayak, then succumbed to the initial stages of hypothermia, as crushing fatigue took hold; I hadn't cared enough to extract myself from the gallons of cold water I was sitting in inside my cockpit. Warm urine pooled in the crotch of my wetsuit, momentarily warming me as I peed in the boat. I'd landed here out of default, and ludicrously bad luck, after paddling nearly forty arduous miles, forced to move on at the twenty- and then thirty-mile mark when mama grizzly bears had trumped my intended campsites. My muscles cramped, my head throbbed, and in spite of a tailwind, my lightweight carbon-fiber paddle felt like a two-by-four and the seas felt like grape jelly. I was completely, utterly spent, and there were simply no other options. I knew that night would be no different from the three previous ones: when I was finally tucked into the thin veneer of my nylon tent, my serial date with the high tide would come knocking at my door. When saltwater began licking at my rainfly under the dark cloak of night I would curse the moon and I would curse gravity for conspiring on a 23-foot tidal exchange. Around three a.m. I would be forced to change back into my cold, wet rain gear and extract myself from my womblike shelter. Then, like a bride snatching up her gown, I'd lift my tent just as the water poured in around my bug-bitten ankles and stand tippy-toed on a piece of driftwood or slippery boulder. Each of those three past nights I stood in a brine-soaked kiddie pool, in the dark, in the pouring rain, and pleaded with the ocean, politely asking her, "Are ya done yet?"

I learned early on in my trip that Mother Nature can be unforgiving. Or she can be neutral, soothing you, enveloping you in her sweet velvety senses. But on that day in Grenville Channel—as I desperately tried to set up camp—she was schizophrenic. She didn't care that I was on the verge of tears, or scared out of my wits. I'd put myself in this position, and it was up to me to put on my big girl panties and figure a way out.

It was then, when I was chilled to the bone, fumbling with the tarp, that an inner pathos hurtled out of me, along with an alarming variety of expletives. My explosive rage made my blood flow hot, pressed my mental reset button, and refocused my intent. Perhaps it saved my life. Miraculously, I was able to tend to all my needs: shelter, food, warmth and rest—at least for a few hours. Praying for sleep to come, shivering inside my slightly damp sleeping bag, eyes wide open, I felt an unease in the pit of my stomach. Would I have the strength and courage to take care of myself throughout the entire journey?

A Sea of Uncertainty

WATER WAS TABOO in my family: a strong river current had snatched my father's five-year-old niece, who had slipped and fallen down a muddy bank while playing along its shores. The river took her and would not let go. My father vowed to never let me suffer from the same demise and forbade me to play in or near water during my youth.

I thought about this as I lay trembling in my tent that night in Grenville Channel and wondered if I should have heeded my father's fears more seriously. But I knew better. Water is my element, where I feel most at home. I have always been attracted to water, seduced by it, drawn to the very thing that my parents tried to shield me from. I was nine years old when I learned that the letters W-A-T-E-R formed Helen Keller's first spoken word. This impacted me in a way I couldn't understand at the time, but now I realize that much like those five letters meant to Helen the wonderful cool something that was flowing over her hand—a living word that awakened her spirit and set it free—so water became for me a substance to love and cherish.

My spellbinding connection to water began with the forbidden tributaries and ponds I frequented as a young girl. I spent countless idle afternoons carefully positioning a toy boat high in the creek below our house—out of my parents' view. The boat tumbled its way downstream, crashing into obstacles, careening over miniature waterfalls, bouncing and free flowing, much like my child's mind. I'd run alongside it, enamored by the forces acting on it. This creek flowed into a small pond where I stashed a dilapidated rubber raft inside a rotten maple log. On quiet summer afternoons I would stealthily retrieve my raft and with my small pink lips sealed over the plastic valve, my pint-sized lungs would exhale air over and over again until the raft slowly began to take shape. Still dizzy from hyperventilating, I would climb in and shove off with my yellow plastic paddle. I'd often stop halfway across the pond, sling one leg over the side of the raft, and, with fishing pole in hand, gaze at the dark watery world below. I'd drift and dream at this most magical time when I truly knew how to relax.

"KEEP YOUR LEGS WIDE," said my friend Bobbie. "And sit tall like your mama told you to at the dinner table." Instinctively I pulled my chin back, my shoulder blades together, and lengthened my spine as my legs assumed a loose frog-legged position in the boat. It was early summer 1991 and was the first time my pelvis had met the low-slung fiberglass seat of a long, tippy sea kayak. As my toes reached for the foot pegs deep within the cockpit, I knew this was for me.

"Don't forget to breathe!" Bobbie said as she watched the skinny kayak beneath my rigid hips respond to every twitch of muscle, and quiver a jig in dead calm waters.

My inaugural sea kayak excursion placed me on the largest lake west of the Mississippi. Bobbie was shepherding three greenhorn paddlers over the glassy waters of Montana's Flathead Lake, across a three-mile freshwater expanse to a large island where we planned to have a picnic lunch and catch glimpses of wild horses and bighorn sheep grazing on the rolling hillsides.

Within ten minutes, my body started to relax and my hands loosened their grip on the paddle shaft. Soon my hips settled deeper in the cockpit and the boat sat quiet and steady beneath me. "Hah!" I yelled across the water toward Bobbie. "She senses my fears—just like a horse. I stop fighting, she stops bucking!" From this low, yet commanding vantage point, I treasured the feeling of cruising along on the water's surface at the pace of a brisk walk. I felt blessed to experience nature's beauty from this perspective, while absorbing all that my senses would allow. I was contained in that kayak, ensconced in a vessel that I literally wore, that suited my body type, my personality, my soul. I radiated a child-like sense of joy and wonder, and embraced a sense of discovery, contentment, and familiarity like none other. I transcended into a secret world, a magical world, a healing world with that first sea kayak experience. I could touch the water at will—and the water could touch me. The kayak was an extension of my hips, the paddle an extension of my torso. I imagined myself as half-woman, half-kayak. I was *Womyak.*

FOR THE NEXT NINETEEN YEARS, my perpetual love of water and this newfound sport led me to many adventures. Being on the water, paring life down to the basics, puts things in perspective for me and illuminates in a very clear and undiluted form what really matters—and who I am. I'd sometimes pack my gear into my kayak and disappear for several days to be alone somewhere on the water. I paddled the glacier-carved lakes of Montana, Idaho, and Wyoming. I paddled with friends in Mexico, Belize, on the Atlantic and the Pacific. I explored the Great Lakes and big rivers, from the muddy Missouri to the class-five whitewater rivers in Montana and Idaho. I paddled lagoons, estuaries, lakes, mill ponds, creeks, rivers, bays, and pools. Laudably, kayaking is a layered sport—it can be whatever you want it to be: gunk holing in protected nooks and crannies; playing in dynamic water; surfing; racing; pushing through grueling, exposed crossings; barreling down adrenalin-spiked whitewater; exploring sheltered coastlines—or paddling the Inside Passage.

My fascination with the Inside Passage began in 1996 when I joined

Jim on a hundred-mile portion of its route in British Columbia. A novice at expedition paddling at the time, I stuck to Jim like the epoxy resin that held my kayak together, mimicking his every move, absorbing his seamanship skills as best I could, and simply learning about the unstable environment of the sea. I took an instant liking to the expedition aspect of sea kayaking. I loved the repetitive cycle of multi-day paddling: setting up camp, exploring, breaking camp, paddling, then more exploring. I reveled in my newfound self-containment—everything I needed to survive was either on my person or in my boat. I remembered falling into a rhythm with the ocean and feeling at peace with my surroundings. Over the years I was slowly introduced to other sections of the Inside Passage, and I felt a deep desire to connect the dots.

FROM A CRESCENT-SHAPED BEACH near Anacortes, Washington, I sat tall in the cockpit of my eighteen-foot sea kayak, ceremoniously dipped my paddle into the vast expanse of the Salish Sea, and sallied forth on an inner and outer journey up the Inside Passage of British Columbia and southeast Alaska, and into the unknown. It was Spring 2010.

My kayak was a beautiful boat: fire-engine red, low-slung and sleek, seaworthy, and tough as nails. Long and lean, she cut through the water gracefully, even fully loaded with kit, food, water, and paddler. She needed a name. I chose *Chamellia*.

Loosely named after the chameleon lizard, whose eyes rotate independently in all directions, I entrusted Chamellia's 360-degree view of all aspects of this journey to watch over me and to help me adapt to quickly changing conditions. When my eyes were focused dead ahead, I'd need her to gently guide me, because part of my quest was to lose that tunnel vision, but not necessarily my focus. With our collective vision, one eye would be looking forward scanning the horizon, the other observing behind or to the side, to keep me—a mere sliver on the sea—safe. Whether we were facing long stretches of monotonous placid seas, or monstrous waves, or butt-puckering tidal currents, Chamellia and I would continuously respond and adjust to the ocean's moods and motions, its rhythms and writhing. Slow and calculating, frozen in anticipation, or gracefully swift, we would meet the sea on its terms—or so I hoped.

I wanted nothing more than to experience the Inside Passage in all her moods, with all my senses. I wanted to feel free, bold, and spontaneous, to be awestruck, and to see in my journey the lessons I needed to learn. And I believed those lessons, and the ability to ponder deeper truths, would best be acquired in solitude. I realized my choice to go solo was risky, but I felt the potential rewards outweighed the possible dangers and accepted the fact that my adventure had an unknown outcome. For that is the ultimate draw of a long journey: the unknown, and all the possibilities of adventure wrapped up in that uncertainty.

"Adventure" implies an element of risk, of gambles and unpredictable circumstances, and one risk I was *not* willing to take was that of staying on shore and then dealing with the rising flood of "what-ifs" that would certainly follow. I didn't want to grow old and look back on my life and feel disappointed that life had passed me by, or that I'd shortchanged myself and missed out on something big because I'd harbored fears of uncertainty. I didn't see my adventure as a foolhardy endeavor or some sort of quixotic dream. It just felt right. The time was right, my dreams and ambitions about it were all right, as though my queries to the universe had finally given me the thumbs up. I needed to trust that all I'd done to this point had prepared me for this journey.

A Sense of Adventure

I DOVE HEAD-FIRST into the world while a blizzard raged outside a hospital window in upstate New York. It was January 14, 1961. As that storm raged on that cold winter evening, my birth mother—a child herself at sixteen—lay stupefied at the thought of a second mouth to feed. Her son, born eleven months earlier, was home with an uncle. Our father, who didn't care much for snot-nosed kids, was nowhere to be found. He cared most for his bottle I was told—so much in fact that he had earned the title of town drunk. My birth mother would bear four of his children before she finally left him for good. Often neglected during those precious formative years, my three siblings and I were wrenched from the arms of our petrified teenaged mother and made wards of the court, consigned to New York State's foster care system. I was three years old.

Meanwhile, in a neighboring county, Helen and William Conrad were busy raising their thirteen-year-old boy, Billy. He was their pride and joy, yet they yearned for a daughter. Unable to conceive another child, they decided to adopt, and placed their order for a blond, blue-eyed girl. Initially, they got two. Another family adopted my one-year-old baby sister, leaving child services hesitant to split up the two older girls. My two-year-old sister and I arrived as a matching set. I can still picture our cherubic little faces, framed with hair so blond it was nearly transparent, our chubby legs swinging in unison, eyes uplifted, hearts eager for this much-needed attention. For a few short months we shared Lincoln Logs, Tonka trucks, and cloth dolls—until a tragic accident separated us for good.

While our new family of five was headed home one summer evening, an accelerating Mack truck crossed the double yellow line and hit our '62 Plymouth Fury head-on. The two drunks in the Mack truck were killed instantly. My new dad was critically injured, his chest crushed by the steering wheel, his right leg mangled by the impact. He held on to life by a thread in the hospital's ICU. Two weeks later he was moved to a private room where he stayed for two more months. His healing period was extensive and, because he was the sole provider (mom didn't work or drive), child services ruled that my parents could no longer support two young girls and insisted they return one of us. My sister was taken away and I remained in their lives; another bond broken, new feelings of isolation and abandonment permeating our young souls. Yet I still had a new family and a new world that would, optimistically, provide me with a sense of security, love, and caring.

Up until that juncture, I had suffered many childhood injustices. I was too young to clearly remember them, but I know they happened. I remember fragments: the glass ketchup bottle hitting my brother square in the head at the dinner table; the Christmas tree smashing through the window, then teeter-tottering on the deck railing, tinsel and shiny ornaments still hanging on its branches; and the yelling and screaming and doors slamming and dishes breaking and babies crying and car tires screeching. A sibling's broken arm, another's walloped head, my severely burnt hand, held to the top of the kitchen stove burner—to learn the meaning of "hot." Details are vague, yet I know these things groomed me into a guarded, if not stoic, young adult. I became an elusive shadow, avoiding all attention, because in my world, attention only meant more pain. These loud and terrifying moments embedded themselves in my psyche and created in me a craving for sacred privacy and stillness. As a teenager, I was safe in my aloneness, in the quiet of my soul.

Yet, in reality, I wasn't *always* safe in my aloneness. My brother had moved in with his girlfriend years prior and I was often home alone on Saturdays when my parents were at work. I was probably twelve or thirteen—old enough to have budding breasts. A close friend of the family often visited on these Saturday afternoons. He'd sit too close to me, stay too long, say inappropriate things, creep me out. As uncomfortable as it all was, nothing happened—until one day something did happen. Breathing heavily, he abruptly turned toward me and forced himself on me, ripping my shirt open, forcing me to the floor, wedging a knee between my thighs. He left marked hand-shaped bruises on both my breasts, which I would hide from my mom for weeks, until thankfully they disappeared. I kicked and screamed and fought bitterly under the weight of his heavy, hairy body until he finally stood up, zipped his pants, and, as if suddenly coming to grips with what he had just done, mumbled an apology and left. I sat trembling on the couch, clutching my torn pajama top to my chest, listening to the crunch of his tires as he pulled out of the driveway. I locked the doors and windows, then sobbed for hours. There was no physical penetration, yet his actions left an emotional penetration that was a significant game-changer for me.

Much like water was taboo in my family, so too, I sensed, was talking about this sort of thing. It was dangerous heresy, and therefore shouldn't exist. I chose not to tell, although my behavior spoke volumes. I awoke screaming from nightmares, grew hugely rebellious, and became savvy at emotional detachment. I'd walk briskly through the kitchen, past this man who had the audacity to take a place at our dinner table, as if nothing had happened. I didn't understand why it happened. I couldn't rely on my feelings, and I certainly couldn't rely on my parents to protect me. I felt betrayed by their inability to provide a safe home, and their inattentiveness to my sudden, erratic behavior. I expertly masked my vulnerability and built skyscraper-high walls, all of which helped make my decision to remain silent easy.

Yet I yearned to be loved and wore my fill-this-huge-hole-in-my-heart emblem on my sleeve, but they couldn't see it, and clearly they couldn't heal it. They provided all my fundamental physical needs, and I viewed them as my true parents, but it was the emotional needs that they had no clue how to deal with.

In fact, about two years later, my father's actions would deepen my emotional detachment and shatter my already fragile confidence. Mom was in the hospital for a brief stay, healing from gallbladder surgery. I voluntarily tried to fill her shoes, and brimmed with pride as I kept up on the laundry, swept the floors, and made dinner for my dad and me. It may have only been spaghetti or mac and cheese from a box, but my domestic contributions mattered a lot to me. The night before mom came home, I was lying in bed reading a book, its pages barely illuminated by the dim light on my nightstand. My bedroom door creaked open and in the sliver of light from the hallway I saw my father standing there in his boxers and a button-up nightshirt that wasn't buttoned, revealing his chest and stomach. The last thing I saw was his penis in his hand. The door opened farther and he walked toward me. *Oh my god, you, too!* I thought, throwing the bedcovers over my head. I held my breath, and prayed he would just go away. He didn't. Instead, he sat down on the bed beside me. I could feel pressure through the blankets; I don't know if it was his hand, or some other part of his body because I numbed out, dissociating my mind from my body. "Go away, don't do this, please go away!" I yelled. "Go away. Go away." And he left as quickly and quietly as he entered. I didn't breathe a word of it to anyone, and nothing of this nature ever occurred again.

THESE EARLY LIFE EXPERIENCES of neglect, abuse, and abandonment led, not surprisingly, to unhealthy behaviors and coping mechanisms as I matured. As a teenager, I was convinced that my parents had conspired to ruin my life, and I ran away from home three times. On my sixteenth birthday, in the midst of a blizzard in upstate New York, I ran away for the final time. With that choice I cheated myself out of much of my youth and innocence and lost a productive young adulthood.

Just as I ran and hid as a teen, I became a runner as an adult. At the tender age of eighteen I ran from my biological brother when he tried to reunite me with my siblings and birth mother. I ran from my feelings when I lost my adoptive brother to a drug overdose, his death the first in a series of tragic losses that I had no clue how to deal with. I ran from one man to the next, one job to the next, one state to the next. I ran from my problems, I ran from my fears, I ran from love and commitment, I ran from myself.

WHEN I DECIDED TO PADDLE the IP, it had been 45 years since I had been separated from my biological family, yet I was still a woman in search of something, still working through many issues from my past abuse, still struggling with the *why* of it all. Over time, I'd proven to myself empirically that my old patterns and strategies didn't work, but I trusted that if I kept at it, truly put my heart and soul into it, that the healing would slowly come.

My personal research into child welfare has revealed that kids who have been abused or neglected tend never to feel attached to anyone in a trusting way and often insist on slugging it out alone. Perhaps this is why I chose to experience the Inside Passage solo. Solo adventures had always pulled me into a realm of solace and healing, an emotional comfort that I hoped the Inside Passage could also impart. The IP felt different to me. Instead of running *from* something, I realized I was running *to* something—my hopes and dreams and desires. And to uncertainty, for I preferred risk over stagnation and was convinced that I'd make peace with that uncertainty, become even more comfortable with solitude, and honor the questions that would emerge from it. Yes, I decided, I would paddle a long, skinny boat to Alaska, and I brought my whole focus to this intention. I was confident about my decision, and in turn, my decision created confidence.

Common paddling wisdom asserts that it takes about 1,000 strokes to travel one mile in a sea kayak, in average conditions, without the assistance or impedance of wind or current. With this math, I would take approximately 1,200,000 strokes. Once underway, in my aloneness, through all those miles I would paddle, and all those strokes I would take, I would have plenty of opportunity for soul-searching.

Mine would be a one-way paddle. Not a circuitous route, but linear— like me. I revel in sequence, preferring things orderly. I call it methodical, goal-oriented. My friends call it anal. I thought for such matters as planning a solo expedition up the Inside Passage, methodical was a good thing. Real dangers existed "out there," and the best mitigation, I reasoned, was proper planning and sensible risk management. A twisted ankle, an errant stumble into a tidal rapid, or an unexpected encounter with a grouchy mama grizzly could abort the trip in a heartbeat. Hypervigilance would be necessary at times. So too would patience.

I had no idea what I was doing, really. I'd figure it out as I went. I knew that certain hardships would manifest and when they revealed themselves to me I believed I would have my own personal ocean of revelations. With these thoughts, I sealed my commitment to myself, my adventure, my friends and loved ones, my safety, my life. I would paddle the IP, one section at a time, one mile at a time, one island at a time, one stroke at a time. And with each milestone, I hoped to move closer to healing my soul and to find answers to all those questions swirling in my head.

SIX MONTHS AFTER COMMITTING to the IP, in the midst of a cold, dreary winter, I watched from my assigned window seat as the tarmac crew de-iced the airplane wings in preparation for a long flight from Montana to New York. Buckling up, I imagined that similar weather awaited me back east. I shivered, picturing a steel-gray sky hanging over low rolling hills, and long rows of barren deciduous trees dusted with snow, flanking the stone walls that were part of the landscape where I grew up.

I cautiously exited the enormous car rental complex at the John F. Kennedy airport and drove ninety miles north to my mom's nursing home in the Catskill Mountains in upstate New York. They call them "adult care centers" now, I was told. I had moved her into this care center a couple years earlier, into the same room with my father, who was dying of Alzheimer's disease. His brain went quickly, followed by his body, which had finally waved the little white flag seven months prior to this visit. I'd long since forgiven my father for the one isolated incident where he breached my trust as a child. I'll never know why he made the decision to enter my room that night in such an inappropriate manner. But through my own perseverance—and years of therapy—I worked through those transgressions, which allowed me to change on the inside so that I could move forward in my life with intent and purpose. The very act of forgiveness had taken away the power of those bad memories, now just experiences safely tucked away in my past.

I HADN'T SEEN MY MOTHER since the funeral, and felt a strong need to visit her before embarking on my big kayak journey.

It was late December 2009, and I was feeling a hint of dread, as I always did, in returning to the nursing home. I was highly sensitive to the sights and sounds and smells that permeated the building, and usually made my visits as brief as possible.

The elevator doors slid open and I walked down the polished hallway toward my mother's room. She stood with her back to me just a few feet away, rummaging through her top dresser drawer. For a moment, I quietly watched her from her doorway. A crinkled-edged black and white photo fluttered to the floor, landing face-up near her foot. That was my cue. "Look Mom, it's a picture of our old house!" I said, snatching it up before she could do so herself. Slightly startled, she quickly turned toward me. Within a split second her facial expression went from surprise to sheer happiness; her eyes twinkled and a generous smile filled her face. After a long hug, we turned our attention back to the drawer of photos, while rain flecked a window that looked out over a small wooded pond.

"DROP DEAD!" yelled an emaciated woman, sitting on the edge of her twin bed, suddenly disrupting our moment. Her long, thin hands clutched the opening of a paisley bathrobe that resembled an old couch cover. A strong urine funk lingered in her corner of the room, which she shared with my mother.

"I HATE YOU!" she angrily lashed out at no one in particular. An intravenous fluid bag dangled from a steel hook above her bed and shook violently from her erratic movements. While the bag still swayed, her head fell heavily forward, and she sat slumped in a catatonic state until her next outburst.

While mom and I visited, the shift nurse came into her room to change her bedding. Soon it would be dinnertime for the residents. Those who were ambulatory, like my mother, would walk to the dining hall on their floor; others were wheeled, and those most incapacitated, like my mother's roommate, would have their meals brought to them.

"See you tomorrow, Mom," I said as I hugged her goodbye. Releasing our embrace, ten plump fingers wrapped around my hands and held me tightly. "See you tomorrow, sweetheart," she said, tears welling up in her eyes.

As I walked down the hallway toward the elevator, I averted my eyes from doddering men in wheelchairs who wanted to reach out and touch me. I walked past the dining hall where my mother would soon be eating, then hurried into the elevator, pressed the ground-floor button, and held my breath against the nauseating smell of Lysol and urine. When the doors finally opened, I stepped through them and watched a black man with white hair expectorate into a napkin. I walked down the hallway past plastic flowers and chunky oil paintings, past silver rolling carts with neatly stacked food trays, past a mop and bucket, to the receptionist desk where I would sign out—quickly. Relieved to be outside in the fresh air, I took a deep, cleansing breath and nearly ran to my vehicle.

In the years to come, I grew to understand that mom was where she belonged, that the care center was her home, that she loved living there and was adored and well-cared-for by the staff. This comforted me, allowing my sensitivities and apprehensions to soften over time, but on that day, I struggled with the intensity of my emotions.

Free to explore the countryside where I grew up, I drove my rental car past stone walls symmetrically lined with maple trees, past forgotten cow pastures and dilapidated barns. I reflected on my visit with Mom as I drove, allowing the strong images to cycle through my mind. Odd, I thought, that my focus was more on her roommate and all the sights and sounds and smells, as uncomfortable as they were for me, rather than the mother/daughter bond one might expect. I realized then that my visits were more out of obligation and relationship than love and connection. Mom had mellowed over time and seemed more insightful and loving than I had ever remembered as a child. I knew in my heart that she was a different person now, but for some reason I was only able to reciprocate that love on what felt like a superficial level. I'd long since stopped running from her but obviously held feelings of resentment that still lingered in my soul; feelings I hoped I could work through in the months and years to come.

I INSTINCTIVELY TOUCHED THE SCAR on my upper lip as I looked down the steep hill sprawling below me. I'd driven to the very spot I had stood, day after day, year after year, waiting for the long, yellow school bus on top of Thunder Hill Road. The road still had gaping ditches and lacked a respectable shoulder, much like the other twisty-turny country roads that it connected to. I spotted thin patches of sand on the pavement, scattered there by the road crew to offset the icy conditions New York winters are notorious for. Those sand patches took me back to the day when I'd slid too fast through one of them on my bicycle many years before, which had sent me into a head-first tumble over my handlebars, resulting in lips and knees colliding with the pitted surface of Thunder Hill Road. I remembered the bicycle I pedaled that day: it was brown with silver sparkles, balloon tires, a rusty kickstand, and a three-speed thumb-shifter that rotated loosely on curved handlebars with pink rubber grips. My wispy blond hair had streamed in the wind, as I stood high on the pedals, the seat post permanently rusted, set too short for my long, skinny legs. I remembered watching my mother's face as she cut away my torn, blood-soaked dungarees with a pair of sharp kitchen scissors. Tears had streamed down my face and rolled over my fattening, bloodied lip, but the thick flap of gravel-encrusted skin that hung from my kneecap—revealing the bone beneath it—took priority.

The gaping wound had taken months to heal and the skin on my kneecap had become smooth and shiny, permanently devoid of hair. Standing on the road I grew up on, I could practically still feel the stiff fabric of my bell-bottom jeans rubbing on my tender skin as I limped through that painful stage of my youth. My scabbed lip, though it healed much quicker than my knee, elicited hurtful remarks from my schoolmates, who claimed among other things, that I'd kissed a horse's ass. At the time, I vowed to myself to be more cautious, but not to allow any of this to quell my sense of adventure.

This strong childhood reflection became proof in my mind that while I wasn't immune to adventurous mishaps, I was also high-spirited and thick-skinned. As a child, I felt that the bicycle represented freedom and exhilaration, much like the kayak had come to embody those things for me as an adult. What I didn't know as a child was that my overly stubborn, I-shall-conquer personality quirks would flow into my adult life, further hone my sense of adventure, and eventually bring me to my choice to paddle the Inside Passage.

Through Hell and High Water

THE INSIDE PASSAGE is an extraordinary coastal route, with some of the most spectacular fjords and convoluted coastlines in the world. It's a narrow artery that connects with and is a part of the 64 million square miles that comprise the Pacific Ocean. Often presented as the most breathtaking—and challenging—paddling trip in North America, it's touted as a holy grail for those accessing it in long, skinny boats.

Seattle, Washington is considered the official starting point and Skagway, Alaska the terminus where one literally runs out of ocean, about 1,300 miles later. After traversing through a snippet of northwest Washington, including an oblique trajectory through the San Juan Islands, the IP extends north along the British Columbia coastline. A fifty-mile-long strait called Dixon Entrance plays sentinel to the Alaskan boundary, and from there the IP snakes its way up Alaska's panhandle, where Skagway waits at the pinnacle like a grand finale.

In addition to providing habitat for bears, wolves, whales, sea lions, a host of other sea mammals, sea birds and birds of prey, the Inside Passage also boasts the largest intact temperate rainforest in the world. I planned on being wet.

As I began to discuss my trip with others, it surprised me how many people thought of the Inside Passage as an easy route through calm, protected waters. That I would simply point my bow north and paddle. Nothing could be further from the truth. Yes, the Inside Passage is an inland route, sheltered in part from the open ocean. But the exposed and often tumultuous sections such as Queen Charlotte Sound, Cape Caution, and Dixon Entrance would demand patience and respect. Even then, I wasn't about to let my guard down in more protected waters. Funneling winds, schizophrenic seas, and unfriendly or nonexistent beaches make even the so-called protected areas problematic. Regardless, it would be my universe for an entire summer—a sea voyage marked by inlets, bays, valleys, peaks, glaciers, towns, inflowing rivers, sounds, islands and the Alaskan peaks looming in the distance.

Once I started blabbing to people that I was actually going to do this, I was thoroughly committed. A rush of fierce determination percolated through me. No turning back now, no matter how many powerful reality checks flashed in front of me. The big "five-O" birthday loomed depressingly close; I was pitifully out of shape and still nursing my wounds from a series of losses that had left me with a raw, lingering ache. In addition to the recent death of my father, a close friend had died, another had moved away, my cat had been eaten by a coyote, and my long-term relationship was falling apart. I had withdrawn from the paddlesports business that had defined me for ten years and felt a strong need to reinvent myself. I was single, jobless, fatherless and restless, desperate for new doors to open. I could continue to throw my chronic pity parties or pull my head out of my ass. I chose the latter, signed up for a triathlon, became a gym rat, and started a regular paddling regime. I was going to paddle the Inside Passage after all.

It occurred to me that I should set a date.

Cinco de Mayo had a nice ring to it. I would launch on the fifth day of May 2010. It'd be early enough in the season to avoid heavy boat traffic on the more populated coastline of the lower route and would put me in Alaska sometime in July, where, I reasoned, I would have a better chance at good weather and calm seas. Depending on the whims of Mother Nature and how my energy level and body held up, my ETA in Skagway, Alaska, would be ten to twelve weeks later.

May 5th would also border on the one-year anniversary of my father's death. Launching into this new journey on this day would, in a sense, commemorate his life. Over time, he and my mother had come to accept and—I suspected—secretly admire, my adventuresome spirit. My pelagic wanderings, and my blatant disregard of their whole don't-go-near-the-water-you'll-drown thing, probably concerned them the most, but other than telling their grown daughter to "be sure to wear your hat," they didn't have much recourse. I wanted my father's blessing on this journey, and had he been alive at the time and cognitively with it, I believe he would have given it to me. I believe he would have respected what I was doing. And my mother would have stood by his side, wringing her hands, her eyes slightly crossed like they do when she grows worried. She would remind me not to "do anything foolish," because she wouldn't know what else to say. But this would not be the scenario. Neither one of them would be there when I launched, because after 62 years of marriage she was alone in the world, confined to her small room in the adult care center. I could never muster up the nerve to tell her that I planned to do this, to paddle the Inside Passage by myself. I didn't want to add any stress to her already enlarged and compromised heart. My friends and relatives back in New York had been sworn to secrecy. All Mom knew was that I was traveling "up north" and that my cellphone coverage might be a bit spotty at times.

With Cinco de Mayo less than nine months out, it occurred to me that I'd never done a solo trip on the ocean. I'd paddled on the ocean with others and had led guided trips in the San Juans of Washington State and the Southern Gulf Islands in neighboring British Columbia. But in the better part of two decades I'd only paddled solo a handful of times, mainly short trips on large lakes in Montana. In his nuts and bolts book *Kayaking the Inside Passage*, Robert Miller lists three essential skills one should have before embarking on such an ambitious journey: a dependable roll, competent navigation, and good seamanship.

As if keeping score, I tallied my strengths. My ability to right a capsized kayak was solid, and I could read a chart, plot a course, and stay found. I knew how to read water and I wasn't afraid to get wet. But having lived in landlocked Montana for nearly twenty years, my seamanship skills were questionable. I understood that good seamanship, in part, is about internalizing the rhythm of the ocean—deciphering, respecting, and accepting her moods, her patterns, her soul. Good seamanship is about making choices—and not second-guessing yourself once you do. It's about good judgment and corralling your fears, of knowing when to push on and when to say uncle—and staying out of the shit in the first place. The upshot of all this is staying upright—and alive. Cold water shock, which often leads to instant drowning, is the number one killer for sea kayakers. Hypothermia, a drop in your core temperature, is the runner up. On the water, the anatomy of a bad or fatal decision is often blamed on hypothermia, which, among a myriad of other symptoms, causes a person to become grumpy, irrational, and seriously brain-fogged. Since falling into the heat-sucking fifty-degree waters of the Inside Passage was not on my to-do list, I needed to be as prepared as possible.

Experience, they say, is the best teacher. I decided that the scattered islands, islets, and reefs of Vancouver Island's west side would be my tutor. A short solo stint in Barkley Sound would serve as an overture and tell me if I could cut the mustard on a longer journey up the IP.

I chose a circuitous hundred-mile shakedown trip in the fall of 2009. It turned out to be the perfect approach to decide which pieces of equipment were working and what needed to be reworked. Forced to paddle through dense fog on a compass bearing, I gained more confidence in my navigation skills. I slowly acquired a keener sense of scale, and grew savvier at converting the two-dimensional chart on my deck to the three-dimensional world across my bow, constantly matching the natural features of the landscape with the chart on my lap. I drastically edited the self-doubt tape that often played in my head. I knew deep down inside that I must trust in my abilities or I would never pull off paddling the more arduous and exposed waters of the Inside Passage.

I enjoyed my own company and traveling solo. When I was sublimely lost in my thoughts or my camera lens, the minutes and hours would melt away. I reveled in the wind, waves, swell, and sunshine bestowed on me on the outer islands and crossings. I dabbled in sea caves, poked into bays, and skipped around rocks and reefs. Once, skittering around a corner of a rocky islet, I came face-to-rump with a sizable black bear, her fur so dark and glossy it contrasted sharply with the monochromatic landscape surrounding us. Rummaging through the beach debris, she pawed at large rocks, moving them as easily as if they were pieces of Styrofoam. I was relieved to be down-wind of her and quietly paddled into deeper water, distancing myself from her. *Note to self*, I thought: *check the expiration date on my bear spray canister before setting off for Alaska and research every drib and drab I can find on proper bear etiquette.* I respected all wildlife and harbored no unusual angst at being in their presence, at least in broad daylight, but I was a firm believer in being prepared.

A few moments later, I was gliding through the water when the glistening, forty-ton body of a humpback whale abruptly surfaced in front of me. I gasped, then watched in stunned reverence. It barrel-rolled, then disappeared, but suddenly resurfaced. She stared directly at me with a large, bulbous eye. Chills darted down my damp back when she slowly rolled away, waving her large, white pectoral fin as if to say goodbye. She dove deep, her tail fluke momentarily suspended above the water. I finally exhaled.

While roaming bears, ogling whales, persnickety tidal surges and growling sea lions kept me on my toes, I had an epiphany. I didn't embark on this shakedown trip to simply sort through issues such as paddling longer distances day after day, or schlepping massive piles of gear without assistance, or coming to terms with camping alone—I had come to deal with my fears. My overactive worry gland was in zero danger of atrophy. I needed to dig deep and figure out where my trepidations were coming from, make some sense of them, and perhaps come to terms with them. Most importantly, I wanted not to allow them to petrify me to the point of questioning why I was going there in the first place.

Was I afraid of dying? Nothing life-threatening had happened on my practice run. Was I terrified of having to be rescued? Was this all a result of my fragile ego? A fear of embarrassment? Was courage the opposite of fear? I knew that a healthy fear—a respect for the power of the ocean and all it could dish out—was one thing, but I also knew it was imperative to get a handle on dealing with my fear in general. So I vowed not to let fear hold me back. I would coexist with the fear—perhaps that would be my courage.

I spent the tenth and last day of my warm-up excursion poking around in protected inlets, nooks, and crannies and I began to lose myself in the rhythm and pace of the islands and to work through my fears with a hint of composure.

On my last evening in Barkley Sound, I soaked up a crimson sunset, sipped burgundy wine, and reflected on the recent chain of events in my life. I hugged my knees to my chest and allowed waves of emotion, and feelings of perpetual gratitude, to wash over me. I listened to my fears and accepted that they were a necessary part of this journey, and every journey to come. I understood that as long as I didn't allow my fears to consume me, they would prompt me to be strong and vigilant—and hopefully safe. I felt fortunate to be sitting on a beach in the Pacific Northwest, slowly healing from a lousy year.

High Tide in Montana

I RETURNED TO MONTANA after that late fall shakedown trip feeling rejuvenated and more prepared for my big journey. Autumn turned into winter and the sun's rays became ever more indirect, skimming the big sky vastness at an almost horizontal angle. Temps dropped well below zero, and the water grew too hard to stick a paddle into.

On a frigid December morning, my hair hung in frozen ringlets, nearly shattering each time it brushed against the top of my down jacket. I shivered, then gently placed my kayak, bow first, into its protective cradles that were attached to my vehicle's roof rack. Once Chamellia's hull made contact with the ice-encrusted saddles, she slid effortlessly into place, and I strapped her down. I'd just finished a two-hour practice session in my local health club's heated pool, refining my rolls, braces, jazzy paddle strokes, and all the other things a prudent kayaker does to ward off unexpected capsizes. I often took advantage of this open-pool session on Sunday mornings throughout that winter. Sometimes I'd share the pool with one or two other paddlers, but mostly I had it to myself, like I did that day. In the comfort of that heated pool, I deliberately created out-of-boat experiences in order to practice climbing back in. Re-entering a capsized kayak involves a blend of coordination, strength, and timing—a conundrum in cold, undulating seas. Falling out of the cockpit is the easy part—getting your butt back in, weighed down with layers of neoprene, thick-soled boots, a sprayskirt, and a personal flotation device (PFD), can be a bloody hassle. Consistent practice, in my mind, was of utmost importance. Occasionally, I noticed spectators peering through the steamed up, thick glass walls that surrounded the pool area. They seemed amused by my body-contorting antics; perhaps they thought I was playing a game of "Aqua Twister," or practicing advanced yoga moves. Although their presence distracted me at times, I was committed to devoting as much time and energy as possible to preparing for the trip, and this included sharpening my rescue skills, boat control skills, stroke precision, muscle memory, and overall body conditioning. I stayed focused as best I could.

After my training session on that sub-zero Sunday, I negotiated the icy roads from the pool to an outdoor store in the nearby town of Kalispell in search of a cushier sleeping pad. I was skulking in the camping gear section when a young, marmalade-haired employee appeared and asked if he could help me.

"No, just looking. Thanks." I wasn't feeling chatty that day nor did I want to go into my whole soliloquy about what I was doing. Persistent in a professional manner, he asked all the right questions, until I finally admitted that I was "going on a longish trip."

His interest deepened. "How long?"

"Oh ... I'm not sure, really. Could be up to ... three months, " I demurred.

His eyes widened as big as saucers as he surveyed the forty-something-year-old woman standing in front of him.

"Wow, where are you going?" he asked.

"I'm going to paddle to Alaska," I answered.

"Alaska?! Whoa, from here?"

I tried not to roll my eyes, although I guess technically it could be done. I could paddle down Montana's lower Flathead River for 72 miles to where it joins the Clark Fork River, which eventually meanders into Idaho. From there I could ride the currents of various tributaries until I hooked a sharp left onto the mighty Columbia River. Eventually I'd get dumped into the Pacific near Portland, Oregon. Heck, then all I'd have to do is hang a right and I'd be on my way to Alaska! Never mind the series of dams, waterfalls, rapids, and gut-splitting portages I'd encounter along the way.

"From Anacortes, Washington," I politely corrected.

"Dude—that's a LONG friggin' trip!" he said as though I'd just told him I was traveling to the moon. "Wow, that's burly!" He gestured with his hands outstretched wildly over his head. I laughed, mostly at his animations, and before he could ask me any more questions, a gangly teenager intercepted him with a pressing inquiry about backcountry stoves. I quietly turned the corner, and slipped out of his view behind a compendium of earth-colored sleeping bags that hung plumb from the rafters.

I didn't buy a camp pad from this store. I didn't buy anything. There was still time, and I had a lot of other things to tend to. I had to calculate how much toilet paper and floss and ibuprofen I'd need, plan food rations and resupply boxes, consolidate my bills, automate my debt, get my teeth cleaned, my pap smeared and my hair cut, order enough contact lenses to last the entire trip, put my car insurance on hold, move out of my cottage, and cram everything I owned into storage. I also had to place my domestic life on hold for six months: February, March, and April I'd be living on Salt Spring Island in Canada to train in a saltwater environment, and, after a brief return to Montana to fine-tune any trip logistics, the following three months I'd be paddling to Alaska.

Thick aromas of pineapple, kiwi, banana, and cinnamon greeted me later that day when I entered my kitchen. For months I'd been dehydrating food for my trip and these fruity odors had alternated with the more acidic fragrances of drying tomato leather, chili, and pork stew, and the wholesome smell of sweet red peppers, snap peas, and juicy tomatoes. Wafting through my cottage 24 hours a day, these were the smells of progress. I dehydrated much of my food for this expedition in order to eat well and to save space in my kayak. The rest of my kit was no different. I'd learned the importance of going as light as possible from my previous trips, and as I prepared for this one, it was imperative that each item that went in the "go pile" had multiple purposes to warrant taking up precious space in my hatches. Empty, my kayak weighed 52 pounds. Full of gear, water, and food it would top the scales at over 150 pounds. On numerous trips I'd experienced heightened annoyance with all the stuff one takes on an expedition and was forever inventing ways to lighten my load.

I regularly refined my urban hunting and gathering skills by sleuthing food co-ops, Asian markets, and wholesale grocery stores. I also frequented farmers' markets and pilfered friends' gardens and orchards, bringing home a wide array of fruits and vegetables that would lie on my dehydrator trays as hot, dry air sucked the moisture out and inhibited the growth of bacteria. I'd be packing up to two week's worth of food in my kayak hatches between each resupply town, so the substantial savings in weight and volume were worth the effort. An entire pineapple fit into a snack-size baggie, and ten medium-size dried tomatoes weighed in under one ounce. I had already vowed not to subsist on preservative-laden canned mystery meats, lifeless sodium-saturated noodles, or bottomless jars of boring peanut butter. I was committed to having quality food choices on my trip—something to look forward to after a long day on the water, to savor and delight in. And as far as I was concerned, chocolate was non-negotiable. This treat consoled me on nearly all my adventures, and would be tucked into every available nook and cranny in my hatches.

THE WINTER SOLSTICE HAD PASSED, and the days were growing noticeably longer—the closeness of spring and the dawn of my trip loomed on the horizon. I grew restless from what felt like hopeless inertia. In my small, snow-bound Montana cabin, I longed to be attuned to the tides and currents, and smell the briny richness of the sea, my wild spirit reawakened. My thoughts turned to the seemingly endless eighteen-hour days I'd spend dipping my paddle along the wild coasts of British Columbia and Alaska. I could already see myself exploring the labyrinthine passages, clicking away the miles as I glided through the archipelago of islands. I was ready for the paddle to be my vocation, my engine, my brake, my steering wheel, my safety net, my rescue device. It was the repetitive, sometimes mundane, sometimes enchanting and hypnotic, stroke of the paddle that would tap the reset button in my mind, body, and soul. It's what would keep me going out there. It would prop up my kitchen tarp, wave to passing fishermen, propel me forward, and poke at kelp beds during those rare times when I practiced the art of doing nothing, an acquired skill I had yet to master.

On expeditions of this nature, particularly solo ones, it seems there is always something that needs tending to. A large percentage of my time and energy would be spent on mere survival. Staying upright, dry, fed, hydrated, warm, alive. Dealing with my fears, doubts, and despair along the way, landing and launching, finding adequate camps and setting up and breaking down those camps, practicing good bear camping etiquette, experiencing many a restless night despite the good etiquette—all these things would occupy my time. But I prepared for these potential hardships and planned my trip around them, through them.

Paddling solo, I shouldered the burden of self-reliance, whereas people who paddled with others had the luxury of divvying things up. They share the carrying; they also share the workload. One person tends to the kitchen area, while the other pitches the tent and fluffs the sleeping bags. One person dips water from a nearby stream while a paddling partner rounds up some firewood. Whoever cooks is pardoned from KP duty. With convenient carrying handles attached to the bow and the stern of each kayak, it's remarkably helpful when there's another body to pick up the opposite end.

But I was choosing to go solo because I believe there is a clarity that comes with silence, a peaceful understanding and heightened awareness with solitude. Just as quality companionship is a gift, so too is delicious alone time. It helps deliver a feeling of contentment and a profound sense of gratitude. The mind-numbing repetition, the familiar motion of the paddle, and the delicate sound of the blade piercing the water—all these things are comforting to me. On a solo adventure I'm alone in my world, free to explore at my own pace; my experience is mine and no one else's. I'm simply a part of it all, and intricately a part of something much bigger. I also felt that in being alone, truly alone, with my thoughts, feelings, hardships, and hissy fits, I could begin to understand the uneasiness I had been feeling, put an end to the self-destructive patterns that were braided through my past, and accept myself fully. I only wanted to be responsible for me, myself, and I—and that at times, was enough of a handful.

I knew this trip would be different from that of anyone who had gone before me: different in my approach and different in what I would take away from it. Before I embarked, that was all I truly knew. The rest would reveal itself to me on a need-to-know basis. I hoped to derive simple pleasures from all that was out there: the creatures, the plants, the water itself that would challenge me with its dance of rising and falling twice a day, every day. I hoped to be more at peace with myself and truly learn to live in the moment. For out there, what else is there? My survival would depend upon "the skill of now."

As the January moon waxed over the Rocky Mountains, I realized it would be the last full moon I would see in Montana—whether momentarily or permanently, I had yet to determine. I was undecided as to whether I would return to this place I had called home for nearly twenty years. I'd always wanted to live near saltwater, and I had an inkling that that desire could grow too strong to ignore. My cottage walls were now barren, closets and drawers empty. Mounds of expedition gear had replaced furniture, and would be leaving with me. My emotions fluctuated like the tides that seemed worlds away. With so many decisions to be made synchronistically, the enormity of it all was hopelessly daunting and hugely gratifying.

Steadfast

WE ALL HAVE GOALS to reach, journeys to experience, and summits to tackle, whether metaphorical or physical. Dan Millman, in *The Warrior Athlete*, writes about how each one of us has been given a different mountain to climb, a goal to reach, during our life. The peak represents our highest potential. Each of us may be at different points in this journey: at the base looking up, on the mountain's shoulders enveloped in the clouds, out on the plains contemplating where your mountain even is, or maybe on the summit, already scanning the horizon for the next peak. Regardless of where you are, Millman emphasizes, one should have a map of the terrain ahead, to avoid drifting or wandering aimlessly.

The complex route I would paddle consisted of 32 maps, or more accurately, nautical charts, each measuring three feet by four feet. Chart number 3462, *Juan De Fuca Strait to Strait of Georgia*, laid crisp and clean on the carpeted floor of my small cabin, which was the only place I could completely unfurl it. My starting point, Anacortes, Washington, highlighted in bright yellow, practically leapt off the paper. To this chart's right sat an unfurled chart of the finish line, featuring Lynn Canal and Skagway, Alaska. Neatly stacked between them were the thirty other charts that would mark the progress of my journey, as would the islands, inlets, channels, sounds, straits, bays, fjords, waterfalls and lighthouses depicted on them.

Months earlier, as part of my logistical homework, I had loosely plotted my entire route on these paper charts hoping I could better wrap my brain around what I might encounter along the way. I tacked a six-foot paper map of the entire Inside Passage to the wall next to my desk and used it as a big-picture planning reference for the charts I'd be using on the trip.

On my hands and knees, I smoothed the creases of the chart I'd hand-numbered "21" and pushed aside a metal ruler, a small plastic compass, and two dog-eared books about the Inside Passage. I laid one of the books on the top right corner of the chart to keep it from rolling back over on itself.

Standing up, I plucked chart number 22 from the stack behind me and tacked it to the wall as Jim nodded in approval over my shoulder. He stepped aside as I hung chart number 23 on the adjacent wall, to the right of number 22.

"The currents will meet and reverse here at Klewnuggit Inlet," Jim said pointing a long, bony finger on the arrow-straight, nearly fifty-mile long Grenville Channel. "If your timing is spot on, you'll get a free ride with both the flood and the ebb." He ran his finger up and then down the length of the fjord, his shaggy eyebrows knitted together in concentration.

That day he had driven ninety miles on icy roads from his home in Eureka to my riverside cottage to help me with some of the trip's logistics. I respected Jim's advice and appreciated his calm demeanor and breadth of experience. A plethora of expedition knowledge and expertise floated around in Jim's brain and I planned on gleaning every last ounce of that information from him. We had all day to pore over the charts, yet I was anxious that it wasn't enough time. I nervously thumbed through the list of questions I had scribbled on a yellow notepad. For the next eight hours on that late January day in 2010, Jim and I worked methodically through those questions, and the entire one-dimensional route. Fat snowflakes piled up outside and a bitter cold wind formed small wavelets on the still open areas of the ice-encrusted river that sluggishly flowed in front of my cabin.

THE 32 CHARTS that captivated our attention that day were the same charts Jim had used on his trip eighteen years earlier. His generosity had saved me well over a thousand dollars, and his knowledge and past experience with the Inside Passage saved me umpteen hours of trying to figure this stuff out on my own. Most of the charts contained his personal annotations—lightly penciled commentaries of particular importance— many of which were derived from his own Inside Passage mentor and

close friend, Audrey Sutherland, the "grand dame of expedition paddling." Just as Jim, with his experience and knowledge of the Inside Passage, was my inspiration and go-to person, Audrey was his. The queen of going simple and solo, Audrey had started paddling in her fifties and remained a hardcore paddler well into her eighties, logging tens of thousands of miles in British Columbia, Alaska, and Hawaii. Prior to Jim's solo 1992 trip, she had requested he mail her all his charts. Within two weeks, they were back on her protégé's doorstep, neatly organized and annotated. Suitable campsites, fresh water sources, refuges, areas where prudence should prevail, lurking dangers, and stern precautions were duly noted, lightly handwritten in a sharp-pointed pencil. The initials A.S. always followed her notations. I was honored that soon those charts would guide me.

I learned years ago to never call a nautical chart a map unless, that is, I wanted to sound like a landlubber. Charts are nautical roadmaps of the water, designed specifically for marine navigation. As if conspiring to confuse a lone paddler, the nautical chart and the marine compass speak different languages. Due north, whether depicted on a globe, a map, or a nautical chart, is shown as true north or *geographic* north—a representation of how the mapmaker sees the world. I was heeding the rules of *magnetic* north—how my deck-mounted compass sees the world, as the direction from my location to the magnetic North Pole, which sits off-kilter from the top of the world. The compass works because the earth is essentially a gigantic magnet, with its floating needle always swinging toward that massive, slowly moving lodestone. I've always wondered why someone couldn't just dig up the magnetic North Pole and replant it on the top of the world. It would make certain things so much easier.

Seafarers call the difference in the readings between true north and magnetic north variation—landlubbers call it declination. Thankfully, a simple element called a compass rose, superimposed on the chart, does the math for you. Nice touch, chart makers.

STUDYING THE CHARTS and reading everything related to the Inside Passage revealed what I considered four "rites of passage," or crux areas I would encounter—four chunks of open water that I would paddle through that had the potential to be dangerous and that, quite frankly, scared the hell out of me. The first was Boundary Pass, which divides the San Juan Islands from their Canadian cousins, the Gulf Islands. The US-Canadian border runs through the middle of this four-mile, open-water crossing, which is smack in the center of a major shipping lane. Beamy freighters, barges, container ships, tugs, cruise ships, ferries and any conceivable pleasure craft frequent these waters. To compound the freakout factor, Boundary Pass is notorious for considerable current and wind.

My second crux area, the Strait of Georgia, carves a gaping hole between Vancouver Island and the mainland, encompassing over a hundred miles of open water. I was warned that "Ms. Georgia," as I called her, could dish up an attitude in the blink of an eye, and I didn't plan on ignoring her reputation.

The third crux was Cape Caution, an ominous headland perched above the northern reaches of Vancouver Island that faced an uninterrupted sea horizon—all the way to Japan. Just uttering the place name conjured up images of scenes from *The Perfect Storm*. Appropriately named, the cape is exposed to everything the Pacific can and will dish out. This is open-ocean padding with the potential for huge swells and raging surf. And, just to access this area, I would first have to cross Queen Charlotte Strait, another serious body of water with a bad-ass reputation.

The fourth crux was where two large bodies of water collided at the Alaskan border: Dixon Entrance and Hecate Strait. Why they were referred to as "the punching bag of the Pacific Ocean" became apparent when I studied their immensity on my chart. As if to appease myself, I drew a dotted line representing where I intended to cross from British Columbia into Alaska. I wrote in whimsical letters, "You're in Alaska!" Of course, it was smack in the middle of the punching bag.

Skedaddling across Boundary Pass, playing hopscotch across the

Strait of Georgia, clearing the prominent headland of the infamous Cape Caution, and putting Dixon Entrance and the Alaskan border behind me would all be necessary evils. Jim warned me that any or all of these known challenges could be pussycats or roaring lions when the time came, and that other less ballyhooed places could take me by surprise. The best strategy was to be prepared for anything at any time.

APPROXIMATELY THIRTEEN WEEKS LATER, traveling the same route I'd driven hundreds of times to reach the sea, Jim and I hammered over two mountain passes, headed west in my ten-year-old Subaru Outback. Generally those rendezvous were aimed at getting a quick saltwater fix. But this one was different, celebratory. We were heading to the starting line—the same beach that Jim had launched from eighteen years earlier, a beach I would take my first strokes from in two days.

The Rocky Mountains disappeared in my rearview mirror; soon the Cascade Range would loom in the distance, and beyond that, the Pacific Ocean; within that, the Inside Passage. My first resupply box jostled in the back of my car, along with all the accoutrements I would need for this adventure. The other boxes were each choreographed to arrive at their intended destinations at the proper time. Logistically, I had broken my trip into seven legs strung between six resupply points—ports of call that I would paddle into to retrieve a box of supplies that would hopefully be waiting for me, care of general delivery, at its respective post office. I'd calculated the distance between each resupply town and then figured how long it would take me to paddle that distance, duly noting such variables as bad weather, illness, or even injury. These six boxes contained essential items for the next leg of my journey: charts, food, toilet paper, and, of course, chocolate. During the last few weeks of packing up I'd nearly worn the cardboard flaps thin, repeatedly opening and closing them, demanding a visual on something I was already fairly certain I'd seen in that box at least twelve other times. Finally, I had to trust that ninety days of food and gear would be where it needed to be when it needed to be there, and sealed the six boxes shut with sturdy strapping tape. It was a ginormous act of faith.

A missed or misplaced resupply box would be a disaster. To circumvent this, I personally contacted each postmaster to let him or her know about the box and to confirm the proper mailing address.

> POSTMASTER: This package contains essential food and gear for an Inside Passage kayaker. Please hold for her arrival around __/__/__.

I had typeset the words in a 48-point font and printed out six sheets on bright white paper. I taped these, along with large address labels, on the top of each box and neatly printed my name and cellphone number on all four sides.

Jim read a tattered copy of *Moby Dick* while I drove, and my mind wandered to all that I had done to prepare for this journey that suddenly loomed so close. I thought about how single-minded I was in my commitment, progressively lengthening my training paddles, early morning runs, and evening power-yoga sessions. I thought about all the books I'd devoured about the Inside Passage and how I stayed up late under the blue glow of my monitor, sleuthing websites and blogs, gleaning any information I could from those who had gone before me. I had schooled myself on weather, tides, currents, and navigation. For months, I had futzed with gear, waded through more websites, and tended to other seemingly endless logistical tasks. In doing all this I believed that eventually I would be incorrigibly, utterly prepared.

Leg 1   ✈   160 miles   ✈   8 days

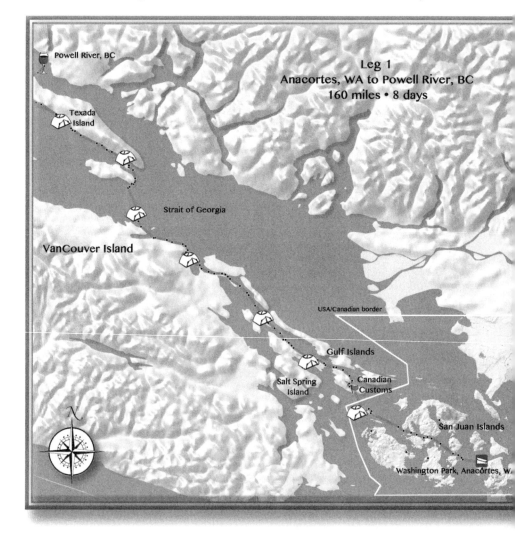

Powell River, BC

Leg 1
Anacortes, WA to Powell River, BC
160 miles • 8 days

Texada Island

Strait of Georgia

VanCouver Island

USA/Canadian border

Gulf Islands

Salt Spring Island

Canadian Customs

San Juan Islands

Washington Park, Anacortes, W.

N

Two

Anacortes, Washington to Powell River, BC

Now is the right time.

—Lotus Sutra

Game On

I STUFFED VARIOUS SHAPES, sizes, and colors of dry bags into my three hatch compartments while six of my best friends looked on. I positioned heavier items such as the tent, food bags, and water as close to the cockpit as possible for ballast; the lighter items went into the far ends. I worked my way through the heaps of gear, squeezing and wedging each item, until it seemed that every molecule of air that was once inside my kayak was now displaced with gear. Meanwhile, my friend Julianna canvassed the area, documenting the dawn of the trip with her camera; her images would provide a glimpse into how this first day was all part of a much bigger thing. A slender woman with deep-set brown eyes and high, angular cheekbones, she had an extraordinary eye for capturing emotions and freezing pivotal moments in a single frame: pensive moments, tear-filled moments, ecstatic moments, milestone moments. Now, on a public beach on the northwest tip of Fidalgo Island, she recorded the manifestation of a journey about to begin.

The sea stretched out before me, the backdrop for my expedition, while Chamellia and I would be the centerpiece. Like a quickly dispersing fog, the weight of ten months of preparation was behind me. Kneeling beside my packed kayak, tending to last-minute chores, my shoulders had lowered, and my smile relaxed, and I looked—and felt—unbelievably happy. It was *finally* time to throw it in the boat and go! All that lay ahead of me for the next three months was the ocean, geography, time—and the gift of possibility.

Every day it would take a leap of faith to push on in a direction I had never been; to have complete confidence in something of which I didn't know the outcome. I was open and willing to accept the risks of being physically, emotionally, and spiritually vulnerable. If a crystal ball had appeared on the beach that day, foretelling my feelings, along with the adversity and hardship I would be encountering, I would have smashed it to smithereens. Uncertainty was part of the adventure and I wasn't about to water down the magic of it all. No, I would simply slide into my cockpit, take my first strokes of the day, and let the boat glide toward Alaska, a chunk of country I had never seen before, and simply let the magic unfold.

Each morning would present me with a clean slate; what I did with my carte blanche was entirely up to me—and the whims of Mother Nature. I had carved out this sliver of time in my life where all I had to do was paddle and tend to the intrinsic chores of an expedition. I had no expectations other than arriving at my next camp for the evening; I fully understood any number of wild cards could change these plans and stop me dead in my tracks.

Still, I felt remarkably confident that day, as if my whole life had prepared me to believe that I could do this. I was ecstatic to start paddling north to Alaska. I looked at my friends standing on the beach that morning and realized what this moment was all about. They'd come from various corners of the earth to be here, to support me, to be a part of this adventure. After christening the bow with the obligatory bottle of champagne, then toasting my safety, my friends stood quietly, clear plastic cups in hand, and patiently listened as I stumbled through a seaside soliloquy:

> *Today I give thanks for this opportunity. To get to this point in time I have built on yesterday's achievements. My mission is to bring all my thoughts, words, and actions into harmony with this journey, this must-do adventure that is encoded within me, this passion, this path that I have affixed my sights on and set my mind to. I choose to accept with a sense of wonder and gratitude the magic of life, and of the experiences I am about to have the privilege of being a part of. I dedicate this day to the expression of that purpose. The Ocean is calling me. This is my Journey. I am forever grateful that you are a part of it.*

Our huddle disbanded after a round of goodbye hugs. It was time to go. I slipped into the cockpit and fastened my sprayskirt around its rim. With a gentle shove from my friend Becky, I left the safety of the familiar behind me, along with the protection of Washington Park and Fidalgo Island. With my bow sighted across Rosario Strait, I swung my paddle in an arc, pierced the water with my right blade, applied power and felt Chamellia glide forward with my first stroke.

Ten strokes later, as I rounded the small public dock, two old salts rigging their fishing boat asked where I was headed. "Alaska," I replied matter-of-factly, with a deliberate pause between my strokes. I could hear my friends chuckle on the beach behind me; my big, toothy grin could have lit up the ocean.

Time to get the road on the show, as my Dad would often say. He was famous for his intentional dyslexisms, no bout adout it. First on the slate; get my butt across the open waters of Rosario Strait and work my way through the San Juan archipelago. Leaving Fidalgo Head and staying well south of the Washington State Ferries route, I made a beeline for the north end of James Island and then ducked into Thatcher Pass. Paddling northwest, I wove my way through the center of the San Juan Islands in a mostly diagonal trajectory. I felt like an adrenalin-spiked greyhound, fresh out of the starting gate. *I'm finally on my way!* I thought. *I am paddling the Inside Passage.* Despite all my nervous energy and my natural high, a sense of calm came over me.

My first official pit stop was at Blind Island, a three-acre marine camping park, designated and maintained by Washington's Cascadia Marine Trail system. Less than twelve miles from my launch site, I was in the middle of the San Juan Islands, one of the most popular sea kayaking destinations in the world, and had the place entirely to myself. I snapped a few photos and shoved off. As I rounded the corner, a Washington State Ferry chugged up the sound on its way to Friday Harbor on San Juan Island.

A patch of bitchy water at Green Point on the eastern tip of Spieden Island snapped me out of my monkey mind, where my body was on autopilot and my mind played hopscotch, skipping from one thought to the next. Like a hyperactive child amped up on Snickers bars, the swirly waters tossed me around as if my boat was a toy, bringing me back to a more attentive state of mind. My bow wrenched first one way, then the other, and I wished I'd paid a little more attention to slack time, that window of opportunity when the tides turn and the waters are the most benign.

Wide-eyed and alert, I lifted my torso tall off my pelvis to afford me the best view of the unfriendly submerged rocks, boils, and colliding currents in front of me. Several hundred strokes later, I released my death grip on the paddle shaft. Before me lay Boundary Pass and Canada; behind me lay the expanse of the San Juan Islands, and to my left lay Stuart Island, the most northwesterly island in that archipelago—and my first campsite of the journey. By seven o'clock that evening I was settled into this inaugural camp, jockeyed for position to cross into Canada the next day. Sublime exhaustion coursed through my body and along with it the satisfaction of knowing I had just propelled my 140-pound body, 52-pound kayak, forty pounds of water, and approximately a hundred pounds of food, clothing, camping gear, electronics, waterproof journals, resource books, first aid supplies, and assorted emergency paraphernalia nearly thirty miles on my first day.

And thanks to a magic orange box that I nicknamed "SPOT," any of my friends who wondered where I was at any point on this journey could have an immediate answer, providing they had a web browser and an Internet connection. About the size of a deck of cards, waterproof, impact resistant—and orange—my SPOT satellite tracking device was a simple yet functional widget that allowed my friends and family to virtually follow me. SPOT functioned like a personal locator beacon so it worked where cellphones didn't. Like having a "Where in the ocean is Susan now?" button, SPOT would send a continuous signal to a satellite, which in turn converted that signal into a single point on Earth. That point on earth and all consecutive points were then converted into a snaking digital breadcrumb trail that was viewable on Google Earth. I could also transmit a canned "I'm OK" message to up to ten of my faithful "SPOT-crew" followers, including Jim. The magic orange box also had a "doomsday button"—a direct line to a third-party search and rescue system. In the event I needed to be seen, heard, or found in an emergency situation, my first line of defense would be my VHF marine radio. If I wasn't able to summon help via this two-way radio or a cellphone, I could summon SPOT's cavalry.

Prevost Harbor, tucked into a northeastern cove on Stuart Island, proved to be a pleasant campsite, and the perfect place to call home on my first night of the trip. Practically a stone's throw from the Canadian Border, I contemplated my first day's adventure and considered what I was up against tomorrow.

One of my four cruxes—Boundary Pass—lurked between my current location and my next landfall. Weather permitting, I would leave the safe haven of Prevost Harbor and check off the first scalawag before the sun cleared Orcas Island. *Goodbye, San Juan Islands, heeellllllo Canada!*

I didn't plan on lollygagging and left early with a slack tide and minimal current. I inhaled deeply, gulped back the lump in my throat, looked both ways and uneventfully slid across the nautical super-highway that had had me skittish for months. All the buildup and self-imposed drama were unnecessary. I wasn't complaining, though—and I wasn't letting my guard down.

I saw a glint on the water, followed by a slight disturbance directly beneath it. As I caught my breath in the lee of South Pender Island, two porpoises oscillated a few paddle lengths from my stern, their small dorsal fins knifing through the water's surface. I wondered if they had accompanied me across Boundary Pass as a token of good luck, then reached for the leather talisman pouch I wore around my neck. It belonged to Jim, and wearing it felt meaningful, perhaps because the items in it were meaningful. They didn't represent luck as much as they represented promise: a raven painted on a small stone from Jim, a quartz pendant from my past, a Guatemalan worry doll from a now distant friend, a silver wave pendant on a black leather cord from a buddy back in Montana. I'd carefully assembled the items in the pouch prior to the trip, and hoped that together they would bring me good fortune. Because the pouch had already safely made it to Alaska and back with Jim, I intended to wear it every day on the water to increase my chances of encountering Lady Luck.

THE NEXT MORNING, while I worked my way toward Canadian customs, Jim sat hunched over his computer, nursing his morning coffee, and posted his first of a long series of what he referred to as "blabs"—informative emails to friends and followers painting a picture of sorts of my adventure as it unfolded.

To undisclosed recipients

Thursday, May 6, 2010
SUBJECT: Susan is on her way

Hi everyone,

I am just sitting here at the computer watching Susan's progress up South Pender Island on her way to Canadian customs. This SPOT is incredible. And just a few minutes ago, got her first "Check-in/OK SPOT message." She will be in Canada now for hundreds of miles, until well north of Prince Rupert.

She got off yesterday morning from Washington Park in Anacortes, launching on the same beach I launched from 18 years ago. The beach seemed virtually unchanged, which is good considering the onslaught some of our wild places have seen in that time span.

She left at about 8:30 in the morning on calm seas, to the well-wishes and not a few tears from six kindred spirits ... It was a joyous, mystical, and spiritual experience to watch one of our own "put to sea," reliving a scene on this planet as old as time. We made sure Susan was sent off in style, with tradition ranging from eagle feathers to champagne.

As she departed, Susan was asked by two fishermen, "Where are you going?" She paused for a moment and then simply said, "Alaska." Did they get it? Probably not.

Before long, Susan had disappeared to a dot on the width of Rosario Strait—having left our world and entered her own. Careful eyes caught the flash of her blade, like the fluke of a whale glistening momentarily in the sun. Then it was time for us to slowly turn away and leave her to her journey ...

Jim
(kinda like the color commentator in the sports booth)

My adventure, you could say, was plugged in, thanks to modern technology, and the SPOT device that made it convenient for my audience to follow along, in real time, whenever they chose. In 1992, Jim had been hard-pressed to find a working pay phone on his trip, and thus was out of touch for weeks at a time. I often wondered how he executed his trip without the technological marvels of Google Earth. My SPOT consortium grew as the trip progressed, and Jim's new hobby of self-proclaimed trip agent further brought my journey to life for many people. In addition to his logistical and resupply responsibilities, he now filled the role of a correspondent of sorts. With a long bony finger on the pulse of what I was experiencing at any given time, Jim had this magical gift of being able to narrate and evaluate my journey as it progressed. He posted emails several times a week, apprising folks of my status. His delightful blabs were filled with warmth and sincerity, knowledge and charm. My fan club seemed to have eagerly awaited each new installment, and they became a collective, remote heartbeat that cheered on my journey as it pulsed up the Inside Passage.

Kayaking Out Loud

"I SAW YOU PADDLING ACROSS," said the Canadian customs agent as he thumbed through my passport. I was standing on a wooden dock in Poet's Cove on South Pender Island. The Canadian and American flags flapped side by side in the breeze directly behind me. The agent directed me to a phone on the outside wall of the small and perfectly square customs building just down the dock, where I spent the next ten minutes answering the usual battery of questions. Although there were several customs agents at the dock, for reasons unknown to me, I still had to be directly linked to another customs agent via phone. I smirked when the voice on the other end asked how long I would be in Canada.

"I don't know exactly," I answered. "I'm paddling through, on my way to Alaska."

"Give me your best estimate, ma'am."

"Sixty days."

"Have a safe trip."

As soon as Canadian customs released me, I slid Chamellia back in the water and eventually rounded the northern tip of North Pender Island. I looked across Swanson Channel and spotted Portlock Point's distinctive lighthouse, perched on Prevost Island. I had hedged my bets crossing the infamous Boundary Pass at slack water, but Swanson Channel, although a shorter, less exposed crossing, was not to be taken lightly. I'd had a hair-raising, heart-stopping encounter crossing this channel a few months earlier, when I was nearly mowed down by a BC Ferry. So close was this ship that I could see the green water split and rise up on her bow, her wake churning the sea like a giant eggbeater, and I could feel the resonating thuga-thug-thug vibrations in my chest from the ship's turbines. This near-catastrophe was a consequence of second-guessing myself—and of my stupidity. Oftentimes multiple ferries cross Swanson Channel, on their way to Vancouver or Sidney, or any number of interisland "milk run" stops. Crossing Swanson's northern end was like negotiating a nautical roundabout. It gave me the heebie-jeebies, stirring up a mixture of dread and urgency.

I fiddled with the squelch button on my VHF marine radio, tuning into channel 11 to monitor the vessel traffic. In this neighborhood, ships transiting busy areas are required to call in, at specific points, to Vessel Traffic Services in Victoria. It behooves a paddler moving at a fraction of their speed to pay attention, because simply looking both ways is sometimes not enough. Failure to monitor the radio had been my previous error, and I wasn't going to let it happen again.

Paddling the Inside Passage isn't exactly a Disneyland cruise around Tom Sawyer Island. To be a prudent mariner other issues needed to be considered, too. What were the currents doing? Which direction was the wind coming from? Would the wind and currents impede my forward progress and prolong my vulnerability to large ships or other hazards? Was there a better area to cross? Should I work the eddies a bit more up or down the channel and then sprint for my life?

All these considerations cycled through my mind. I decided to work my way down the coastline of North Pender Island toward Stanley Point, reasoning that this path would buy me a little more time with ships coming out of Navy Channel and put me just south of the imaginary roundabout. BC Ferries' *Queen of Nanaimo* chugged around the corner, its whirling turbines resonating across the water until I could feel the vibrations beneath me, reminding me of my previous close call, and putting me back in near-panic mode. Although the ferry passed safely in front of me, I switched my radio to channel 16, turned the volume up, nervously stuffed it in my PFD pocket, then snapped the plastic fastek buckle closed with a forceful click. Channel 16 is the go-to channel: all ships are required to monitor this distress, safety, and calling channel around the clock. I rehearsed what I would say in the event I found myself on a crap-your-pants collision course with some behemoth's bow: *To the southbound ship just east of Portlock Point, this is a red sea kayak approximately one mile off your port bow. Please confirm that you see me.* I looked both ways and gave myself a green light, then sprinted to the other side with my hairs standing straight on the nape of my neck.

While I was catching my breath in the safety of Prevost's shoreline, I noticed that the ferry traffic had picked up. My timing had been good— rush hour had just begun, with a parade of ships coming and going. Large, fast, and heavy, these ships commanded two hundred yards to make a course change and nearly a mile to come to a stop. The law of tonnage applied—I knew I'd better stay on my toes and out of the way.

Within an hour I was enjoying buck-naked yoga poses at my campsite on the north end of Prevost Island, embracing the warmth from the rocks beneath me. My muscles, sore from the day's repetitive motion, quietly rebelled. Water gently lapped in James Bay as I settled into a series of downward-facing dogs to work the kinks out of my lower back and shoulders. It was only my second day paddling, but I'd already logged nearly fifty miles. In spite of my aches and pains, I felt strong and was reveling in my solitude. I was in the middle of the southern Gulf Islands, with nary a ship in sight, and it seemed as if I had the ocean all to myself.

Ravens cawed overhead and a slight breeze began to chill my skin. That meant it was time to get dressed. My floating suitcase held a paltry supply of clothing options. *Gee, what to wear tonight? Hmmm, let's see … there's black fleece … or there's … black fleece. Oh wait, here's some blue fleece!* Nonetheless, it was warm and dry, and the setting sun and sea breeze felt pleasant on my now-clothed body. The sun disappeared behind the trees, and I gently rocked back and forth on the ground in my soft camp chair, swaddled in my fleece du jour. A cozy merino wool hat rounded out my ensemble.

Salt Spring Island, named by officers of the Hudson's Bay Company for the cold and briny saltwater springs on its north end, stretched out before me. I looked forward to paddling through familiar waters the next day, weather permitting. I knew Salt Spring Island well, having spent nearly three months there that previous winter. At that time, I was focused on beginning my expedition as fit as possible and the harsh winters and often iced-over waters in Montana made winter paddling problematic. So, I had put out feelers for house-sitting positions on the West Coast, honing in on BC's southern Gulf Islands, an area I had frequented via sea kayak many times on short trips. Soon I had connected with the perfect house-sitting arrangement on Salt Spring, a commitment conveniently encompassing the three months directly preceding my launch date. This small but welcoming home, nestled in a thick grove of massive cedar trees, sat two steep blocks from a mucky lagoon named Walker Hook, where I would often begin my daily training paddles at high tide. When not paddling, I would jog with Tess, a loyal, if not slightly demented Blue Heeler that I was also responsible for. My intention while living on Salt Spring was to train and prepare for the Inside Passage mentally, physically, emotionally, and spiritually.

Tomorrow I would paddle along the striking shoreline of this largest, most populated, and most eclectic of the southern Gulf Islands, past Walker Hook, and past all my old stomping grounds. From my perch on Prevost Island I scanned Salt Spring's eastern coastline, nearly five miles from where I sat. I could barely detect Walker Hook's sharp-cornered headland created by the ninety-degree hook protruding from the northern end of the island. I peered through my binoculars and saw that Walker Hook's long sandy beach was choked with logs, evidence of the power of southerly storms that would thrust anything caught in their fury into the littoral zone. It felt surreal to be heading north through this area where I had dipped my paddle many times in recent months. This time I wouldn't be ducking behind the little hook of land to haul my boat out, like I had so many times before. I wouldn't be hucking my kayak on top of my Subaru and chugging back uphill to the small cedar-shake house to take Tess for a jog. Not this time. I would paddle right by, grateful for the memories, and for the new journey I was on.

A Magic Carpet Ride

I DIDN'T GROW UP around mountains or the sea. I first laid eyes on the vastness of the Atlantic Ocean as a teenager. It was an eye-opening, sunburning, bologna-and-Miracle-Whip-sandwich-eating three-day foray with my mom, her girlfriend, and her girlfriend's daughter. I stood mesmerized on a bright and bustling North Carolina beach, letting my fifteen-year-old eyes and soul absorb the hugeness of it all. The sound of the surf, the soft white sand between my toes, the taste of salt on my tongue, the breeze on my face, and the smell of fish in the air were all new to me. The wide sandy beaches and warm water that I remembered seemed worlds away from where I was now, paddling the fifty-degree waters of the Inside Passage alone, beneath towering cliffs, rain-nourished forests, and soon, tidewater glaciers.

I paddled past shorelines pockmarked with intricate eroded sandstone formations; unusual shelves of rock scoured by water, wind, and sun. Arbutus trees—Canada's only native broad-leafed evergreen— and Gary oak thrived in the sandy, briny soil. I lingered for a short while, then paddled along the privately owned Secretary Islands, finally swinging out to the middle of the channel, and making a beeline toward Reid Island, where I wanted to camp.

With two hours of camp chores ahead of me and a quickly disappearing sun behind me, I gave up scouring Reid Island for possible campsites and settled for a small cliffy islet a stone's throw from its southern tip. Lugging as many gear bags as possible, I negotiated my way up and over a mishmash of rocks and ledges to the top of the island, the only flat spot suitable for camping. At least the tide wouldn't flood my camp—a luxury that I didn't know would be sorely missed later in the trip.

On my third lap down to my kayak, I slipped on a greasy rock. My body went THUD as I landed hard on the unyielding bedrock. I lay unmoving for a moment, no longer admiring the view, stuck in a quasi- crumpled position. Pain seared through my right leg, and I wondered if I had broken it. *Sloppy, Susan, sloppy,* I silently admonished myself as the possibility of aborting the trip on day three fleetingly crossed my mind. "Dumb-ass," I muttered and pulled myself into a better position to assess the damage. I unzipped the leg of my wetsuit and found a gash in my shin oozing bright red blood. A knot the size of a large marble had already formed beneath the gash and bulged above my pasty-white skin, which was hideously pitted from the compression of the wetsuit.

Grunting, I pushed myself up from the ground and put weight on my injured leg. It throbbed like hell, but I confidently diagnosed it as *not broken*. The trip could go on. I continued my descent to the boat, this time a tad more cautiously, to retrieve my first aid kit and water bottle.

I squeezed a stream of water on the gash, irrigating the dirt and debris out of it as best I could, then dabbed on some Neosporin and covered the gash with a super-sized Band-Aid. I may have felt graceful as a swan on the water, but I was a genuine klutz on land. My mind flashed back to the pinched face and beak-like nose of a well-meaning aunt, reminding me I was a child who could, and repeatedly would, trip over thin air. I could never prove her wrong.

I limped back to my camp chair, poured myself a snort of dark rum, and settled in for the evening with my chart on my lap. *Oh my god, I've arrived in Oz*, I thought, finally taking stock of my surroundings and the magic that was exploding all around me. This was not the rum speaking. I was amidst the most incredible plethora of wildflowers I had ever witnessed. My islet was carpeted in colorful masses of purple and yellow wild iris, indigo mountain lupine, and red columbine. Everywhere I looked, I saw an artist's canvas, and I felt deep gratitude to be camping in the middle of it.

The view from camp was equally stunning. My eyes darted east over the water, up and over the jade green knolls and hummocks of Galiano Island's northern end. Galiano blocked my view of the Strait of Georgia, which lay like a sleeping giant on the other side. My awareness lifted higher to Washington state's Mount Baker, standing proud and stark white on the mainland in its 10,781 feet of grandeur. The *Great White Watcher*, or *Komo Kulshan*, as the Salish call it, is one of the snowiest places in the world. She was watching over me, perhaps to keep me safe, in spite of my clumsiness.

Porlier Pass, a pinch of water between Galiano and Valdes Island swirled to the east. Four purple exclamation points were splattered on my chart throughout the pass—printed symbols that generally indicate a warning or a hazard. Over the years, I learned that the more colorful and complicated-looking a chart appears, the more interesting and inherently dangerous it will be to paddle. On a falling tide, the current pours into Porlier Pass from the Strait of Georgia, racking up speeds of eight knots and generating overfalls several feet in height. When the tide floods back into the Strait, it picks up another knot, stirring further trouble in the half-mile opening. Porlier Pass is an area to be traversed with extreme caution. Several ships have met their demise here: The *Del Norte*, a steam schooner, struck a reef in 1868, and the *Point Grey*, a 110-foot steel steam tug, collided with a rock on the western side of the pass. The tug ran aground in 1949, and stood as a stark reminder to passers-through for another thirteen years until a stiff gale decisively rolled it off its perch, where it sank to its final resting place, lying upside down on a forty-foot ledge. A diver's mother lode, both ships are blanketed with anemones, basket stars, sponges, and a wide variety of marine life. In 1972, the *Del Norte* was declared a protected Heritage Site by the BC government. Her wooden hull has long since disappeared, but her paddlewheel, boilers, and engines still lure divers from all over the world.

Trincomali Channel flowed on both sides of me, extending sixteen miles south to Prevost Island, where I had camped the previous night. To the north, the channel flowed about twelve miles until it met the De Courcy island, merging into Pylades Channel, and eventually squeezing through False and Dodd Narrows, two slim fingers of ocean wedged between Vancouver and Gabriola Islands. The water in this area constricts, builds momentum, and spurts forcefully in a focused stream; picture a child holding her thumb over the end of a garden hose. If not navigated at the proper time, it can deliver butt-puckering results. I chose the mile-long False Narrows, the longer and safer of the two, and would pick my way through at the tail end of the flood early in the morning. Then, I figured, it would be smooth sailing for the seven miles to Nanaimo. But slack wouldn't last long, so once again, timing was critical.

Fortunately, I could benefit from the knowledge and observations of thousands of mariners on these waters ahead of me, their knowledge all distilled into one of the great books of this planet, the half-inch slim volume, *2010 Current Tables: Pacific Coast of North America and Asia.* This book is a compilation of numbers and times that describe the behavior of the waters in these parts of the world, and I closely examined the pertinent sections that night.

I wiggled into my sleeping bag as the sun melted into the sea. I intended to study my chart a bit further and propped it against my cocooned thighs so the beam of my headlamp could illuminate its squiggly lines and pale colors. I awoke a few hours later with the chart on my chest and dead batteries atop my head.

Tides and Tribulations

EARLY THE NEXT MORNING, Jim sat rooted in his office chair, coffee cup in hand, his eyes fixed on my SPOT blip that was slowly advancing northward. Well aware of the ticking salt-water clock, he felt compelled to educate my followers on what I was up against that morning and summed up my present state with another email "blab."

> *To undisclosed recipients*
>
> *SUBJECT: Timing*
>
> *Morning everyone,*
>
> *The "clock" is everything on the Inside Passage. One would think that the further from civilization that one progresses the less need for watches, clocks, schedules, departure times, check-ins, travel times, etc. Well, to a certain extent that is true. The trappings of humans do tend to fall away with the simplicity imposed upon a person by a journey on a very large body of water in a very small boat ...*
>
> *Where Susan is, the waters move up and down and back and forth based upon such natural phenomenon as the Earth's distance*

from the sun and the moon. In effect nature does its thing, and we adventurous humans try to keep up with 'er. Sometimes that will mean Susan is up at 3 AM, sleepily stumbling through sopping wet vegetation, gathering her things for a daylight launch. Sometimes that means she must sit for hours to await the return of the water that has vanished with a low tide. Waiting like that is when the paddler intimately gets to understand how a barnacle works or gets incredible insight into the hunting prowess of a bald eagle. Sometimes the clock of nature will force Susan into a dash to catch a break in the weather—even if she is dreadfully tired.

Today Susan will bump up against two of the many time-related phenomena she will encounter this summer. Just before arriving at Nanaimo, she'll slip through a passage called False Narrows in order to avoid another "tidal squeeze point" called Dodd Narrows. These two places are called tidal rapids. They are rapids exactly in the sense that a whitewater river is to a kayaker. In some places they flow at speeds of nearly 20 miles per hour and when they go around an obstruction, such as an island, the water behind the obstruction is perhaps 4-6-8 feet lower than the water before it strikes the obstruction. A kayaker can literally fall down these watery cliffs, which of course is a disaster designed to ruin your day .... They do not suffer fools kindly.

Tidal rapids are truly chameleonic. In most cases, they change their nature four times a day, flooding and ebbing twice each 24 hours. Susan's intention is to go through False Narrows nearly at slack, just before the current changes from the flooding direction (her direction of travel) to ebbing. Knowing her, she will time it perfectly. While the current tables are there, it does truly become a combined skill and art to travel these waters. Susan's route will take her through fewer than five rapids, the most severe coming between her first and second resupply at Hole in the Wall. We'll talk about that in a couple of weeks.

Jim

At 3:30 in the morning, on my fourth day at sea, I crawled out of my tent on my hands and knees to tend to my pint-size bladder. If the seawater in Trincomali Channel was moving at all, my senses could not detect it. Everything around me seemed tranquil and hushed. A golden banana moon dangled from a shimmering sky over Galiano Island. Babying my sore leg, I limped a few steps from my tent and surveyed my surroundings. I noticed, in a very abstract way, that I was completely in love with life and all that surrounded me. I was seeing my world with newly thankful eyes. I saw beauty in everything and fleetingly remembered a time when I did not—a time when I had forgotten how to live in wonder and awe. Now I was able to paddle a marathon; negotiate a difficult landing; haul up mountains of gear; competently set up my camp; enjoy a wonderful, much-earned meal; nurse my wounds; and still maintain a good attitude. The secret, I had learned, was to create this moment not just once, but over and over again. I ducked back into my tent, snuggled deep into my sleeping bag, delighted in how camping is like sleeping with the window open all the time, and drifted back to sleep.

I CRINGED AS MY WARM, DRY SKIN met the cool, clammy rubber of my wetsuit later that morning. It felt like putting on wet underwear every day, only worse. As the rising sun replaced the sinking moon, I enacted the contortions required to put on a rubber suit: I stretched and tugged and yanked it up over my knees and thighs, wriggled it further up my hips, over the bruises and welts and bug bites and aching muscles of my entire body, until my arms slipped through the armholes. In less than a minute my body heat warmed the thin pocket of air trapped between my skin and the cold rubber. I zipped it up, patting all the bulges smooth into place. *There*, I thought, *ready for another day*. Well, almost.

I had arrived at my postcard islet confronted by a series of challenges, and evidently I'd be departing in the same manner. The tide was still rising, quickly covering the nearly nonexistent beach I had landed on the day before. All that remained were the same cliffs I had scrambled over less than ten hours earlier. Boat packing conditions were undesirable at best. My tender leg—and my aunt's voice—reminded me to be careful.

I pondered two options for loading more than one hundred pounds of gear, food, and water into my kayak so I could safely depart. I could carry all my gear down to the sea and precariously perch it on some pointy rocks while I stood in the cold, nearly waist-deep water and packed my boat, or I could pack my boat on a modestly inclined but smooth slope and then slowly and rather carefully lower it the rest of the way. The second alternative seemed more reasonable because it would, in theory, keep me from getting wetter. It turned out that option B had its own set of challenges. Right off, I watched one of my dry bags roll down the hill, bounce off a large boulder, ricochet off another boulder, then promptly plunge into the sea, where it slowly bobbed and wobbled farther from shore. Cussing, I climbed back down to the water, extended my paddle out and coaxed it back in.

On my hands and knees, with my gear bags lined up in a tidy row beside my kayak, I began stuffing the hatches. The slope was narrow and wouldn't accommodate an eighteen-foot kayak sideways, so I was forced to orient it with the bow pointing downhill, facing the sea. Like an unattended vehicle that had slipped out of park and into neutral, my kayak began sliding down the grassy slope without me.

With my best MacGyver impersonation, I rigged a trucker's hitch on my towbelt and tied Chamellia's stern to an uphill tree. Satisfied, I finished shoving gear into the hatches, filling every nook and cranny. I sealed the hatch covers, untied the rope, and assumed a wide-legged stance on my butt near Chamellia's back end. With the stern carry toggle in my hand, I gave her a gentle shove. She started sliding down the grassy slope toward the cliffs as I controlled her descent and speed from the stern. I already had the path picked out once we got to the cliffs—a short, but steep stretch of rocks that were relatively "friendly," smooth, and rounded, avoiding, as much as possible, the barnacle-encrusted nemesis on either side that would halt the descent and could seriously damage a fully loaded kayak. Aided by gravity and still holding onto her stern, still on my butt, I lowered Chamellia down, cringing as her loaded hull creaked and bent over the boulders, until her bow nosed into the seawater. She was floating!

Since I was now six feet above her, getting in was another challenge. Even though I was wearing a perpetually damp wetsuit, the thought of starting off a 21-mile day dripping wet did not appeal to me, so I was determined to not get any wetter. With paddle in hand, I climbed a few steps down toward the water and plunked myself on a craggy rock about four feet above the waterline. Using my paddle to draw Chamellia in parallel to the shore, I jockeyed myself into position to board the vessel. I slowly transferred my weight from the boulder to the cockpit, pivoting my torso toward the boulder as my legs dangled closer to the seat. Once I made contact with my right toe, I wheedled the kayak a tad closer and, thankful for my upper body strength, lowered myself into the cockpit. Lastly, I snapped on my sprayskirt, bid adieu to the postcard islet and paddled toward Nanaimo. Starting off the day with dry feet was my *pièce de résistance.*

My homework from the previous night paid off, allowing me to coast with the flood current through False Narrows. Slack showed up right on cue, but was accompanied by a stiff head wind and an annoying assortment of chop and tide rips that persisted up Northumberland Channel. I'd been spoiled with an easy five-knot speed ever since leaving camp that morning, but for the next ninety minutes I struggled to keep a two-knot pace against the ebb current as I worked my way up the channel. Long, slender kelp fronds formed dense underwater forests, living curtains that streamed toward me, reminding me I was bucking the current, and would be for a few more hours.

In the ninety miles since I'd left Anacortes, I'd slowly worked my way, in an oblique westerly angle, toward Vancouver Island. Now that nearly three-hundred-mile long island was just a few feet off my port side.

Just south of Jack Point and industrial Nanaimo Harbor, an

alarmingly large BC Ferry pulled into the Duke Point terminal about a hundred yards directly in front of me. The *Coastal Inspiration* is one of only three coastal-class ferries, currently the largest double-ended ferries in the world. The "Painted Ladies," as the locals refer to them, operate on the three busiest routes connecting the lower mainland to Vancouver Island.

The surface of the water turned into a froth of white foam, whipped up from the ship's turbines, as if someone had put too much soap in a dishwasher. I paddled a wide arc behind the docked vessel to avoid its raucous backwash. My bow pierced through the suds and the world beneath me was momentarily muffled as I glided over a mumbling sea, toward the city of Nanaimo and my next campsite.

Beyond Duke Point, a flurry of activity and obvious signs of civilization began to assault my senses. I crinkled my nose in disgust at the emissions wafting toward me from two large industrial complexes. The prominent chimneys of the Harmac pulp mill and Canadian Occidental Petroleum, along with cranes, barges, and smaller smokestacks became part of the skyline. I maneuvered around massive log booms, floating rusty barrels, pilings, buoys, and crabbing boats. Float planes buzzed the harbor, small ferries tacked back and forth, pleasure boats and working boats scooted at every angle; we all shared the water beneath mini-skyscrapers looming in the distance. People were everywhere. Laughter and the sound of clinking glasses emanated from the docks, which were redolent with the scent of cheeseburgers and french fries. A middle-aged couple sitting at a round glass table on the dock, dressed in crisp pastel spring attire, smiled and waved at me. Waving back, I breathed deeply and kept paddling.

Under a temperate blue sky, I paddled into Nanaimo, Vancouver Island's second-largest city. Layers of beer-bellied clouds hung over the distant mountains, mimicking fluffed up crocodiles, brontosaurs, and peregrine falcons. Newcastle Island, a provincial marine park, was a stone's throw from the city and would be my home for the evening, and my first developed campsite since leaving Anacortes four days earlier. I chose a campsite close to the water, with a gently sloping, unimpeded foreshore. After last night's landing and this morning's launching debacle, I was grateful that camping here would be a piece of cake. Other than a few tourists who came over on the small foot-passenger ferry from Nanaimo to have a quick look around, and the caretaker who took my camping fee, the place was deserted.

I had balked at the $16 camping fee, but once I soaped up and began reveling in a long, hot, heavenly shower, I knew it was worth every copper penny. Blow-drying my hair under the hand dryer was priceless. I surveyed myself in the warped bathroom mirror and noticed about sixty percent of my body covered in a rash. The combination of nasty neoprene, the constant movement that produced constant heat, and the salty sweat that mercilessly mixed with saltwater was to blame. My hands, blistered and swollen, were raw and bloody, and my shin was slightly infected. I dabbed some more Neosporin on it, got out a fresh Band-Aid and called it good. Jim had warned me that my body would rebel, but he also told me it would slowly adapt. I fervently hoped it would do so soon.

Back at camp, towel still in hand, I toyed with the idea of making the two-minute paddle back to the marine pub I had seen earlier. An adult beverage and juicy burger sure sounded good, but I had packed plenty of tasty, nutritious food and needed to eat down some of my reserves to lighten the load. Besides, having a picnic table to set my camp stove on and eat at were additional luxuries I needn't take for granted. While I was chowing down on buttery pasta wheels with rehydrated snap peas, peppers, and tomatoes smothered with parmesan cheese, I watched my first cruise ship ply north up the Strait of Georgia.

A few hours later I was treated to a flaming sunset while the same banana moon dangled above a swirling tapestry of clouds and a peaceful sea. The island was all mine for the night, an amusing contrast to the bustling city that lay behind me.

I nibbled on a hunk of dark chocolate infused with cherries and almonds, studied my charts, tides and currents data, and began to worry about crux number two—getting my butt across the Strait of Georgia.

I was on the verge of dealing with one of the most significant passages in my entire journey, and it was coming tomorrow, day number five. I would paddle a total of 64 miles from my current campsite to the mainland on the other side; nearly eighteen of those miles were open water. I was poised to cross from south to north, and intended to break this section into several chunks as needed. This crossing had been in the back of my mind since the inception of the trip, and I'd been paying daily attention to the forecast, looking for a safe weather window. I wasn't entirely certain that I had it. I listened to my marine weather radio: *Wind variable ten knots increasing to southeast ten to fifteen early this afternoon then diminishing to light Monday morning. Wind becoming northwest fifteen Monday afternoon.*

The weather report sounded reasonable, but I was feeling a bit uneasy knowing that distance was a prime player. I wasn't dealing with a rigid time factor that currents can impose, but instead I was dealing with what my reference book, *Kayaking the Inside Passage*, called a meteorological phenomenon responding to actual solar conditions. In other words, the conditions change during the day as the air heats and causes wind and, ultimately, waves. The most unstable times for this generally are in the afternoon, so logically on a crossing of this sort, one tries either for early or late in the day. The latter sometimes pushes a camping kayaker up against darkness—a potentially serious situation.

Dire Straits

I'D ALWAYS BEEN A DEFIANT LITTLE SHIT. I was a tough and resilient tomboy, full of piss and vinegar, having grown up with an older brother and a host of rowdy male cousins. Girls my age were scarce in my neighborhood, and I knew nothing about the boundaries of gender, defying my parents when told I couldn't do something simply because I was a girl. *Phooey,* I had thought and tenaciously held my own with all the rough and tumble boys. I'd ride my bike on the road even though I was frequently scolded to stay in the driveway. I'd march straight down the hill, through the meadow, and into the woods to the brook I was forbidden to visit. With squinting eyes that matched my furrowed brow, hands shoved in pockets, feet rooted to the ground, I appear boldly disobedient in many a childhood photo. It's not clear to me where this defiant gene came from, but gearing up to tackle Ms. Georgia's moody waters, I wondered if I was being dumb-assed defiant in paddling the IP solo. Would piss and vinegar mix with saltwater?

For the next three days, I leapfrogged my way across the Strait of Georgia, using various islands as stepping stones, safety nets, and respites. Blue sky, waves, swell, sea birds, seals, and a beautiful archipelago of islets and islands were part and parcel of my crossing—as were a strong in-your-face wind and opposing tide. As I stabbed my paddle into the water, I laughed at my naiveté and mocked the words I had written the prior year regarding my hopes for this adventure: *...To feel the rain on my eyelashes, to hear the thunderous boom of crashing waves, to taste the saltwater on my lips, to breathe in the pervasive aroma of the sea ...* Hah! Well, Susan, how does it feel to have cold bucketfuls of saltwater slap your face and sting your eyes every few minutes? Taste good? Like that salt caked on your eyelashes? Nice. The thunderous boom of crashing waves? A bit unnerving, eh? Careful what you wish for, girl. Enjoy the dead fish odor, and for god's sake, keep paddling.

When a windsurfer blew by me at breakneck speed on the first day of the crossing, his red and white sail filled with the wind blowing through Nanoose Harbor, I had a hunch I was in for a rough ride. Hooting and hollering, thumbs pointing up, caramel-blond hair streaming back, he was having the time of his life. I, on the other hand, had a white-knuckle grip on my paddle. Before I left the shelter of Vancouver Island's shoreline, I wondered if committing to the crossing at this moment was a bad idea. Whitecaps were building out in the main channel, but the wind didn't seem atrocious and the weather report still sounded reasonable. I decided to go for it.

I looked both ways, then up at the sky and down at the water, and pushed off, ready to deal with whatever Neptune tossed my way. I needed a block of time with decent conditions—like an interstate running through eastern Montana—straight and clear where I could just floor it. I didn't get it.

Thick, swollen waves rolled under my hull, yawing me back and forth. The wind and opposing tide began to freshen. My spirits sank with the deep trough of each passing wave and my speed steadily grew slower. I knew it was going to be a long slog. I was nearly overcome by the gut-wrenching effort I had to sustain, yet if I stopped paddling I would be pushed backward, like a bully's target on the playground, losing all momentum and the little bit of ground I had just gained. My dreadfully slow pace felt like a seafaring deadlock, advancing me less than three inches on the chart, equivalent to about four miles in real time. Technically, I wasn't even truly in the thick of the strait yet; I was merely crossing Ballenas Channel, and it was giving me a run for my money.

I surveyed my options: Keep going, or go back. It seemed pretty simple. I could propel myself into an escalating, potentially deadly sea or I could high-tail it back to Southey Island, safely tucked along Vancouver Island's shoreline. If it was that simple, then why was my decision so difficult? After all, it was only my life at stake. Being alone in rough seas, on a long crossing, in a major shipping channel—this was all serious business. The annoying critic lurking on my shoulder said to buck up and push on. The voice of reason chattered incessantly about how this was a bad idea, and implored me not to push my luck.

I remembered my friend Doug's advice on my last visit to upstate New York. We stood next to each other in his driveway, snow shovels in hand, having just freed my rental car from the confines of the previous night's blizzard. The engine idled, the wipers flip flopped, and snowflakes landed and melted on the black vinyl of the open car door. With a concerned look in his eyes, Doug placed both hands on my shoulders and said, "When you find yourself in a crisis situation, Susan, slow down, study your options, and be patient!" I gave his wife Linda, my best friend, one last hug and slipped behind the steering wheel, soon merging onto the New York State Thruway.

I had told Doug that I would heed his advice when dealing with adversity, and now I was faced with honoring that promise, and allowing the sea to teach me patience. After clawing my way across the open water for more than two hours, I called "uncle" on South Ballenas Island. The small cove and sandy beach on the northern end of this chunk of rock was protected from the northerly winds by North Ballenas Island. I was dispirited by the piffling distance I had covered, but thankful to be off the water and out of the wind. I quickly set up camp, grabbed a chocolate bar, and whisked my cellphone out of its protective case. It was Mother's Day and I had two bars on my cellphone. Sea lions barked in the distance below the lighthouse on North Ballenas Island. I dialed the New York nursing home and settled into my camp chair.

I could hear the phone clatter to the floor on mom's end as it slipped out of her hands, like it often does. I could also hear her labored breathing as she bent over to pick it up and bring it to her ear. "Happy Mother's Day!" I said, with the most upbeat tone I could summon.

"Hi sweetheart. How are you? Where are you now?" her raspy voice asked on the other end.

"I'm doing wonderful, Mom," I said. "Really enjoying my trip." Then I quickly diverted her attention by asking her about the weather. I half-listened to her response, half-poked at the bandage on my shin, and kept a wary eye on the sea. After a few more moments I told her I'd call again in a couple of weeks, reminding her that my cell coverage might be intermittent for a while. I tucked my phone back in its case, happy that I'd made contact with her, but worried about the longer periods ahead when I would have no cell coverage, and how that would affect her anxiety.

After dinner, as two squares of dark chocolate melted in my mouth,

I ducked into my tent, physically and mentally exhausted from my most arduous day at sea thus far, suspecting worse was yet to come.

The wind blew strong out of the north all night. At five a.m., I climbed out of bed to assess my situation. Whitecaps surrounded me, whipped up from the 25-knot winds—too much for my comfort level. The sea's scare tactics were working. I sighed and went back to bed. Restless, I got up again at six o'clock and listened to my marine radio. The digital voice on my hand-held device sounded somewhat reassuring: the barometer was holding steady and conditions weren't predicted to worsen.

I paced like a caged cat up and down the beach, ignoring the knots forming in my stomach, then climbed to the top of a rock outcropping to better scan the ocean's mood, all the while singing the lyrics to The Clash's *Should I Stay or Should I Go*.

I hemmed and I hawed, dithered and dallied, but finally, after much deliberation, I decided to leave the safety of the Ballenas Islands and head into Ms. Georgia's maw for the second time. A six-mile open-water crossing lay between Ballenas Islands and Lasqueti Island, my first planned landfall that morning. The southeast tip of Lasqueti Island was almost due north of me according to my plastic-encased chart and was perfectly positioned for a break about two-thirds of the way across the channel. If conditions remained stable, I planned to make Lasqueti a rest stop, before continuing on to Texada, another four miles away. The largest island in the strait, Texada spans nearly thirty miles northwest to southeast, with an average width of five miles, and would hopefully cushion the wind as I drew nearer to it.

The variation for my current location was 22 degrees. I was forced to offset my bow another twenty degrees to the west to compensate for the northwesterly wind that was blowing down the strait. If I tried to shoot straight across, the wind and tide would flush me too far south and east, where I would be dangerously exposed in the more open waters. I ferried my way across, combining the heading and speed of my boat with the direction and speed of the wind and current so I could cross in a relatively straight line to my destination.

I paddled those six miles on a 312-degree bearing, constantly eyeballing the big numbers on the dome-shaped compass mounted on my red bow, as waves crashed over it. The wind had picked up again, ushering in a light rain. Conditions deteriorated as I neared mid-channel, and my GPS registered the hundred-mile mark. There was no time to enjoy my first milestone, because now, instead of the constant headwind I had endured the day before, Mother Nature and Old Man Sea joined forces, treating me to stern quartering seas—a sea kayaker's nemesis. Three-foot waves heaved up my stern and skidded it sideways, while the splash from subsequent waves slapped the side of my face. I reminded myself to keep a wary eye out for the bigger sets.

Suddenly a rogue wave hissed and broke underneath my hull. I instinctively slapped the water with the back side of my blade, a stabilizing maneuver referred to as a low brace. In between bracing, I was forced to crank out starboard sweep strokes as hard as I possibly could, lest I miss my mark on Lasqueti by miles.

I rotated the knob on the right side of my cockpit to lower my skeg deeper into the water, hoping it would counteract the effects of the wind and waves and allow me to travel in a straighter line. A fin-like device that deployed under Chamellia's hull near the stern, the skeg was virtually useless that day. Unlike a rudder, I couldn't steer with my skeg; it merely helped with directional control. On that particular day, on that exasperating stretch of water, I would have *killed* for a rudder to save me the inordinate amount of time and energy I spent on edging and bracing, sweeping and power paddling. Steering with my feet and putting all of my energy into simply paddling forward all of a sudden made a lot of sense.

The effect of the wind and tide against my hull was like paddling on a sea of maple syrup; all the tedious body-English in the world helped diddly-squat. My bow was stuck in one direction but I needed to point it further north and lessen my exposure—and mental anguish—in a major shipping lane. The Strait of Georgia was kicking my butt!

My hardscrabble effort lasted three strenuous hours, but I finally made it to the southern tip of Lasqueti, and soon after, to the protection of a smattering of islands in Sabine Channel, between Lasqueti and Texada Islands. But my paddle was still far from a cakewalk. The wind, although somewhat buffered, did not relent. It wasn't until I finally scraped up on Texada Island, pitching my tent in the shadow of Mount Shepherd, that the wind no longer cuffed my ears.

My campsite that night, on a cobble beach wedged between rocky bluffs, provided me with sweeping views up and down the strait. Ms. Georgia's mood had softened, as if she'd finally exhausted herself and decided to hang out like a dog, tongue lolling, at my feet. My beautiful surroundings and a respite from the wind imparted a deep sense of gratitude in me—perhaps more than I ever had before. That night I wrote about this gratitude in my journal:

It is beautiful and quiet here. I have not felt lonely whatsoever, rather I am enjoying magical moments of solitude. The journey thus far is amazing. I had no idea it would feel this way. So freeing. So independent. So grateful. I feel so small, but so grand. I try not to look at the big picture too often as it sometimes overwhelms me— this whole grandiose scheme. But tonight, from the perspective of where I sit—the idea of the grandiose layout is what's intoxicating for me. I envisioned this ten months ago. I planned it. Now I am living it! This is my Life. One section, one day, one stroke at a time. Stay focused, Susan. Stay in the moment. Cherish every moment. Be grateful. Be full. Be alive. Live. Breathe. Paddle.

Emerald Jell-O and Short Stacks

"CAN YOU GUYS EVEN SEE US, or are we just speed bumps out there?" I asked Captain Lance Lomax, who piloted the *Northern Expedition*, one of the largest vessels in the BC Ferries' fleet. Lance had tracked me down at Shelter Point Regional Park, my second campsite on Texada Island. I was erecting my tent when a blue Ford pickup rolled slowly into the campground and wound its way toward me.

"Are you the woman who's paddling to Alaska?" asked the man stepping out of the truck and gently closing the door behind him. He wore rust-brown Carhartts, a dark blue T-shirt, and tan leather sandals.

"Wow, word travels fast in these parts!" I laid my tent poles back on the ground. "Yup, guilty as charged," I quipped and turned to face him. He was a tall man with broad shoulders, nut-brown hair atop an oval face, and a convivial smile that matched his unassuming manner.

"My name's Lance. I ran into Reg and Denise at the store and they told me about your trip. I was curious to meet you." He surveyed my kayak bow to stern.

Reg and Denise were a middle-aged couple I'd met earlier that day at Shingle Beach, during my lunch stop on the west side of Texada. I had been sitting on a stump, balancing some cheese and crackers on each thigh, when their rusted white pickup came bouncing down the dirt road toward the ocean. Clearly curious about what a lone kayaker was doing out there, they had walked down to chat for a spell. It occurred to me that since I'd left Anacortes, other than a brief conversation with the customs guy at South Pender, I had yet to converse with strangers about exactly what I was doing. As I rattled off the details of my trip to Reg and Denise, I was amazed at how relaxed and matter-of-fact I sounded. How I was going to paddle to Alaska, that I wasn't going to stop until I ran out of ocean in Skagway. I could hear and feel the passion in my voice that I felt for the journey, still in its infancy. They were astonished that I had started in Anacortes; they were amazed I had made it to this point on Texada in seven days; they were dumbfounded that I chose to paddle solo.

Later that day they had run into Lance somewhere on the island and told him there was this wild woman paddling a red kayak all the way to Alaska. This must have kindled Lance's interest and prompted him to take the time to find me.

While we visited, I learned that Lance owned a house on Texada, in Gillies Bay, but that he had recently moved to Nanaimo, and just happened to be back on the island checking on the house. At first, Lance casually mentioned that he *worked* for BC Ferries. It turned out he was in ultimate command of a whopping 507-foot ship, taking up to six hundred passengers and crew on the fifteen-hour cruise from Port Hardy to Prince Rupert and back, with stops at Klemtu, and Bella Bella, all ports of call I would stop at on my way to Alaska. Lance's ship was built in Germany in 2008 and arrived in British Columbia in March 2009, and was regarded as the "crown jewel" of the BC Ferries' fleet. It weighed eighteen thousand tons.

It blew my mind to visualize the difference in size of his vessel compared with mine. If we placed them facing bow to bow, Lance's ship would loom over me by nine stories, blinding me with its massive white hull. Resembling a spacecraft, its crisp bow could part the seas—and my kayak—like a Pulaski on steroids. It was capable of 21 knots, while I muddled along at three or four.

At that moment, my childhood school bus driver's large thumb flashed through my mind. I remembered this now because he would crush the bodies of unsuspecting wasps with it. When some kid shrieked in fear, Clarence would park the bus, raise his large frame up out of his cracked vinyl chair, and slowly, in an almost terrifying and painful way, walk down the aisle, then reach over the now-hushed child. While the wasp thorax rattled against the pane glass window, he would place his robust thumb squarely on the trapped wasp and crush the life out of it. The *Northern Expedition* could crush my kayak much like that thumb if I failed to respect the law of tonnage.

Since a big portion of my route up the IP was also a major thoroughfare for ferries, I bombarded Lance with questions, eager to allay my fears about run-ins with big ships. *Can you see us? Do we show up on your radar? How quickly can you alter your course? How long does it take you to stop that thing?*

But Lance's answers and gentle demeanor immediately put me at ease, assuaging most of my fears of getting run over by big ships. He told me the bridge is the room from which the ship is commanded and is manned by an officer of the watch (OOW). The mission-critical component of this OOW is to look for what doesn't belong. This guy or gal is always on the bridge looking for obstacles in the ship's path, such as kayakers, drunken recreational boaters who decide to take a siesta in the middle of the shipping channel, or stalled fishing boats. Skinny fiberglass kayaks are poor reflectors for the ship's radar, Lance told me. I could only hope the OOWs were keen on scanning the water's surface in front of that gargantuan bow for our presence.

"And don't be shy about using that radio of yours," he urged. "The sooner you can make us aware of your presence, the better. Besides, we enjoy the communication," Lance said with a wink. He helped me set up my VHF radio so I could easily communicate with the bridge of these big ships, and refreshed me on proper radio protocol. Then he handed me his business card and cordially offered a tour of his ship if the opportunity presented itself.

"I'd be honored, Lance!" I said, envisioning following this handsome man dressed in a crisp white shirt beneath a jet-black jacket, adorned with four gold stripes on each sleeve, as he explained the functions of a myriad of panels and instruments on the bridge and in the main control room.

With a firm handshake—and knee-buckling eye contact—Lance said goodbye and wished me a safe trip. "I'll be sure and tell the Navigating Officers to keep a look out for any 'speed bumps' trying to hail us on the VHF." I stood motionless beside my half-erected tent, holding his business card in my hand, and watched this man entrusted with a $133 million vessel, disappear from my view in his tumbledown truck. I tucked his card into my wallet, behind my passport and Montana driver's license and stashed it deep inside my day hatch. Then I walked over to my tent, snapped the shock-corded aluminum poles together, stuffed them through the nylon sleeves and finished the job.

THAT NIGHT MS. GEORGIA remained serene. Her emerald-Jell-O waters had transitioned to muted bronze and gold as the sun set deeply behind Vancouver Island. Tomorrow, weather permitting, I'd paddle into Powell River, my first resupply town. I had chocolate ice cream on my mind.

But the Strait of Georgia hadn't let me out of her grip just yet, and I would work for that ice cream until the bitter end. Gearing up for another stint of rough water the next morning, I slid my dry top over my head, carefully separating the latex neck gasket with my fingers to reduce the tugging effect on my long hair. I stepped into my neoprene sprayskirt, pulling it up well above my waist, and then completed my ensemble by donning the PFD. Attached to the front of my PFD was a large diver's knife, storm whistle, and hand-held compass; a long black antenna stuck out of the pocket that housed my VHF radio; and perched on my shoulder was a bright orange strobe light. A 1.5-liter hydration bladder was attached to the back of the PFD with black webbing. Tucked into the holster that held the bladder were "bail-out items" which theoretically would keep me more comfortable or perhaps even alive in the event I became separated from my kayak at sea. Chemical blocks of fire starter, a flint lighter, a butane lighter, a silver space blanket, a nearly microscopic emergency stove that ran on pellets, a handful of pellets for said stove, a small metal cup, chia seeds that were rumored to have kept Aztec warriors alive during their conquests, iodine tablets to treat questionable water, and one high-calorie energy bar were all strategically wedged into two quart-size Ziploc bags stowed inside the holster on my back. I resembled the female mariner version of Rambo.

From the northeast tip of Texada Island, keeping an eye on the small ferries going back and forth from Blubber Bay to Powell River, I set a twenty-degree bearing and bounced across the remaining four miles to Willingdon Beach campground with choppy quartering seas and enough wind to keep it interesting.

Making it to Powell River was one of many milestones I would experience on this trip. I was in great spirits regardless of the inevitable aches and pains I'd suffered by wrenching my body from civilization. Up until that point, Powell River had just been a pushpin on a six-foot map on my wall. Now I stood, elated, in line at the post office to retrieve my first resupply package, tangible proof that I had made it this far. Others were buying stamps or mailing utility payments while I, on the other hand, was in the midst of an adventure. I immediately recognized the large cardboard box the clerk carried from the back of the post office and managed to restrain my euphoria as he handed it to me over the counter. Christmas in May! With a bounce in my step, I carried the heavy box back to the campground, all of it downhill with one slight detour—the ice cream stand I had spotted on the way up. I ordered a large chocolate cone dipped in chocolate and savored every lick and bite as it melted down my face and dripped onto my shirt. I didn't care one iota how sticky my face got because the stream of a hot shower would soon be spilling over it.

Entry to the small cement building that housed the showers and laundry room at Willingdon Beach Campground required a four-digit code that I had acquired from the campground host when I checked in after arriving at the beach. I punched in the four secret numbers, pushed open the heavy steel door and entered the tiny room. Standing on cold concrete, I fished an assortment of electronic devices and respective chargers out of my daypack as I commandeered the washroom. Steam filled the room while my clothes spun in the washer, I scrubbed in the shower, and my gizmos charged on the back of the toilet. I threw back my head and laughed at the luxuriousness of it all.

The next morning found me holding a sticky menu encased in thick plastic that showcased pictures of country-fried steak and eggs, lumberjack omelets, and a hungry mariner's short stack. Dishes clattered in the background, the smell of cheap coffee filled the room, odd snippets of conversation floated toward me, and Steppenwolf's *Magic Carpet Ride* blared from the kitchen of Starvin' Marvin's, Powell River's finest greasy spoon.

I was ravenous and would have eaten my napkin if it had been dusted with chocolate. And I was almost giddy that I had a napkin in the first place, along with a real plate, sparkling silverware, and a thickset water glass. I ordered coffee, a cheese and mushroom omelet with hash browns and crunchy sourdough toast, a side of fruit, and a short stack of pancakes. I also asked the waitress if she could bring me a blueberry muffin right away with my coffee—as a sort of an appetizer. As she approached with two platters of food, she awkwardly glanced sideways, probably wondering where this other person was that I had also ordered for. Considering the large amount of calories I had burned in the last eight days, I figured a little proportion-distortion wouldn't hurt anything. I used my fingernail to peel open the single-serving containers, slathered my three pancakes with butter and maple syrup, then smeared my toast with peanut butter and strawberry jam, followed by a thin layer of orange marmalade. Then I rolled up my fleece sleeves and dug in. By my third cup of coffee, my blue-speckled formica table top was littered with sugar packets, individual creamer cups, containers of jam, peanut butter, honey, and butter. Feeling sedated from my food overdose, I sheepishly apologized as the waitress cleaned up the aftermath around me. I'd done enough damage by then and practically waddled over to the public library to rent a computer and fill all my faithful followers in on my adventure thus far.

To undisclosed recipients

May 13, 2010
SUBJECT: Gratitude from the intrepid paddler

HELLO TO EVERYONE FROM THE INTREPID PADDLER,

This is Susan—alive and well and having the time of my life! I am taking a much needed rest day in Powell River, my first resupply point. ...I am holding up well. Body is adapting to the aches and pains that move around. The first fifteen minutes paddling each morning my shoulders and back scream, but then the body parts get into a groove and the pain miraculously dissipates.

...My good friend Jim Chester has a new hobby and I am elated about it! My personal correspondent—who woulda thunk? He is doing a great job and I hope you all will encourage him to continue being the verbose and enlightening chap that he is.

...I feel blessed that I am capable of doing something like this. I am making good progress. 139 miles so far—only about 1100 to go! I paddled 26 nautical miles the first day—basically a marathon on the water, followed by seven more 15- to 20-mile days, without a break. I am nine days into the journey and it seems like it has just flown by. It will go soooo quick. I intend to cherish every moment. Weather looks like it is going to hold for about another week. How lucky is that?!

...David—I am honored that your fifth-grade class is following the trip. What a fantastic class project! I feel like my friends and loved ones are tuning into "Susan's Adventure Series," as narrated by Jim Chester ... "Tune in tonight to see where she's at, what her trials and tribulations of the last day or so were, and what she's up

against in the near future ..." LOL :-)

Darn, time's up, gotta go. Love you guys. Will stay in touch as much as I can.

XOXO Susan

Leg 2 ⟶ 175 miles ⟶ 7 days

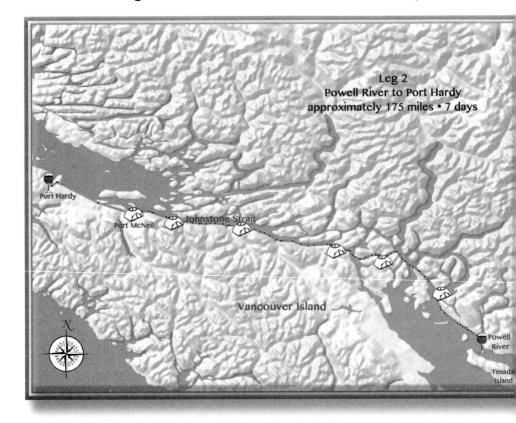

Leg 2
Powell River to Port Hardy
approximately 175 miles • 7 days

Port Hardy

Port McNeil

Johnstone Strait

Vancouver Island

Powell River

Texada Island

Three

Powell River
to Port Hardy

*Beyond the very extreme of fatigue and distress,
we may find amounts of ease and power we never dreamed
ourselves to own; sources of strength never taxed at all
because we never pushed through the obstruction.*

—William James

Slack Tide

PORT OF CALL, port of entry, port in a storm, port side, port wine, strong and sweet from Portugal. Ports, also referred to as harbors, docks, havens, marinas, anchorages, and moorages lie scattered along the Inside Passage. Seen from a satellite on a black night, they look like single stars, street-squared constellations, or fragments of the Milky Way fallen to earth. To list them all sounds like the Johnny Cash song, *I've Been Everywhere*, just with different place names.

Associated with ports are cranes, tugs, harbor pilots, canneries, canals, customs, cruise ships, ferries, yachts, and every recreational and working boat imaginable. Ports are strategically positioned to serve that interface between land and sea, to optimize access to land and navigable water for boats both big and small, as well as to provide shelter from the storm, a place for seafarers to resupply, reintegrate into society, and socialize.

Ports also bring in a promenade of cruise ships filled with people—sometimes thousands of people—that I needed to plan around. Most cruise ships offer lavish suites, sophisticated five-star dining, extensive entertainment, infinity pools, spa facilities, gambling casinos, and a host of endless amenities. Some of the bigger ocean liners boast tennis courts and golf courses on their top decks—a fetching piece of real estate for patrons wishing to work off some extra calories. These ultra-luxury vessels, with their own water desalination and sewage treatment plants, don't need to resupply en route. The only reason their passengers have for interacting with ports is to briefly enjoy the tastes of local geography, local history, local kitsch, and the more tangible tastes of local food and beverages. As if modeling themselves after nature, the ships berth, and the people flow down the gangplank like a flooding high tide. Then, when their port time is up, like a departing tide, the travelers ebb back onto their mother ship until the next port. As a solitary kayaker, I quickly learned the best time to accomplish my goals while in port was between these human tidal exchanges.

I have yet to hear of a kayak expedition up the Inside Passage that was totally self-contained, although there may have been some that I'm not aware of. For most paddlers, including myself, ports are resupply depots—where we replenish our food, booze, toilet paper, coffee, and energy level. Ports are where we ship back failed equipment and seek out replacements if necessary. They are where we gather in a new set of navigation aids and return those we've exhausted. And perhaps most importantly for some paddlers, ports allow a brief reconnection with civilization that reminds them they are not alone. For me, this was a mixed blessing because solitude was at the heart of my journey.

At Powell River, the first of my six resupply ports, I promptly gathered the last leg's flotsam and jetsam to mail back to Jim: seven nautical charts, a broken NavAid held together with tape, a Newcastle Island Provincial Marine Park brochure, some personal notes and mementos, six pieces of sea glass, and five pretty stones.

Over the course of the summer, if all went as planned, I would stop at five more ports: Port Hardy, Shearwater, Prince Rupert, Ketchikan, and Petersburg. These six locales, custodians of my respective resupply boxes, would champion my adventure paddling north. Unlike IP travelers who entrust their route and logistics to a cruise line or ferry, I was completely reliant on myself and on all the advance planning I had done. I relied on my boxes arriving on time and intact: the next leg of my journey depended on it. I wouldn't have the time or the money to scurry around one of these unfamiliar ports to round up replacement items. The biggest catastrophe, had a box not shown up, would have been the loss of Jim's charts. The charts could be replaced, but his and Audrey's priceless annotations could not.

RESUPPLY CHORES WERE an important part of my routine and a welcome break from paddling and camping every day. Routine tasks included a trip to the post office, a trip to the neighborhood grocery store, eyeballing the charts for the next leg, making minor boat and gear repairs, washing my putrid clothes, soaking three layers of dirt and grime off my body, sleeping with a pillow beneath my head, and consuming untold calories. "Port-sport-eating"—eating my way through these ports of call—became an immensely satisfying pastime during these brief pauses in my journey. I ate as though I was refueling my tank for the next leg of my journey, seeking foods with a high fat content, and chowing down on more cheeseburgers, french fries, and pizza than I'd consumed over the previous decade.

But ports are not all fun and games. The transition into ports can be problematic at times. Pulling into an unfamiliar port, I must first find a place to park my home. My food, water, clothes, medicines, books, bed, transportation—essentially my whole existence—is suddenly a disconnected burden. I can't carry it around with me. I can't pitch my tent on front lawns. I have to leave everything I own out on a dock assailed by rain, wind, saltwater, seagulls, and the eyes of strangers. The post office is often miles from the marina. A hotel costs upwards of $150 a night. There are tourists crawling all over the place. The bank machine wants to charge me for withdrawing my own money.

And I sometimes tired of answering the same questions over and over: "You going to fit all that into *there*?" (Invariably, the guy asking has a hundred-foot yacht.) "Where do you stay in between towns?" "How long is your kayak?" "Have you seen any bears?" "Aren't you scared?" "Are you lonely?"

Some folks thought I was crazy attempting something like this by myself, others respected the journey I was on. And others, I could tell, were seduced by the romance, the sheer adventure of it. I routinely answered their questions with patience and pride, but sometimes I hurried through an explanation, too tired to care, or not wanting to share the emotional highs and lows in the fleeting moments of those brief encounters.

Sometimes I considered avoiding ports altogether, but the fact that I usually hadn't showered in at least a couple of weeks mattered a lot. So I learned to dash in and out of ports more quickly, becoming more efficient in them. Happy to be clean, dry, rested and restocked, I was equally happy to be settling deep into the cockpit again, paddle in hand, pushing away from port. *Ahh, back in the saddle*, I'd think. On the watery trail again.

This antisocial behavior on the water was not entirely disparate from the rest of my life. I had always craved solitude, and I often got it. My mask, developed at a young age to camouflage my true feelings, allowed me to be a shadow, to stay in the background, to be alone. My coping mechanisms taught me that if I was elusive and didn't bring attention to myself, didn't offer an opinion, that I wouldn't be hurt. Like many people, I justified the existence of my masks for a variety of reasons: an inability to deal with my feelings, to avoid closeness, to protect myself, to manipulate others, to hide my insecurities or inadequacies, to maintain a so-called image. By projecting my character armor for so long I had lost touch with my true self. As an adult, I genuinely wanted to be heard, to be acknowledged. But how to get the ears, eyes, hearts, and souls of others pointing my way escaped me. While on the IP, I didn't feel like I had to protect myself like I did as a child, yet I still yearned to be more complete, more tuned in to who I was as a person, more capable of giving back to others, and dealing with life's day-to-day challenges. I knew there was no silver bullet for these quests, but I hoped that all the time for reflection and soul-searching I'd experience on the IP would help.

As a child, I wasn't one for entertaining others and struggled with connecting with other people. I'd grown up like an only child; my adoptive brother, ten years older than I, had moved out of the house before I turned nine. A latchkey kid, I essentially did what I wanted, when I wanted, at least until my parents returned home from work. I was fanatically independent, horribly defiant, painfully shy, and hopelessly stubborn. I was often alone, but seldom lonely. I *wanted* to be alone. When my school bus stopped in front of my house, I couldn't escape its confines quickly enough. If my solitude had to be interrupted by companionship, I insisted it be on *my* terms.

Two sisters, two school bus stops away, would often visit me, unsolicited, happily traipsing down Thunder Hill Road from their house to mine. I'd peer through the dusty, aluminum kitchen blinds, pushing one finger down to get a better view, and spot them skipping down the road, eager to visit with me. Sometimes I accepted their company and even delighted in games of Yahtzee or Parcheesi, but most times I just wanted to be left alone. Those times I'd lock the door, draw the blinds in my bedroom, and hide. Eventually they'd go away and I'd plop back on the couch, eat fried bologna sandwiches, and watch cartoons, or read a book in my solitary bliss.

At many points on the Inside Passage I was indeed alone, but rarely lonely. It was a palpable feeling—being out there in the thick of everything—as nature unfolded, leaving me wide open to fully experience the awe of it all. To paddle for days on end, with no form of human contact was empowering, ever-deepening, at times surreal. Who could be lonely with all this at your fingertips? Henry David Thoreau had devoted an entire chapter to the subject of solitude in his classic book *Walden*. Lonely is a state of mind, he deduced and further wrote, "I find it wholesome to be alone the greater part of the time ... I love to be alone. I never found the companion that was so companionable as solitude ...." Although he was a celebrated hermit, I took Thoreau's words to heart, and also believed that solitude is not about seclusion or loneliness, it's about introspection and self-harmony. Being alone wasn't so much a state of being as it was a place where I could retreat, where I could feel safe. Where no one would hurt me. I could feel real, be myself, and not have the burden of putting on a mask to appease whoever I was charged with entertaining.

AS A KID, I was the textbook klutz. Gym-class team captains typically picked me third from last, right before Fat-Judy and Nervous-Nelly. I couldn't dribble a ball, swing a tennis racket, or slide into home base to save my life. I enjoyed running, but someone had to be last, and I fulfilled that role quite well in school track and cross-country practices and meets.

But I could paddle. I wasn't pretending to be a paddler. It was *finally* something that spoke to me, that I was halfway decent at, that I picked up quickly. Perhaps my attraction to the sport was its potential for solitude, that sublime feeling that would wash over me within a few strokes, and along with it a sense of respect, magic, and discovery.

As much as I value my solitude, I'm really an introvert soul trapped in an extrovert personality. Since teaching is often the best way to learn and excel at anything, I began sharing my passion with others early in my paddling career. I found teaching empowering because it helped bring me out of my shell. I teamed up with naturalists, astronomers, geologists, photographers and yoga instructors to offer kayaking and complementing fill-in-the-blank activities. Over the years, I'd guided groups of people through insanely beautiful waters, watching their transformation as they discovered the wonderful world of paddling. I helped them pitch their tents; plied them with wine and cheese; ignited their salivary glands with bubbling cauldrons of dutch oven chili, cornbread, yummy stews and steaming lasagna, all prepared at the water's edge. We'd toast sunsets with crisp chardonnay, and sunrises with chilled pulpy orange juice and hot black coffee. In between, we'd paddle and laugh and sleep. And then paddle some more.

It became a passion, a love, a lifestyle. And it worked. I did it for people, hoping they would emulate my passion. I did it for the sport of kayaking. I did it for love. I did it for money. I did it to further the paddle-sports business I owned. I did it for my partner at the time. We did it together. But now I was doing it for me. It was Susan-time. I'd earned it. I deserved it. And I was ready for it. Perhaps for the first time in my life I was in the driver's seat, doing exactly what I wanted, when I wanted. My actions were not dictated by parents, an authority figure, or a man in my life.

This was a rare time where I found myself single—an atypical circumstance, as it seemed I'd always been under the auspices of a man ever since I'd left home at the age of sixteen. "Rebound" was my nickname. Looking back, I now realize that it was when I was without a partner that my existence felt more justified, my purpose further vindicated, that I didn't need a man in my life to feel whole. It wasn't until I began to prepare for this expedition that I truly understood the many doors kayaking had opened for me and the possibilities when life is experienced at the pace of a paddle stroke.

On Gratitude and Stability

K-A-Y-A-K. THE WORD IS A PALINDROME. It reads the same, forward or backward. That in itself makes it a balanced word in the English language. Over time, I'd come to understand that kayaks don't tip people over; people tip over kayaks. As a paddler, paradoxically, my body-English must be toward the direction of the threat, whereas my instinct is to recoil from it. If a wave is about to overtake me, I brace into it with my paddle. By moving in the direction I least trust, I maintain stability. Trust is ballast. By moving in the direction of doubt, I have hope. Through years of practice I gained stability in this fluid environment yet strove for stability in what often felt like an unstable world.

Feelings of trepidation, excitement, fear all flowed within me at times throughout my expedition. Their intensity depended on the day, how the seas appeared, what the weather forecast was, how well I had slept—or even whether I had slept—if I felt strong that day, or vulnerable. I often worried about the expanse of water I had to negotiate before darkness fell: Was it open, exposed, or did it promise to be languid and non-adrenaline-provoking?

ON MAY 14TH, with mostly calm seas, sunshine, and temps in the low sixties, I methodically broke my Powell River camp, meticulously packed my kayak, and paddled contemplatively into another day and the second leg of my journey. It had been ten days since I'd left Anacortes and the next 175 miles would take me from Powell River to Port Hardy, where I would meet my dear friend Becky. She and I would travel as a team, experiencing the third leg, approximately 150 miles, from Port Hardy to the First Nations' community of Bella Bella together.

North of Powell River, sandwiched between the finishing touches of the Strait of Georgia and the sometimes ill-tempered waters of Johnstone Strait, lay the Discovery Islands and Desolation Sound, a fairly protected and therefore less treacherous stretch of water. The currents from the north and south met and mixed here, forming tepid, quasi-swim-friendly waters, sheltered from the southerly blows of Ms. Georgia. It was here that the intrepid adventurers of Vancouver's expedition of 1791 to 1795 discovered that Vancouver Island was in fact an island, and the name Discovery Islands stuck.

Chained together in the shallow waters near shore, thirty minutes from Powell River, floated the rusting hulks of a dozen World War II ships. They served as a breakwater for one of the world's largest paper and pulp mills, which operated on the shoreline behind them. Beside them, dozens of well-fed, blubbery sea lions lolled and belched on an old tire raft, under a cloud-blotched sky, lackadaisical about my passing by so closely. The tires, floating on their ends, were lashed together vertically in the mercury-colored water like one large axle, ready to roll up on shore. I estimated the raft to be about 75 feet long, and guessed it served as a makeshift jetty for the paper mill. A large bald eagle perched nobly on an iron rail two ships down.

Floating beneath a cement-hulled ship's mammoth bow towering forty feet above me, I craned my neck to look up at a monster-like chiseled face of stone. The ship's blunt nose dropped vertically to the water's surface, and two eye sockets eerily stared down at me. Once the anchor holds, they now oozed rust and muck from their dark recesses, painting the creature's cheeks a sepia tone of burnt sienna and caramel. Its face, once painted light blue, was now daubed with puffs of white, where the lighter color of the cement had worn through. The colors and patterns nearly mirrored the blue sky and its tufts of bluish grey clouds. Heavy chains hung from the eye sockets; I pictured the creature as shackled to the ocean floor, crying rusted tears for eternity.

In the unadulterated joy of simply floating on that glassy surface, in the shadow of those time-worn ships, it occurred to me that nature, even in the midst of chaos, is always seeking equilibrium—as was I. The moon gracefully transitions from waning to waxing. The tides ebb and flow. The seasons come and go. Rains pour from the sky; then the sun appears and dries the earth. I breathe deep, my diaphragm flexing both in and out. I push and I pull on my paddle. My body breaks down and repairs itself at the cellular level. My kayak glides forward and advances beyond where the paddle pierced the water. My muscles contract and elongate, and balance a 21-inch-wide boat beneath me, as I paddle through the yang and yin of mystery and magic. I rest and I move. I entertain the questions fleeting through my head.

I reflected on the rhythm and balance of all this and realized that the key would be to surrender to it, to sink into it, to live in a state of silent wonderment.

The ocean, and all that it embodied, was my inspiration. It is what compelled me to keep going, to get up in the morning, to live large, to have faith in living my dream. This I knew, but what I didn't know was whether it was faith in myself or faith in something *out there*. Was something or someone, some higher entity perhaps, looking out for me, keeping me safe? I'd often struggled with the concept of spirituality, but I knew what *gratitude* felt like, and presumed I would experience several large doses of it before the trip was over.

Full Speed Ahead

ON DAY TEN I PITCHED my tent in the cleavage of two small islands, on a welcoming beachfront, safely above the encroaching tide. A nice push from the flood tide and a slight tailwind had allowed me to put in an easy-breezy 23 miles that day to this charming pair of islands nearly kissing the south shore of the much larger West Redondo Island.

I had originally intended to make camp within a cluster of islands in Copeland Islands Marine Provincial Park, but when I arrived there earlier than expected I realized I had miscalculated my traveling distance for the day; it was only sixteen miles, not the 21 miles I had geared up for. Bonus points, I thought, to have erred on this side. If my math had been wrong for that day's paddle, then it stood to reason that it was probably wrong for this next stretch too, and I thought it wise to double check before I pushed on.

Drifting along the passage between the Copeland Islands and a massive peninsula, I took the string on the handheld compass that was tethered to my life jacket and measured the distance from my current location on the chart to West Redonda Island. I did this by laying the string on the plastic chart case and twisting and nudging it to lie directly over the route I intended to paddle. Pinching off the start and finish points between the thumbs and forefingers of both hands, I then took that stretch of string and laid it straight on the left side of my chart on the latitudinal lines that also served as a mileage scale. In addition to the tick marks indicating nautical miles or fractions thereof, the corresponding numbers indicated my position of latitude, designated in minutes, degrees, and seconds. Since a minute of latitude equals one nautical mile, a math-challenged navigator like me can find this especially convenient.

A nautical mile is sailor-speak, the language used at sea. A mile at sea is a smidgen longer than a mile on land, because the nautical mile accounts for the curvature of the earth while the land mile does not. In other words, a straight line between two points is shorter than a curved line between them. More sailor-speak: If I paddle one nautical mile in an hour, my rate of speed is calculated as one knot. An average pace in a touring kayak not impeded by wind, current, or beautiful views that encourage gawking and poking about is three knots. I was warned early on in my paddling career to never-ever say "knots per hour." Not only is it redundant, it screams greenhorn.

Using my string measure, bobbing my head up and down, I counted, one, two … seven nautical miles. Yahoo, wrong again in my calculations from the previous day! Heck, I had another seven miles left in me. Feeling strong, I opted to keep going, which would eliminate another camp setup, and more importantly, position me for a better run through my next tidal rapid—Hole in the Wall.

SOMETIMES LAND COULD BE A ROYAL PAIN in the ass, and I often felt paddling was the easiest part of the expedition. Hauling gear, setting up and breaking down camp, and all the other minutiae associated with on-land survival often wore me down, whereas the steady rhythm of paddling imparted a feeling of being fully alive on so many levels. I was wired to be a long-distance paddler, enamored with the full-body conditioning that comes from propelling a boat over twenty to thirty miles of water, and the focus of having a defined goal. Had I explored every island and inlet along the way, I could find myself weeks behind schedule, or caught in bad weather on the more exposed portions. Time and weather were a gamble, and sometimes I felt like an arrow being shot from a bow: I'd just keep going until there was something to slow me down. Since I was not tied to a specific itinerary, I pushed on most days, clicking off as many miles as I could, without much in the way of exploratory side trips or lengthy rest stops. This approach presented me with a conflict between mitigating the on-land chores and resisting my propensity to push through the trip. I ached to be able to let go and follow the course intended for me. Each time I passed a potential campsite, I'd have pangs of guilt wondering if I was pushing too hard.

Simply finding a campsite was problematic at times, and once on land my over-active imagination would turn to a new series of potential risks: a twisted ankle, tumbling rocks, boisterous ravens, marauding raccoons, curious bears and tenacious tides, to name a few. My badly infected shin from my little skirmish the previous week reminded me of these possibilities. It seemed that on land my guard was always up.

That night I drooled in my synthetic sleeping bag, lulled into the complacency of deep sleep. Then my subconscious detected a vibration in the ground, followed by the snapping of twigs, followed by my heart rate skyrocketing from a restful fifty-some beats per minute to about two hundred in a fraction of a second. With adrenaline-induced alertness I bolted upright, snatched my headlamp out of its mesh pocket, hastily zipped open the nylon tent door, and shone 2000 lumens into the opaque recesses of the forest. I could hear my heart beating loud in my chest while my eyes scanned the trees. My spotlight met the brown rump of my intruder—a large black-tailed deer stood innocently chewing on its midnight snack, unaware of my presence, and oblivious to having scared me nearly to death.

"Shoo, go away, Mr. Deer," I said, as my heart rate slowly came back from the stratosphere. I saw the deer's big brown eyeball indignantly look my way before it bolted into the woods. Since I was now wide awake, I figured I might as well pee. While I drained my bladder, I remembered, as I often do while peeing, why I seem to have to do this more than the average person.

"Donald, stay on the road!" was the last thing I remember screaming before my yellow 1977 Chevy Nova wrapped itself around a large maple tree, immediately resembling a smashed banana. It was four in the morning, I was eighteen years old, and my nearly-fatal mistake of climbing into the passenger's seat alongside my drunk boyfriend resulted in an unforgettable consequences-of-my-actions lesson. I spent much of that spring in the hospital healing my broken bones: multiple ribs, collar bone, tailbone, pubic bone, and pelvis. These all eventually healed but my ruptured bladder has never been quite the same. Punctured by one of my pelvic bones, the upshot of the emergency surgery was a smaller bladder lined with layers of scar tissue that seem to constantly give me the sensation of fullness.

As I peed outside my tent, I got this bright idea to squat in several places around my tent in a half-serious effort to mark my territory, and ward off potential four-legged intruders. But it didn't work, because later that same night I was also visited by a tribe of pillaging raccoons. *Where am I, in the Garden of Eden?* I thought as my flashlight beam bounced off the masked bandits' beady eyes. With their high degree of dexterity and relentless, underhanded behavior, raccoons can, and will, get into everything. They were up in the trees, they scurried around in the bushes, they promenaded on top of my kayak, their muddy little footprints embossed on the red gelcoat as a reminder to batten down the hatches every night.

Tending to my homework was another critical in-camp task. Each night in camp I would transfer the data from my GPS to my waterproof journal. I recorded the distance for the day, cumulative distance, average speed, maximum speed, and my moving time. Each journal entry started with the date, the time, how many days into the trip I was thus far, and the starting and ending points for that day. I'd note such things as the weather, wind, temperature, wildlife if any, moods, and feelings. And, of course I'd write about what had transpired that day: the beauty I saw, the drama I created, the aches and the pains I endured. Some days I would write reams of stuff in my journal. Other days, either because my hands were too raw from paddling or I was simply too exhausted, I would write *too damn tired, will write more tomorrow.*

But at the end of each day, when the camp chores and homework were tended to and Chamellia was safely stowed above the high tide line, my belly full, and the sun setting, I often felt more complete than I ever had in my life. My body felt tauter with each passing day, and I experienced not only a deep hunger to replace the thousands of calories I had burned that day but also an insatiable craving to discover what was around the next curve in the coastline. My spirit of adventure was in full swing—I was in the midst of my own Nancy Drew narrative.

AFTER I MADE THE JOURNAL ENTRIES, I would switch to the tide application on my GPS and note the time and height of the low and high tides for the next 24-hour period. This data was important for choosing campsites that weren't underwater or didn't entail inimical carrying distances— sometimes a half-mile-long portage. If the next day's paddle involved potential fast current or tidal rapids, I would consult my current tables as well, noting this data on the outside of my plastic chart case with a black grease pencil. These were skills I would hone—yet often struggle with—as the trip progressed.

In the Inside Passage the currents slosh back and forth fairly predictably four times every day. They flood, they ebb, they flood, and they ebb. Then they tirelessly start over. Sometimes they squeeze large volumes of water through constricted channels and passages; they speed up or slow down, depending on where they're at in that six-hour cycle.

Tidal currents are, in essence, a form of rapid transit. I like to think of them as the BART, the Metro, or the T-Train. I think of the tide tables as the schedules and the current tables as the routes. Slack, the period of time when the train is not moving, is when it stops to change tracks—and directions. As a passenger, this is when you want to board. It's important to time the routes accordingly in order to catch the right train and go with the flow.

It was imperative that I ride my Hole in the Wall train westbound on an ebbing current. Slack was at 6:50 p.m.—the train only stopped for a few short moments. Once through Hole in the Wall I would intentionally derail, hang a left out of the west end of the channel and paddle south in calmer waters to pitch camp. This timeframe pushed me into a late evening paddling situation with little time before darkness to find and set up camp. If anything went wrong, I'd be paddling beneath dusky cliffs through this narrow passage—alluring during daylight hours but fraught with danger otherwise. Paddling solo in unknown waters in pitch black scares the bejesus out of me; doing the same through a tidal rapid that can reach a maximum speed of twelve knots was not on my bucket list. Good timing would be critical.

Jim knew this, and on that day he sent an email hell-bent to enlighten my followers on this very issue:

> *... This process (tidal currents) has been going on ever since there were oceans. Men and women, either bored with their lives or answering to a higher calling than most of us, have sat like the Copenhagen Mermaid on rocks, on ship bows, and now on office chairs before computer screens and recorded these movements. This hard-earned data is available to us in a variety of printed and digital resources. Susan, you, and I can buy the fruits of their labors at the start of each year for about $13.95 (what a bargain) and hopefully convert the facts and figures therein into a stress-free passage.*
>
> *I will guarantee you that Susan has pored over this slim volume with a fine-tooth comb leading up to her expedition, even when the snows were flying fast and furious in Montana. I will further guarantee you that the Current Tables will head her reading list until safe passage is achieved on Sunday or whenever. Consulting these resources is relatively simple and straightforward, but the process of safely passing through tidal rapids is an art. There are places one must make judgment calls. It is best to make those in the comfort of the planning process, not as a whirlpool sucks one end of your kayak into its vortex.*

With no need to leave my camp at the break of day, I eased into my cockpit at the leisurely hour of eleven a.m. Working my way up a series of channels, I kept my eyes peeled for the sharp left turn where I would enter the infamous Hole in the Wall. A small pinch of water between Sonora and Maurelle Islands would be my "turn here" indicator. I didn't want to miss that exit. A slight headwind slowed my progress, putting me anxiously behind schedule. As I swung into the channel, I noticed the ocean had already turned itself around; the ebb current had started without me and began to quickly lead my boat through the slot downstream.

Paddling, I watched the speed on my GPS incrementally increase: four knots, five knots, six knots. Soon a localized wind stirred up in the canyon—a wind from the southwest that opposed the northeasterly ebb current. Waves tend to stack up whenever wind opposes current, and now my concern was the narrower pinch point on the western end of the passage where the crux of the rapid lay waiting to gobble up untimely paddlers. In less than three miles I would be in its jaws. As I approached, I heard the rush of whitewater and watched standing waves erupt like mini-geysers, adding spice to the mix. Unlike whitewater kayaks, which are short, responsive, and maneuverable, negotiating an unruly patch of water in a heavily-ladened, straight keeled eighteen-foot sea kayak is a different boat to float.

The walls in the canyon narrowed, and suddenly I was the stone in a slingshot, hurtling through the salty rapid, disembarking at the west end— unscathed—where the water relaxed and the sky yawned wide. Darkness even seemed less imminent. I didn't have much time, though, and at nine p.m., with less than an hour to set up camp before nightfall completely blotted out the light, I landed on Francisco Island, a small, shielded island just around the corner from Hole in the Wall. I could still hear the rapids churning out of the pass and heading north into Okisollo Channel.

Camps such as the one on Francisco Island could spoil a girl. The pint-sized gem of an island—only a couple of acres—had everything I needed nearly at my fingertips. This convenience was a pleasant contrast to some of my other, more arduous, setups. On Francisco, I enjoyed a succinct twenty-foot carry from kayak to tent site, with no danger of the tide flooding me out. Setup and breakdown were a snap. Bears were not an issue here so I plunked my kitchen setup close to my tent. Other amenities included zero danger of falling off a cliff and evening accommodations that were relatively flat, protected, incredibly scenic, and relaxing. Or rather, *could have been* relaxing, had there been more time to enjoy the solitude and beauty. More rapids were on the agenda for the next day, and my homework awaited. Dutifully, while eating dinner by the light of my headlamp, I thumbed through my current tables to apprise myself of tomorrow's agenda.

My notes, taken from the *Sailing Directions of British Columbia*, stated that the rapids in Okisollo Channel could reach a maximum rate of nine knots and that "overfalls and eddies are extremely dangerous." I then realized I needed to be paddling by 6:30 the next morning in order to catch the right train and get through the next stretch safely. That meant crawling out of the tent no later than the ungodly hour of 4:30 a.m. *So much for beauty sleep*, I thought as I wrestled with the zipper on my sleeping bag. I was asleep within minutes.

Patience, Grasshopper

IN THE SILENCE OF DAWN I slid my boat into mirror-calm water and glided into my twelfth day on the IP. Soon I was cruising at speeds averaging eight knots on my way to the more open waters of Johnstone Strait. The ocean bed passed swiftly beneath my hull and I began singing and humming as the scenery raced by. I rode the ebb current at mock speed for three days, clocking in seven to eight knots of mostly effortless paddling—"butter paddling," I liked to call it. When the current slowed, my pace did, too, and I settled into a more pensive state of mind.

Alone on the sea, I thought about the challenges I had already faced, and of those certainly still to come. Dealing with challenges on the water, I had learned, is about approach and perspective. Finesse and strategy, more so than brute strength and power, are the keys to managing spirited water. It's about finding the path of least resistance, much like water itself does. I reminded myself of the written words I had shared with my friends back home regarding my intentions for this journey: *I am doing this because I can. Because I deeply want to. Because my spirit is telling me to. I will follow my heart and soul on this journey. I will try not to lead and control every aspect like I so often do with my life. I will let go and follow the course intended for me.*

Hours later, while sipping spiced rum at my next campsite, I wondered if I was indeed letting go, if I was navigating the twists and turns of my life with finesse and compromise, much like I was striving to navigate the IP. I wondered—now that my days were quartered by the tide and currents, my progress dictated by the moods of the sea—if I would stop trying to shoehorn everything into tidy little corners, forcing my ideal vision of order on the universe. Not one to languish in calm conditions, I'd always felt a need to take advantage of good weather, to push on to the next safety net, to outrun the storm that I felt was indubitably behind me. I was feeling those same pangs of guilt I'd felt a few days earlier, of my tendency to rush through things. I didn't want to push through this trip like I so often pushed through life, yet I often struggled to sit still long enough to genuinely soak up every experience. I wondered if the wild disorder of nature could tame my obsessions, or at least dampen my inward need for control? Could I step back from my dogged efforts to keep life on an even keel? I realized these questions couldn't be answered in an immediate fashion. And I knew that I still had an insatiable curiosity to find out what was around the next corner; I knew that that curiosity would keep the mystery alive for me, and it would sustain my forward momentum, right here, right now, and moving forward, in the adventure of life.

Rum sipping helped my introspection. I had squatter's rights to this Forest Service campsite at Little Bear Bay, a vehicle-accessible campground just around the corner from the official entrance into Johnstone Strait. I had arrived at Little Bear Bay at a ludicrously low tide. The pull of the ebb had nearly drained the bay, as if someone had yanked the plug on a bathtub. The foreshore was the length of a football field pockmarked with mucky suck holes, slippery seaweed, and an energy-zapping slightly uphill cant. I made two trips with all my gear and then hoisted Chamellia onto my right shoulder, the top rim of the cockpit resting on my strong neck muscles. I dreaded this part. Chamellia teeter-tottered back and forth, and as my feet sank deep into the quagmire of low tide, I would have given my left knee cap for a helping hand on the stern end. I winced in pain as the bottom of the cockpit rim banged against my bony pelvis, leaving a black and blue mark that would stay with me for a solid week, turning mysterious shades of green, purple, and black.

My reward for this true bitch of a carry was a spacious and level spot to pitch the tent; a lovely amenity juxtaposed with a blackened fire pit, a rickety and half-rotten picnic table, and a nearby fetid vault toilet, with a surplus of slightly damp toilet paper and sizable spider webs.

I held the rum flask to my lips, tipped my head back, and let the mahogany liquid, with hints of cinnamon and vanilla, slide down my throat and warm my chest. As I took in the lovely view of the western fringes of the Discovery Island archipelago, I delighted in these little things I had sometimes taken for granted. The tradeoffs for these creature comforts were people, noise, and the smell of progress from the annoying clang and din of a nearby logging operation.

I relaxed in my campsite, gobbling down a succulent orange and chomping on the end of a king-size dark chocolate bar, compliments of Gladys and Frank, an elderly couple vacationing in their RV three fire pits down. Squinting through birding binoculars, they had evidently watched my thirty-minute drudgery of hauling one hundred pounds of gear, and eighteen feet of kayak above the wrack line. I wondered if they had seen the sweat on my brow and the occasional foul word coming across my lips through their lenses. Curious, they had wandered down and visited for a spell.

"Where'd you come from?" Gladys asked, concerned that I was out there all on my lonesome. Both she and Frank sported clean silver hair, denim shirts that appeared freshly ironed, and taupe slacks with a crisp crease smack down the center of each leg.

"I camped at Francisco Island last night," I said, then added, "I shoved off from Anacortes, Washington, twelve days ago."

There was a pause as both their faces filled with amazement. Then they nodded in unison; they knew where these places were.

"I'll be right back," said Gladys. She turned on her heel with her index finger in the air, leaving me at the picnic table to chat with Frank. Within minutes, she returned with a clear plastic bag filled with two large oranges and three Hershey chocolate bars. I gushed with gratitude, eager to be plied with nourishment from sources other than my token dry bags. As they walked back to their camp—and as orange juice dripped down my fingers—I thought how uncanny it was that they knew chocolate and oranges were, hands down, my favorite food combination.

I dabbed my red bandana in a cup of cold water and wiped off about three layers of dirt, sweat, chocolate, and orange dribble. My next move was a date with my tent for a long-anticipated nap. I slipped into my cleanest dirty clothes and swallowed a half quart of water with the intention of turning my bladder into a built-in alarm clock so I didn't oversleep. I zipped myself inside my tent, lay on top of my sleeping bag, pulled my baseball cap over my eyes to block out the sun, and passed out for about ninety minutes. This was to be one of only three blissful naps I would sneak in on the entire trip. Delicious respites.

As I packed up the next morning, Gladys and Frank came bearing more tasty gifts: strawberries, bananas, granola bars, and a massive chocolate chip muffin. I gratefully devoured most of the goodies while they amusedly observed, then tucked the granola bars and one banana away for safekeeping in my day hatch. It would all be gone by lunchtime. I only needed to carry my kayak and gear a short distance, thanks to the high tide, a welcome contrast to yesterday's arrival. I bid farewell to Gladys and Frank and paddled out of Little Bear Bay.

I entered the 68-mile-long Johnstone Strait and took advantage of the ebbing current once again—another stint of "butter paddling," a free ride that lasted for hours. A small black bear scrounged on a rocky beach, oblivious as I paddled by. *Oh, what a beautiful, fat, fluffy creature,* I practically said aloud. *Gosh, I hope I see more of those.* Stupid, naive child. Excited as I was about my first bear sighting, I didn't know then that as the trip progressed I would encounter more bears than I would ever care to, including grizzlies with cubs. I didn't know that bears would be like multivitamins, one-a-day, sometimes more. Enough for me to develop a bona fide bear phobia. But I thought this first bear sighting was pretty cool and snapped a round of photos to document my good fortune while I inconspicuously floated by.

Making my way further up the strait, I saw no sign of the legendary winds I had been warned about, but that would soon change. My VHF weather radio crackled to life and indicated a southeast wind of ten to twenty knots beginning tomorrow. It began to sprinkle.

The next two days on the water unsettled me. I had just emerged from the beautiful, intimate channels of the Discovery Islands and now found myself on a much larger and unprotected body of water, notorious for its erratic winds and big waves. Up until this point, the IP was my best friend, lying down like a puppy with all four legs in the air for me. (Well, other than during my crossing the Strait of Georgia—there my best friend was barking and lifting his hind leg to piss on me.) Now its other moods—on its dark side—were manifesting. The trip began to take on a new dimension, and my anxiety levels skyrocketed. Johnstone Strait was under a strong wind warning, which remained true almost the entire time I was on it. I'd read accounts about it being schizophrenic, and now, as I experienced the reality of that statement, I understood.

Today, tonight and Wednesday strong wind warning in effect. Wind southeast fifteen to 25 knots becoming fifteen this evening then increasing to twenty to thirty early Wednesday morning, said the tinny voice reverberating from my weather radio. I scanned the shoreline and it confirmed what the chart on my lap showed—not much in the way of landing. Impatient to clock some miles, I chose to keep paddling in spite of this warning, treating it like it was just a little flatulence in the atmosphere—and my first lesson was about to be curtly shoved in my face.

Nearly a thousand miles away, Jim and most of the remote support crew were glued to their computers watching my progress. Jim spied on SPOT and me as we slowly pulsed our way up the satellite imagery of Johnstone Strait. I'm sure he sat in amazement and secretly wondered what the hell I was doing, and in an effort to educate my followers and possibly ward off his own nervous energy, sent another email "blab" to the troops.

To undisclosed recipients

May 18, 2010
SUBJECT: I'll Huff and I'll Puff

Holy Cow! Get a load of the weather (more to the point, the wind) today where Susan is paddling. Today, the Environment Canada marine weather map is shockingly red, the only area that is not so, is strangely enough the vicinity of Cape Caution.

For better or worse, wind is an "actor" in this journey, and will be until the final stroke of Susan's paddle, later this summer .... When you see red all over the place, like you do today, the mariner is being told to pay heed. Other categories of information are marine watches, indicated by yellow on the above maps and special weather statements. The former indicates potential for trouble; the latter, an unusual development worth paying attention to.

OK - those of you on-line with Susan's SPOT will note she is paddling today, with a strong wind warning in effect for Johnston Strait. To be on the water today would violate MY criteria for moving. The fact that she is moving in no way means she is being unsafe. It simply means she feels the conditions are suitable for her *skills. She is on the water, we are sitting here in our chairs, in some cases thousands of miles away. There is no way we have the capability to second-guess her decision ...*

A final little bit of perspective on today's conditions. They are certainly not beyond the capability of good paddlers like Susan ... Did Susan's criteria work for her today? Only she will be able to tell us. Stay tuned.

Jim

Sharp green seas marched toward me like angry soldiers. Cold, snotty water bitch-slapped the right side of my kayak while a steady rain poured off the brim of my rain hat. My bow veered strenuously into the wind as my stern skidded out beneath me, putting my kayak in an unstable broadside position to the waves—and the fifty-degree salt water beneath me.

Moments before, a band of jagged, menacing clouds had descended over Johnstone Strait. Black and blue, the clouds matched the sea's ornery mood. Oily, rolling waves laced with whitecaps dominated the water's surface and conspired with the northeasterly wind. I was paddling through a deep, glacier-carved passage, through wildly remote waters teeming with the largest population of killer whales in the world. But at that moment, I didn't want to see a killer whale—I just wanted to get off the damn water.

I scrunched up my nose and sniffed the air—it *smelled* different. The weather front was catching up with me, and I could practically hear Jim's voice: *Get off the water NOW, Susan. Get off the water!* Whitecaps grew more numerous, adding to my alarm. The waves came from behind, at an annoying quartering angle, with no reference for me to maintain balance. I had no choice but to crank out aggressive sweeping strokes on my right side, over and over again, in a valiant attempt to steer the boat toward shore and to keep from capsizing in this miserably confused sea. A cubic yard of water weighs nearly a ton, and I knew I'd be in for a good clobbering if any mistakes were made. But I didn't focus on the potential mistakes, I focused on where I needed to go. Paddle, paddle, brace, brace. I kept my gaze on the lumpy, steel-gray waves ahead of me and repeated my mantra, *You got this Susan, just keep moving. You can do hard. You got this.* I hoped that if I kept moving, one stroke at a time, one breath at a time, I'd make it. Maintain my stability, sustain my buoyancy. *Keep moving. Keep breathing.*

Conditions became more volatile, and I just kept paddling because there was nothing else to do. I picked my way through the clear, cold sea as it became alarmingly shallow and strewn with rocks, toward a tiny cove hemmed in by towering trees and chunky boulders. The ocean floor raced under my hull. Capsizing in these conditions with a 150-pound boat on top of me would make this bad day even worse. A broken bone or wrenched muscle out here would surely be disastrous. Best to stay upright.

A rogue wave picked up my stern and lurched me sideways. With my jaw clenched, and my thighs locked under the cockpit rim, I braced into it as it steamrolled under my boat, nearly capsizing me. Rattled, but still determined, I worked my way in to shore with a death grip on the paddle. Like a drunken sailor I back-paddled to let the waves go under my hull instead of torpedoing me uncontrollably forward, then slapped the water with the back of my blade to maintain my balance, then paddled forward again in the hopes I could soon fall on my hands and knees and kiss the ground. With my body in constant equipoise, I made deals with the water gods, thanking them in advance for their kindness and generosity. Ahead and to the side, water crashed in mysterious, ominous patterns. *Look where you want to go*, I told myself. *Stay focused.* Johnstone Strait was throwing tantrums all around me. Nasty things groaned and twisted at me as I fought to stay upright.

As my bow scraped bottom, I furiously released my sprayskirt, pulled my legs out of the cockpit, and braced myself for a crash landing. I straddled Chamellia, stood up, and leapt to her upwind side to avoid the blunt trauma of the heavy kayak careening into my legs, bending my knees in a direction they weren't meant to bend. I grasped the carry handle on the bow and, running, started to drag her onshore—just not quickly enough. The next wave lifted her up and hurtled her forward, wrenching her bow out of my hand, and my shoulder nearly out of its socket. Then, like a horizontal yo-yo, she surged backward with the next wave, listing to the starboard side. Gallons of seawater flooded into the cockpit before the next wave thrust her forward again. I watched in horror as she smacked sideways into a boulder and unceremoniously capsized. Poor Chamellia went THWACK when she and the rock met, and I feared she was either scarred for life or broken in two.

Like wrestling a greased pig, I tipped her one way, then the other until the last of the saltwater sloshed out, then turned her back upright and finally dragged her out of reach of the crashing waves. *Lovely. Fucking lovely*, I said to myself. No time to complain, though. I gingerly turned her over again to inspect her wounds. Amazingly, other than a few deep nicks and scrapes, she was mostly unscathed. The previous winter I'd had a beefy keel strip professionally installed on Chamellia's hull. It paid off.

Chilled to the bone, I knelt beside my kayak in the wet sand, still pumped with adrenaline, and watched thirty-knot winds barrel down the strait and whip the sea into a frenzy. It was time to set up camp and get on with the evening. My trembling, pruned hands wiped away the salt caked stiffly on my face, and I slowly rose to a standing position. It had been a long day and Mother Nature was, once again, reminding me who was in charge. She didn't care that I was frazzled and frightened. She didn't care that my parents were inept or that I'd suffered childhood injustices. She was indifferent to the fact that I was a runner from my problems, from my fears, from love and commitment. She didn't give a rat's ass that this time it was different—that I was running *to* something, and that I was on a journey that I hoped would change me.

I trudged up the beach with my gear to a tiny spot high in the cliffs, where I would be out of the wind and safe from the impending tide. I focused on my camp chores, knowing the sooner I got them done, the sooner I could get out of my stinky, clammy wetsuit into dry clothes, and snarf down some hot food.

After putting the finishing touches on my tarp, I looked out at Johnstone Strait from my higher vantage point. My jaw dropped. In the thirty minutes since I'd come ashore, the breakers had tripled in size, and the ocean appeared possessed. Monstrous waves now crashed where I had landed, sending a six-foot spray of whitewater into the air. The sea was foaming at the mouth, and I was grateful to be on shore. Safe landing spots further up the strait were dubious at best. I realized if I had not landed when I did, I could have been in *serious* trouble. I had gotten off easy. I shook my head and vowed to stop my cavalier attitude. I was a woman paddling solo out here, for crying out loud. Why was I taking such risks and pushing so hard? *If you're trying to prove something, Susan, the only thing you'll fucking prove is that you know how to kill yourself.* I berated myself, both fearful and infuriated. Fearful that my inability to listen to my voice of reason and to relax would render me dead. Infuriated because I didn't know why I did this, why I always felt time was of the essence and that I must always be on the go.

The sea was teaching me patience—and I still had much to learn.

Attitude Adjustments and Course Corrections

THE NEXT MORNING, from the safety of my tent, I peered out at Johnstone Strait as I tuned into the weather forecast on my VHF radio. More southeasterlies were predicted, kicking up to fifty knots that night and continuing into the next day, but from my tent the seas appeared much less agitated than when I had arrived less than eleven hours earlier. In these conditions I thought I could at least make it to Telegraph Cove, a colorful, touristy boardwalk community nestled inside a protected inlet, in a couple of hours, well ahead of the next weather front. By 7:30 a.m. I was pressing ahead cautiously as a frisky breeze scudded me up Johnstone Strait.

Blinkhorn Peninsula, a nubbin of land a mile or so east of Telegraph Cove, lured me in for a quick break. I snuck into its lee side and stretched my legs on the narrow cobbled neck of the peninsula and looked out at the steady whitecaps beyond the point. I delighted in the blue skies to the west, but feared the impending storm coming from the east. Once back in my boat, still in the lee of the land, I began to have strange sensations in my body, and the hair on the back of my neck stood on end. I choked back tears that came out of nowhere. I thought about the extreme fortune I'd had over the two-week journey thus far, and how I had come to an uneasy truce with these waters.

Suddenly I felt that I was part of a much bigger thing; that this unfolding trip was a part of a much bigger thing. Perhaps more expansive than just myself in a kayak on the Inside Passage. I sensed a timelessness about it, an internal feeling of free-floating like something magical was carrying me through on this adventure, a feeling that I thought I could ride into eternity. I felt profoundly protected, as if angels were watching over me. Tears slid down my face and mixed with the seawater on my cheeks. Layers of selfishness were washed away and replaced with a heightened sense of gratitude, humility, and awe—an awe that I was here, doing this, living this. I was adapting to it, accepting it. I sat in complete surrender. For the first time, I trusted that there might be a divine plan and felt some sort of connection with whatever greater powers might exist. That I was being guided and looked after, kept safe. I was grateful for all the circumstances that had put me right where I was at that moment, with my paddle in my hand and my boat beneath me.

I DECIDED TO BYPASS Telegraph Cove, setting my sights on a wilderness camp Jim had marked on my chart further up the strait. A poor decision, as it turned out. After three days of bucking temperamental winds and confidence-killing waves, a couple of near capsizes, an ugly surf landing, a chilled-to-the-bone feeling that would not subside, magnified by getting the last of my dry clothing wet, I finally made a judgment call. On the south side of the strait, a few miles past Telegraph Cove, and a solid day's paddle shy of Port Hardy, I snuck into a port-in-a-storm, with my tail between my legs. Thankful to be out of the boat, out of the wind, and out of the pelting sideways rain, I pulled into a protected cove at Alder Bay Fishing Resort, on Vancouver Island, and walked purposefully to a faded gray building with a blinking office sign. I surveyed the camping area on my way up and noticed it didn't have much in the way of good sturdy trees to rig a tarp. With gale force winds beginning to build, camping would be problematic.

I entered the gray building and stood at the counter bedraggled, trying to ignore the effluvia wafting from the PFD and sprayskirt I was still wearing. I licked the saltwater off my lips, and felt cold water squish between my toes while small puddles formed around my neoprene boots.

"You haven't been out kayaking in this, have you?" asked John, the gaunt-faced man behind the counter. He squinted over his glasses and listened as I gave him the *Reader's Digest* version of the last few days. Sensing I wasn't too keen on pitching my tent in an ever-brewing storm, John mentioned a camper trailer he could rent to me. The price seemed a little steep for my budget, but what the heck, I'd take a look. I followed him around the back of the building and up the hill to where a white camper stood just behind a cement shower building. He swung the door open and motioned for me to go in. I climbed up the stairs and stepped onto a clean linoleum floor and into a small but immaculate kitchen. I looked down the short hallway to the bedroom at the back of the camper and saw a queen-size bed decadently covered with a pouffy emerald green comforter and a ridiculous number of even pouffier pillows. The electric heater kicked on, sending its blast of delicious heat against my chilled, clammy skin.

"Where do I sign?" I immediately asked.

Gale force winds, averaging forty knots, howled through the night and the camper shook and creaked. I snuggled deeper under three layers of comforters in my single-wide palace. I fell asleep with my head cradled in a down pillow, still feeling the sea rolling under me. The next morning, I listened to the weather report while I boiled water for coffee in the camper's kitchen. More wind. More rain. Duly noted.

I spread my chart out on the square kitchen table and reviewed the remaining route to Port Hardy. I had 26 miles to go; the last seventeen were moderately exposed. I knew Becky was already en route and an idea flashed through my mind. She could pick me up here in Alder Bay!

WHEN I FIRST CONSIDERED inviting someone to join me for a portion of the trip, Becky had immediately come to mind. I felt my criteria for an intrepid partner needed to be specific for the safety, success, and enjoyment of the trip. In addition to being a strong paddler, this person must not be averse to strong odors emanating from her clothing, or a little fungus and mold growing in her neoprene footwear. She must not be chatty in the morning before strong coffee is served. She must be able to put up with my unbridled need to paddle long distances day after day and not be prone to losing her lunch when conditions got a little lumpy. Her equipment must be seaworthy and she had to have the seamanship skills to keep it properly afloat as much as possible. Prowess in backcountry camping was paramount; being savvy with tarp rigging and fire making were extra bonus points. Of course, it was important that we enjoy each other's company, especially with the potential for being stormbound together in one location for extended periods.

Becky fit the bill perfectly, and then some. Nine years my senior, she was as committed to the success of this trip as I was. Born and raised in Texas, she was a hardy gal with loads of built-in courage. Her 25 years of delivering mail in northwest Montana, along the fringes of Glacier National Park, redefined the word "rural route." And she brought even more fine qualities to the table confirming a good fit: she loved good conversation, dark chocolate, and copious amounts of red wine. We'd get along just fine.

Becky answered her cellphone on the second ring and patiently listened to my plan.

"Of course I'll swing by and pick you up, Suz," she said. "I've been watching the weather, and your SPOT, and I'm surprised you made it as far as you did. Christ, you must be spent."

I'd just finished packing my gear when I spotted Becky's forest-green Toyota pickup rolling through the campground. Within minutes

Chamellia was loaded on top, alongside *Eagle*, Becky's seventeen-foot yellow, kevlar sea kayak. By five o'clock that night, we were swilling Shiraz and savoring copious amounts of salmon and pasta in the small seaside community of Port Hardy, the last bastion of civilization on the remote northwest tip of Vancouver Island. The fact that I had skipped paddling 26 miles out of my proposed 1,200 did not trouble me. I came to terms with the decision and resolved that there was no need to feel guilty or that I had cheated on anything. Plan B was a grand idea.

Leg 3 150 miles 11 days

Leg 3
Port Hardy to Shearwater
approximately 150 miles • 11 days

Four

Port Hardy to Shearwater

*There is a spiritual presence which can aptly cushion
our every fall, bringing comfort and subtle meaning
to our lives. However, we'll not feel this gentle comfort
unless we attune ourselves to the others in our
company. It's within another's soul that we sense
the beacon of light which illuminates the way we're
traveling.*

—Anonymous

Two Slivers on the Sea

I T WAS TIME for Becky and me to stir up the seas together. After two rest
and resupply days, I was ready to begin paddling again—and excited
to have my dear friend accompany me. Since I had 260 nautical miles
under my hull, Becky was concerned that she'd never be able to match
my pace and that she would hold me back. For months she had been
paddling tenaciously, trying to whip herself into shape. I did my best to
assuage her fears and focused on the fact that we were now a team. This

leg of the journey was no longer a solo endeavor—we were sisters of the sea, after all. I had no intentions of leaving her behind.

This section had the potential to be the most dangerous leg of the entire trip because a good chunk of it is essentially not on the "inside." First we had to get ourselves across Queen Charlotte Strait, or the "Queen's Pond" as the locals referred to it. Named after the wife of George III, this large, often moody, body of water concerned us. Its long fetch, the distance traveled by wind or waves across open water, provided more opportunity for problematic conditions. With a fetch to the south of nearly forty miles and a fetch to the north of over a thousand miles, our eighteen-mile crossing was not to be taken lightly. The next 25 miles would entail paddling an exposed coastline, including working our way around the infamous Cape Caution—my third crux and the trip's true rite of passage. Windswept trees warned mariners to take heed of this coastline, where large ocean swells often galumphed unimpeded for thousands of miles across the mighty Pacific until they finally collided with the Cape.

Our progress across Queen's Pond soon reached a crescendo. Ominous swells eight to ten feet high rolled under our hulls, lifting us skyward like a nautical roller coaster, as they marched their way south down the strait, a continuum of rolling energy. We paddled a few wave sets apart on these hilly seas, with no illusion of a safety net. In all reality we knew that if one of us capsized, it would be an arduous task for the other to effect a rescue without going in the drink herself. Becky would occasionally disappear in the trough of the wave she was riding, and I would lose sight of her for long seconds. Now, with another paddler beside me, for the first time I had a mind-boggling sense of scale—and a sobering sense of vulnerability. It seemed more foreboding having the frame of reference of another kayak near me, rising and falling with the mercury-colored water.

"I think they're getting smaller," I yelled to Becky, but my words were swept away by the galloping wind.

"What?" she yelled back.

"THE WAVES—I THINK THEY'RE GETTING SMALLER," I repeated, trying to maintain a veneer of calm and suppress my jangled nerves. She just shook her head, clearly annoyed with my flawed optimism. Later she admitted that she wanted to wring my neck. She knew the conditions were deteriorating and although not scared for her life, she was intimidated.

Halfway across, we snuck into the lee of a group of islands to take a much-needed breather. A fishing boat with a weathered white hull and black trim was anchored nearby and the two men on board waved us over.

"Would you like some fish for dinner, ladies?" one fisherman asked, holding a meaty, partially filleted, just-hauled-out-of-the-ocean cod by the tail.

"Ummm, sounds great!" we said in unison, flashing the fishermen big toothy smiles. He finished filleting the cod on the boat's deck, stuffed it into a large plastic sack, and handed it overboard to me. I quickly popped my sprayskirt and placed it between my legs in the cockpit. With the water temp hovering around fifty degrees, my kayak was a spacious floating cooler, keeping anything that touched its cold hull nicely chilled.

The Queen wasn't letting Becky and me out of her moody grip until our bows touched ashore at the appropriately named Shelter Bay, a surf-free zone on the mainland tucked behind a small cluster of islands protecting the foreshore. In camp, I unwrapped the fish and realized it was enough to feed four or five hungry paddlers. I whacked it in half with my diver's knife and threw the other half back to the ocean. Better the crabs devour it than some nosy bear. Between our two small cook pots, we managed to whip up a scrumptious supper al fresco, centered on the fresh catch of the day. Tonight's menu was sautéed cod, brown rice drizzled with olive oil and dusted with parmesan cheese, and a green salad. I assembled the salad in Becky's helmet, lined with a plastic grocery bag, and placed two individual servings of blue cheese dressing next to it. Becky's coffee cup served as a makeshift vase and she filled it with a rainbow of wildflowers, resting in sea water. I augmented her creative touch with a few seashells, and our centerpiece was complete. We poured two glasses of fine boxed red wine and settled into our soft camp chairs, level with the ground, to enjoy our feast.

The next morning, day nineteen, we paddled side by side in light winds out of the southeast. Becky's silver hair sparkled in the sunlight, and she sat tall in her bright yellow kayak, her slender figure ensconced in a blue drysuit. We paddled under steep granite cliffs, rimmed in white, their lower portions littered with colorful bursts of sea anemones, starfish, sea cucumbers, and other intertidal life, all simultaneously hanging on to the ocean topography and reaching out to the rising tide. A lush, fecund forest towered above us, its deep green contrasting with the smoky-white layer of featureless clouds suspended overhead. We were relaxed and cheerful; the ambiance that pervaded the flat, friendly water all around us was a welcome reprieve from yesterday's white-knuckle-butt-pucker paddle.

The only place we encountered rougher waters that day was crossing the entrance to Slingsby Channel, a short stretch of water that Jim had warned me about. Patches of foam, indicating turbulent water, met us at its shallow mouth. The colliding combination of the tide ebbing back to sea and the northwesterly swell fluffed up the water like a master chef stirring her pot. The world beneath our hulls went silent as we glided through the billowy foam, much like a skier glides through soft, powdery snow.

Soon the two-mile-long sandy crescent-shaped beach of Burnett Bay came into view. Its long arc of brilliant white sand was hard to miss. If it had been located in a warmer clime instead of the remote windswept coast of British Columbia with its fifty-degree waters, it would be stuffed with resort hotels.

We anticipated a surf landing on the north end of this unprotected, wave-battered beach and had brought helmets for this very reason. Fortunately, we didn't need them. Two sets of small, lethargic waves lapped the shallow foreshore, then melted into the sand, allowing us to coast in sans drama. We'd paddled fifteen unhurried miles that day, compared to the eighteen arduous miles our first day together.

Feeling empowered by our successful landing, we struck Xena:

Warrior Princess poses—one neoprene-bootied foot planted firmly on our stern decks, paddles held triumphantly overhead, exuding our best look of defiance, and snapped photos of each other, giggling and reveling in our silliness.

The Magical Cabin

Illustration by Jim Chester

I HAD A TREASURE to share with Becky—a treasure referred to in certain paddling circles as "the magical cabin." It stood humbly alone in the forest, at the end of a serpentine trail, not far from where we stood, waiting to accommodate those who would respect and honor it. Soon after landing at Burnett Bay, Becky followed me down the trail and after a few moments we stood together and admired the magical cabin from a distance. Proud and enchanting, with a patchwork of new and weathered cedar shakes on the roof, it beckoned to us. We ducked our heads and stepped inside.

A small wooden bunk bed filled the length of the back wall; a compact table and wood stove graced opposite walls. Two half-burned candles sat cemented to the wooden tabletop in a puddle of cooled wax, and a handful of mouse-eaten books were stacked in the windowsill. An improvised shelter outside served as a kitchen area, and a discreet outhouse was a short distance away on a spur trail heading south. Most notably there was no graffiti. This place was too magical and mystical for that nonsense.

This tiny cabin was built in 1985 by Randel Washburne, a kayaker, for kayakers. As paddlers began to stumble upon this gem, mostly via tips from other paddlers, many inquired about the story of the building, wishing to know who built it and if this person minded others using it. In 1987, Washburne scrawled this note and hung it on a nail above the stove:

> *NOTICE: This cabin was built by a kayaker for anyone who paddles, rows, or swims along this coast. As builder I have NO proprietary feelings here (guess I enjoy the building as much as staying)—this place is everybody's. I haven't been back here for two years. The stovepipe is in its last stages of life, so be very careful and keep a small fire. Pass the word south for someone to bring up four lengths of 4" stove pipe and an elbow when they come here! Take the pipe down (new pipe, that is, don't disturb this) and cover the hole when departing and it will last much longer.*

Audrey Sutherland, Jim's IP mentor, and the grand dame of expedition paddling, clearly had a soft spot in her heart for this cabin. I'd noticed her lightly penciled annotations on my charts ever since leaving Anacortes, but the eleventh chart in my 32-chart lineup had a particularly lengthy comment. Squinting in the cabin's dull light, I read Audrey's annotation from chart number 3551 as Becky peered over my shoulder:

> *Tiny magical cabin, 6x8' built by a kayaker with tools carried in kayak. It's for the use of kayakers who treasure and care for it. A.S.*

Audrey had penciled in a perfect square, indicating the cabin's position. Two other notations mentioned small streams and wolf tracks.

We'd found nirvana in the forest and began nesting, as women will often do. Our lively chatter filled the forest while we made several trips back and forth to the boats for our food and gear. I threw my sleeping bag on the upper bunk, placed my headlamp on top so I could find it when darkness fell, dug out my flask of dark spiced rum and poured us both a snort. Due to space and weight limitations, we had to skimp on some gear, but rum, take-apart acrylic wine glasses—and chocolate— were nonnegotiable items on all our adventures. I smiled at Becky as we toasted the magical cabin and our good fortune, our plastic glasses ceremoniously thudding together. Luscious dark rum met our lips, and we both sighed deeply. With beverages still in hand, we ducked our heads under the low-hanging doorway and stepped back outside into an enchanting rainforest.

High winds, big seas, and unfriendly surf kept us in and near the magical cabin for the next three days. What a wonderful place to be stormbound! We took long walks and long naps, caught up on reading and journal writing, and simply enjoyed our surroundings. We had no choice but to wait for our window of opportunity to contend with our next crux move—the cat-and-mouse game around the infamous Cape Caution.

The name is in fact historically rooted and venerably sourced by none other than Captain George Vancouver. In an "Aw shucks, I was afraid this would happen" moment on July 6, 1792, his ship was "suddenly grounded on a bed of sunken rocks." It was a Monday afternoon proving that Mondays apparently were no better in 1792 than in 2010. In the ensuing melee between ship and ocean, Vancouver's *Discovery* was laid on her side in the outgoing tide to the extent that, as Vancouver wrote in *A Voyage of Discovery* "… the starboard main chains were within three inches of the surface of the sea."

Fortune smiled on the expedition though. "Happily, at this time, there was not the smallest swell or agitation, although we were in the immediate vicinity of the ocean. This must ever be regarded as a very providential circumstance, and was highly favorable to our very irksome and perilous situation," Vancouver penned. They were faced with "…nothing short of immediate and inevitable destruction …" until "…the returning flood, which to our inexpressible joy was at length announced by the floating of the shoars, a happy indication of the ship righting."

"Oh dear Lord, get me to Tuesday," Vancouver doubtlessly muttered. "And … note to cartographer … call that place Cape Caution!" This prominent headland is damnably shallow—less than forty feet deep over a mile offshore. Any wind, waves, or ocean swell coming in off the vast expanse of the Pacific collides with this shallow ocean topography. The result is a witch's stew, a concoction that can boil up yet another nasty little ingredient: fierce winds. Winds going around a corner are called—not surprisingly—corner winds. Corner winds by dint of physics are up to 25 percent stronger than winds in the same vicinity not trying to race around points of land. Cape Caution is a corner.

The cape itself, a low rocky headland bare of trees, is nondescript. There is no Hardy Boy cliff topped with a lighthouse casting its searching beam out to sea between sheets of rain and flashes of lightning. Neither is there a lighthouse keeper, sporting a yellow slicker and sou'wester hat, clinging to storm-tossed iron railings. No, there is just a stocky metal tower that serves as an automated navigation light. Decidedly uninspiring.

Nonetheless, caution is advised and Becky and I knew that getting around the cape safely required some strategy and patience lest we find ourselves perched like a weather vane on top of the navigation light. So we waited. And we ate.

On paddling days, breakfasts typically consisted of something quick and cold, so we could get on the water and put in some miles. On rest days, whether intentional or imposed upon us by Mother Nature, we could indulge in a warm and nutritious start to our day. Extra bonus: not burning off the calories in the first hour. On our first morning at the magical cabin we dined on rehydrated hash browns and powdered eggs scrambled with bacon bits, dehydrated veggies, and melted cheese, washed down with dark coffee in which floated lumps of powdered creamer. Only on land-bound days like these could we enjoy the luxury of a second cup.

It started to sprinkle just as we were finishing breakfast, so we retreated into the cabin. I settled into a paperback book I had brought along for days like this, while Becky sorted through some of her gear.

"Okay if I turn on the weather radio for a spell, Suz?" she asked after a while.

"Sure," I replied, listening with one ear as I perused *I Heard the Owl Call My Name*. The weather report dictated that we would stay put. Thirty-foot seas dominated the cape and huge breaking surf had rolled in like a locomotive train, reminding us who was in charge.

Later, beachcombing, we watched forty-knot winds shear off the tops of waves, sending spindrift high into the air. Whirling winds flew through our hair, and sand stung our faces. We climbed onto enormous stumps heaved up on shore from previous storms, attesting to the power of the Pacific Ocean, and attuned ourselves to the otherworldly aura of Burnett Bay: a two-mile patch of wildness rimmed with Doctor Seuss-like trees and dense clusters of vegetation resembling Japanese botanical gardens that withstood Mother Nature's ferocity. We refilled our water bladders, took scads of photos, and stumbled on wolf tracks. According to the journal entries in a stash back at the cabin, there are always wolf tracks on this sickle-shaped beach. One citation noted grizzly bear tracks on the south end, and another mentioned bear tracks just outside his tent.

Lying in my top bunk that night, with the wind howling and the surf raucously pounding the beach, I wondered whether a grizzly bear could get into this cabin if it really wanted to. I knew the answer, but drifted off to sleep anyway.

When morning came, there was no need to check the weather report. Gale force winds blew stiffly outside the cabin, and Burnett Bay was a froth of white. We were cabin-bound for another day. As wonderful as the magical cabin and Burnett Bay were, I was growing restless again. I reprimanded myself, then ran my usual self-help tape in my mind. *Patience, my dear. Read your book. Write in your journal. Revel in those long walks. Relax. Surrender. You are exactly where you need to be for this adventure, this coast, this body, this life.*

When Tides Collide

AFTER BREAKFAST ON OUR THIRD DAY at the cabin I climbed back into the upper bunk, a process more closely suited to a six-year-old, and snuggled deep into my sleeping bag. It was May 25, day 21 of the trip. Still wearing her pajamas, Becky sat cross-legged at the small wooden table and read aloud various entries from the cabin log books, notes, and cards left by other kayakers. It was remarkable to sift through these chronicles and read about the adventures of those traveling before us. Like a child being told a bedtime story, I listened to Becky's voice as our small fire crackled in the wood stove and the wind whispered through the trees.

June 12-16, 1988

Paddled from Port Hardy via Deserters Group. Having a cabin is wonderful! I brought the lengths of 4" stovepipe and a cap, but didn't know about the elbow so it is still a makeshift. I'll take down the top section when I leave and cover the hole. A fire is laid ready to light in case you arrive cold and wet. There's a lighter and some tea in the cupboard. I laid a new floor, scrounging 2-by lumber from the far reaches of the beach. It isn't nailed down. The owner should approve first. For nailing, there is a vertical strip of 1-by at 2' intervals. There also is a layer of black plastic on the ground under the 1-bys to keep out the damp. If nailing in, shove it all toward the door to close any cracks. The door was binding and I put a spacer under the top hinge and waxed it. Now it neither squeaks nor binds, and the sliding bolt fits better. Cleared some brush, planted some ferns, stacked lumber, and brought in firewood. The stream to the north is a good little one. Not much rain as glad not to be dependent on catchment.

—Audrey Sutherland

Audrey visited the cabin again in 1990, adding more flavor to the log books:

May 22, 1990

En route from Port Hardy north, going toward Ketchikan, going as far as the boat, the body, and the weather permit. Today 30 knots from the SE. Yesterday 25 knots from the north. Tomorrow? Great to read all your notes. New elbow installed and spare under the bunk. The strange piece of plywood on the woodpile is a mast step/ foot brace. Decided it was more liability than asset. Use that nice 7-ply mahogany if you can or feed it to the fire. That dead tree by the back right corner is a worry. Could two strong guys with ropes pull it down and over away from the cabin? I didn't dare try. This place is always the high point of the trip. "Once upon a time there was a tiny magic cabin in the forest and ..."

—Audrey Sutherland & Kayak "Diodon" (the balloon fish)

Becky read another entry that further piqued my interest:

June 30, 1992

Greetings Cabin Denizens. We surfed our kayaks in here yesterday under a bright, blazing sun. Our friend Jim had already arrived earlier in the day due to us being gobbled in the ebb just past the Fox Group. This cabin is really funky—yet another reason for us to stay an extra day ...

—Jason

It would be nice to spend more time here but the northward urge is pulling us on! I could easily find myself happily stuck here for weeks if I didn't have the idea of a trip to Alaska stuck in my head. The cabin is telling me to mellow out, but I'm curious to see the rest of the coast. Luckily everybody who has been here makes me feel welcome to return. I'll see you soon!

—Robson

I quickly realized it was *my* Jim the authors were referring to. Jim's 1992 trip was mostly solo, but I remembered him telling me about running into a young threesome of paddlers named Robson, Jason, and Christy. Jim's entry soon followed:

July 1, 1992

A landlubber from Montana on a vision quest via kayak on the sea. Hello to you all, past and future. A rare privilege indeed to be here, at this tiny desk, in this wonderful cabin, in the shadow of Cape Caution; the sound of the surf and wind as one … For the moment, I have companions — three friends who graciously allowed me to share their camp at Shelter Bay, and fed me, too; a happy chance encounter in the cosmos [...] It's hard to leave such a place. For me it's as though I've finally found "home" after so many, many years of looking. I will leave a part of my soul here and will return to the "unreal" world clutching a bit of this place to my heart—a sort of talisman against the "craziness" out there. Thank you little cabin and all of you, my companions on this journey of life! Thank you Audrey for the tip on this place.

—Jim & kayak "Ghost," Eureka, Montana

1993 (month unknown)

"Cabin Builder" returns after five years absence! Can't believe it's been so long. I am pleased to find the place in such good shape and to see that so many people have enjoyed it through the years.

Traveling solo, it feels really companionable to read the log and see the touches, big and small (Audrey's especially), and offerings left behind. Anyhow on my way from Bella Bella to Port Hardy via West Athelone, Goose Island, Triquet Island, and West Calvert ... Don't know when I'll get back up here, so I'll write some ideas for building a simple breakdown [stove replacement] one to bring up in a kayak.

—*Randy*

April 25, 2002

Two Kiwi kayakers traveling from Victoria to Juneau and back. We realize that those are the destinations but it is the journey that is most important. Here at Burnett Bay we have started to find the true wilderness we were seeking. Although the last week has had strong northwesterlies and has hampered our progress, we were unable to resist the charms of Burnett Bay and spent a wonderful two days enjoying the sun, exploring and trying to interpret the animal tracks in the sand: deer, wolf and what appeared to be cougar tracks following one set of deer tracks. Reading through the journals reveals a who's who of sea kayakers, some of whom have written books that inspired our trip – Audrey Sutherland, Byron Ricks, and Randy Washburne. Thanks for this treasure in the woods.

—*Garth*

"You might want to read this one yourself, Suz," Becky said, handing me the tattered journal. Taking it carefully in my hands, I took a deep, slow breath, quickly scanning the words before reading them aloud.

July 1996

Greetings again little cabin. You and I first met in July 1992. I was headed north to Alaska. After a most interesting summer that year,

I'd in fact made it to Juneau. This year, I am traveling south and on only a 10 or 12 day journey from Finn Bay to Port Hardy. I have my wife Susan with me this time. She was only an undefined dream back then. Now she is reality and it's my sublime pleasure to share with her some of my magic moments and places I'd experienced. We've been to Fury Island, Cranstown Point, the Golden Sand Beach, around the Cape, and walked this beach, experiencing the pleasure of place and one another. You, little cabin, are wonderful as always. Never change. Always be here, for the next time! To all our fellow paddlers, rowers, etc, it is a great pleasure and honor to meet you here through these pages once again. And, to one special one who also loved me, maybe still does, you've been on my mind since the moment I set foot on the beach. Your spirit pervades the place and everywhere where the wind meets the sea and the sea meets the land.

—*Jim & Susan Chester*

I was that Susan Chester. At one time, Jim and I had been married. On New Year's Eve 1992 I sat in the back seat of Jim's Toyota Tercel wagon, directly behind his long, weathered neck. My bald tires and rear-wheel drive lummox of a vehicle were no match for the snow-packed passes of the Canadian Rockies. Fate had decided that I would carpool with Jim and two others, all of whom I was meeting for the first time, from Eureka, Montana, to Banff, Alberta, for five days of backcountry hut skiing. At fifty years old, he was fresh off his solo Inside Passage trip from the previous summer. I, on the other hand, was a greenhorn kayaker, living in landlocked Montana, and had no clue as to what the Inside Passage was. As far as I was concerned, it was an esoteric chunk of water "out there" somewhere on the West Coast, and Jim, having paddled it, was way out of my league. But as I learned more about his passion for adventure, for the magical waterways of the Inside Passage, for the Great Bear Rainforest, for life and all that is right, I was mysteriously taken by this man.

Three years later, as a harvest moon climbed above the Canadian

Rockies in northwest Montana, we exchanged vows beside a small lake, while friends—mostly dressed in shorts and sandals—looked on. Together we failed miserably at five years of matrimony and pulled the plug just days before the 21st century roared into our worlds. Though we bonded on many levels, it wasn't until we divorced and became separate entities, tied only by friendship and our ineradicable knowledge of each other, that we became closer. A platonic intimacy that couldn't be skewed by sex. We broached the subject all right, and mutually decided that door would remain tightly shut. "Unless, of course, you change your mind," Jim couldn't help but add. After all, he was a man. But we both knew that an act that may seem innocuous at the time could have toxic consequences in the end. Still, we continued to tell each other everything, confessing past, present, and even future sins, hopes, and desires.

If I'd had a crystal ball to peer into when I first met Jim, I would have been shocked to see myself, eighteen years later, armed with his wisdom and experience, strength and support, his charts and his good luck talisman, paddling north to Alaska prior to turning the big Five-O myself.

LATER THAT DAY THE SEAS flattened out. The barometer rose steadily, and the sun shone intermittently. The surf no longer sounded like a freight train, the wind no longer howled through the trees, and cavernous thoughts of fear no longer lurked in the recesses of my mind. That fear had relocated itself front and center. I was mindful that the cape loomed just four miles to the north. We couldn't see it from this beach, but we knew it was there waiting, quietly, moodily.

"The weather report should be updated by now," I said to Becky as we finished our walk and cautiously worked our way over the massive piles of driftwood that blocked the trailhead to the cabin. Our boats were pulled up high on the logs—and tethered—out of reach from a boat-stealing high tide. I retrieved the marine radio from my PFD pocket, stashed deep in Chamellia's cockpit. Our spirits soared as we listened. Wind predictions were scaled down to ten knots, seas only one to two meters. Our window of opportunity was finally about to be pried open. In my mind I could hear Jim's voice loud and clear with his advice for rounding the cape. "Go with the flow, when everything is traveling in the same direction—the wind, waves, swell, and tide. Go early. Swing 'er a mile wide."

"I think a celebration is in order," Becky said, cradling her flask of rum in both hands.

"Is it rum-thirty already?" I smiled. We had more to celebrate than just our meteorological fortuity—it was also Jim's birthday. We toasted Jim and discussed our plan for the next day. Weather windows, skill, and good luck were one thing, but both Becky and I were firm believers in positive visualization. We jointly envisioned a safe landing at our next campsite, the cape behind us, elated, triumphant, and pressing that "SPOT OK" button. Our friends back home would be watching and cheering, and Jim would be clicking the reply-to-all button and messaging the group about a job well done.

Burnett Bay had been good to us. After dinner I strolled back to the kayaks to stash a few items, feeling more prepared for the morning's launch. I noticed wolf tracks less than twenty feet from my boat and watched a cruise ship slip by about two miles offshore, with a large Coast Guard cutter close behind. Earlier that day we had seen the blue-hulled Alaska State Ferry go by. These were all good signs that others were out and about.

That night, I slept restlessly in my narrow upper bunk, which was not much wider than an ironing board. Sporadically, I'd pry open one eye to see if it was daylight yet and strain both ears to listen for surf. I awoke at 5:15 a.m. and immediately walked the trail to an open area to assess Mother Nature's mood. Thick clouds hung over calm seas; light fog drifted slowly toward me. The tide was out and still dropping, exposing a glistening sand mirror reflecting the clouds and jagged shape of the coastal forest. The two-hour pack up, entailing carrying our kayaks and gear nearly the length of two football fields, put us on the water at 7:30.

With apprehensive sidelong looks at each other, we pushed off from the sandy beach, swallowing back the lumps in our throats, leaving the magical cabin behind, and paddled into what seemed like a false, disquieting calm, toward Cape Caution. We spoke in hushed tones—not wanting to awaken the sleeping giant who had the power to turn our world topsy-turvy—and paddled almost directly under the navigational structure crowning the most westerly point of the cape. It seemed nearly disrespectful to be paddling so close. Our patience paid off; the big bad cape ended up being a total pussycat. We snuck right on by.

Cocoa and Puff

NORTH OF CAPE CAUTION we paddled through ivory spume laced with viridescent seaweed, like fresh grass clippings sprinkled atop new snow. Large incoming swells tickled the tops of submerged reefs and exploded violently, opening a cauldron of hell below and erupting spray high above. These suspicious pockets of saltwater energy are called boomers, and along this tangled coast they leapt all around us, window-shading into breakers, then cascading white and frothy against the rocky bluffs, dripping down like milk from a baby's face. Preferring our skeletons intact, we hurried through this gauntlet, dodging these minefields as best we could, focused on keeping a buffer between the rocks and our boats. We danced among a myriad of boomers and reefs at Hoop Bay and rode tidal surges that kept company with our adrenaline surges and pushed us along at nearly six knots as we eyeballed the ocean floor careening much too fast beneath our boats.

We were in the thick of wild country, a veritable Eden for wildlife. Both grizzlies and black bears roamed the beaches and pawed at huge boulders, barely noticing us as we paddled by. We didn't see any of the coastal wolves that travel in packs throughout this temperate rainforest, but felt certain they saw us. We did see dolphins, sea otters, sea urchins, and, finally, whales. Humpbacks. Together we enjoyed leisurely paddles along a rugged, dramatic coastline, caressed with sunshine and light winds. The rising tide gently pushed us north, over beds of eggplant-colored mussels, vibrant green anemones, and orange sea stars. We paddled away from the more open waters of Hoop Bay, Smith Sound, and Kelp Head, and crossed the fishing mecca of Rivers Inlet. All five species of salmon fatten up in these nutrient-dense waters; legendary chinooks have topped the scales at sixty pounds. We worked our way toward the numerous smaller islands, channels, and coves of Penrose Island Marine Park and came ashore at the angelically beautiful Fury Island. White shell-midden beaches lined Fury Cove, and had it not been for the frigid water and a north latitude of 51°29', we would have sworn we'd paddled into a tropical paradise. When the tide calmly engulfed the dazzling white crushed clam shells, it transformed the water from a dark blue to a deep turquoise.

We pitched our tents at the top of the midden, with open views to the west into Fitz Hugh Sound and into the quiet easterly lagoon created by Fury Cove. Tall stands of red cedar and hemlock graced the interior of the island, lending it a prehistoric feel. *Grizzly Bear*, an eye-catching fifty-foot schooner, all wood construction and emerald green trim, floated in the small harbor. As the tide lapped toward our bare toes, we lapped up vodka and orange juice, graciously supplied by Tom and Rena, *Grizzly Bear's* liveaboard owners.

They both wore mukluks (soft, knee-high boots indicative of sea-faring adventurers), jeans, and long-sleeved fleece shirts. Rena's thick brown hair danced in the breeze around her tanned olive skin and deep-set dark brown eyes. She had an air of refinement, incongruous with the rough-around-the-edges exterior some liveaboards maintain.

"You know, those tents of yours will be underwater with the midnight tide," Rena casually mentioned, her Canadian voice carrying just a hint of French. She sensed our disbelief. "Every last spec of the clam shell beach was underwater last night." That night would bring a full moon— and with it a fifteen-foot tide. We decided not to take any chances. Off into the woods we went with our nylon homes.

Later, Tom got to asking about my route further north. He and Rena often chose life afloat over a terrestrial existence and lived on their sailboat for years at a time. They knew these waters well. Tom, with his obvious passion for all things nautical, struck me as an old salt who still lived with one foot in the maritime past, a modern-day mariner, transplanted from another time, another ocean—perhaps born a century or more too late. A handsome, silver-bearded man with a headful of matching bushy hair, he pointed out a glut of places on my master chart that he thought I should visit. Intrigued, I watched his finger trace long passages, bays, and indentations in the coastline as he spoke of hot springs, waterfalls, and the Kermode spirit bear. Rena gathered firewood and kept our adult beverages thriving.

Just as Rena and Tom were retiring for the evening, a small yacht pulled into our quiet harbor and anchored fifty yards from *Grizzly Bear*. Yachties, sailors, kayakers—all sharing the same chunk of real estate, dipping into similar magical experiences for a speck of time. We were all mortals of the sea, here for similar reasons: a love of nature in her raw and natural beauty, and a desire to live simply and peacefully.

I'D TUCKED A SMALL BOTTLE OF SHAMPOO into my toiletry kit for the rare, hot shower. Becky and I had hoped that our self-imposed layover day on Fury Island, with a side trip to Buck's Trophy Lodge, would be such an occasion. The next morning, each armed with trial-sized containers of thick golden shampoo and small camp towels, Becky and I hugged the shoreline of Penrose Island where we aimed to duck into Finn Bay, a large indentation at its north end, and find civilization. We weren't stopping at just taking showers either. We'd also packed a dry bag full of grimy clothes, our Canadian currency, and our garbage. I'd read in my guidebook that the Finn Bay Resort and Buck's Lodge were the last of the Rivers Inlet fishing resorts, boasting many amenities. In our minds danced visions of silky clean hair, freshly laundered fleece, an empty garbage bag, and bellies full of fish and chips—and beer.

But instead we sat at Buck's Trophy Lodge, on a wooden bench, beneath a placard on the boardwalk that read "BULLSHIT BOULEVARD," with no humans in sight. Turns out we were a few weeks ahead of the season and the lodge was still shut tight. Only two forlorn calico cats, left to their mousing, kept us company. Still sporting grungy hair, dirty fingernails, and over-ripe armpits, we ate our humdrum lunch together, laughing on Bullshit Boulevard. Our consolation was trusting that we could properly freshen up at Namu, a former cannery town about a two-day paddle away.

When we were done eating, we wandered around the floating camp, peeking through locked glass windows into homey guest cabins, a tackle shop, and a laundry room. A dozen fishing boats with Honda outboard motors sat dry-docked, side by side. In the main lodge, tawdry plastic palm trees decorated with strands of chili pepper lights, a pool table, and a cast iron wood stove occupied a large, open room. A hot tub and sauna, to provide relief to the sore arms of anglers who had battled giant salmon for hours—and paid good money to do so—sat forsaken in the corner. In the back stood an oversized varnished bar, where we imagined a few oversized paunches had bellied up. An adjacent room housed a commercial-sized kitchen, brimming with propane tanks, chest freezers, and Formica counter tops. We fantasized about the aroma of cheeseburgers and fish and chips that would permeate the air when Buck's came to life, when scores of sport fishermen would spend their vacations here, living the beauty and wildness of coastal British Columbia for a short week, maybe two, if they were lucky, sharing their fish tales on Bullshit Boulevard. We, of course, would be long gone by that time.

NORTH OF QUEEN CHARLOTTE SOUND, the Inside Passage winds 250 miles through the Great Bear Rainforest, the largest intact coastal temperate rainforest in the world. Becky and I paddled beneath old-growth western red cedar, western hemlock, and Sitka spruce forests where cougars, wolves, bears, and Sitka black-tailed deer call home—a home that boldly fills twelve thousand square miles and 21 million acres.

While I was researching for my trip, I had learned that bears come in three colors in this fragile ecosystem: brown, black, and white. The white Kermode bear, also known as the spirit bear for its role in First Nations' lore, is often erroneously thought of as an albino bear, but is actually a black bear with a double recessive gene, which renders its coat white. Both the mama and papa bear must carry the recessive gene in order to produce the white cub. An Oreo-cookie litter often results, with both black and white cubs born from the same pregnancy; one in ten cubs born in the Great Bear Rainforest is white. Resembling a small polar bear, and found nowhere else on earth, the highest populations are found on Princess Royal Island and nearby Gribbell Island, an area I would be passing through soon after Becky and I parted in Bella Bella.

The Kermode bear symbolizes not only what is great about this magical place, but also what is threatened. In my research, I had learned how profit-driven trophy hunting of bears and wolves was upsetting the web of life in this forest. But that is just the tip of the iceberg. The wild salmon population, a vital link in the food chain of a healthy rainforest, was threatened both by overfishing and fish farming. Scientists believe sea lice and other parasites, often rampant in the concentrated environs of fish farms, infect the migrating juvenile wild salmon, enroute to their spawning grounds, which then die in huge numbers. This eventually results in bears and wolves, standing side by side in riverbeds, awaiting their much-anticipated seasonal fall buffet, often going hungry or even starving to death.

I also learned that this area is under threat from a proposed oil pipeline that would ultimately put up to 225 supertankers per year on the narrow arteries of the IP. These colossal ships, some as long as the Empire State Building is tall, would carry up to two million barrels of the world's dirtiest oil from the Alberta tar sands through this portion of the Inside Passage. This jarred my memory back to 1989 when the *Exxon Valdez* ran aground and dumped eleven million gallons of crude oil into the sea in Prince William Sound. Years later, an orgy of greed focused on short-term "benefits"—and the next election—evidently still hadn't learned from past mistakes.

There are simply some places where oil tankers should never go—the Great Bear Rainforest is one of them.

BECKY AND I FELL IN LOVE with the Koeye River, where we camped at its outlet on Heiltsuk First Nations' property, pitching our tents alongside a sun-bleached longhouse, embellished with First Nations' graphics. Bold black and red shapes formed whales, wolves, ravens, and eagles on exterior walls of the building, embodying, I assumed, specific meanings and purpose of which I was ignorant. The Koeye, a massive watershed that dumps into Fitz Hugh Sound, lies directly across from Hakai Passage, the opening between Calvert and Hunter Islands, two large landmasses responsible for deflecting the ocean swells from hitting the mainland.

To the west of the longhouse, in a clearing on a point guarding the entrance to the Koeye River, sat an L-shaped lodge. The lodge served as a base camp, along with three riverfront cabins, for the indigenous children of nearby Bella Bella, healing retreats, and eco-holidays for the public. The caretaker was away for a few days, but his two bear dogs enjoyed our company—and our beef jerky. That night they slept in the sand beside our tents; the lighter one guarded Becky, and the darker one guarded me. We were, after all, in dense grizzly country, and they

Wood, stone, feather and bone,
Spirit of the Ocean
going to carry you home.
River, Sea, Cedar Tree,
Spirit of the Wind
going to set you free ...
Angels singin','
Angels are singin'
in your soul,
in your soul.
  ~ Native saying

Becky riding the swells of Queen Charlotte Strait.

One of about a dozen
World War II hulks
anchored in the
shallows north of
Powell River,
British Columbia.

Above: Extreme high tides forced me deep into the forest at this campsite.

Below: 56 days at sea and still smiling.

Above: Paddling, spellbound, amidst icebergs in Holkham Bay that calved from the glacier.

Background: The base of Sumdum Glacier creeps down to the sea.

Majestic Sumdum Glacier robed in clouds
as seen from my cockpit.

High winds, angry seas, and rough surf
kept us stormbound at Burnett Bay
for three days.

The calm before the storm at Burnett Bay.

Dragging my heavy, loaded kayak
to the water's edge at low tide
as I continue north after the storm.

Above: A sunwashed Heiltsuk First Nations longhouse and canoe at the Koeye River.

Below: In a downpour, I struggle to wedge the last few items into the hatches as I prepare for the longest leg of the journey.

The topography starts to narrow and steepen at the southern end of Grenville Channel.

The six-foot-high dorsal fins of frolicking orcas surround me.

Above: Humpbacks play outside my tent. Note the heart-shaped whale breath.

The abandoned seaside village of Butedale.

Butedale Falls plummets into the sea.

After dreary days of rain, the sun burst through the clouds and turned the peak behind my campsite golden.

Hitching a ride on the *Pacific Coast*.

A magnificent Alaskan sunset greeted me as I arrived in the 49th State.

Above: Just a couple days out of Juneau, happy to be warm and dry.
Below: I chose a picture-perfect place for my last campsite!

had a job to do. I named them Cocoa and Puff to complement the color of their fur.

Sea Diary

May 30, 2010, day 26, Koeye River

Lying in my tent, 10 p.m., catching up on some journal entries while a crimson sunset lingers outside my door. A cruise ship just floated by about a mile offshore, lights all aglow. It resembles a floating city, loudspeakers blaring, informing the thousands of tourists aboard about the remarkable area they are passing through.

This "lady of the sea" struts about in front of me, a buoyant land of milk and honey—and for one brief moment I am jealous of their decadence. By shifting my perspective I realize that I am the lucky one here. The cruisers only see the big picture. It's a beauty all right, but what they miss is the micro view. The details. By virtue of my kayak, I'm privy to an intimate perspective not seen from bigger craft. The pervasive aroma of the cedars and spruces offers no redolence to them. They cannot breathe in the stillness of a starry night. They cannot study the imprint of a wolf's foot or tickle the underside of a sea anemone. Do they pine, I wonder, to lie on their bellies on cedar boughs, peering up at a bald eagle, camera perched, lens zoomed? Click—they missed it. They are missing the intimacy of the interface between land and sea, they lose a sense of detail, a sense of scale. Nor do they feel the coolness of the seawater as it trickles through fingers while washing a dish up after dinner. Or feel the utter satisfaction of delirious exhaustion from self-propelled power. How unfortunate, I thought, to not intimately tune into the rhythm of the sea, to experience the deep ebb and flow. I understand, however, that the only way some people can experience these magical places is to travel onboard these larger, self-contained vessels. I don't wish to diminish their experience by reveling in mine. Each traveler will come away with a distinct vision, and leave their own unique thumbprint on the Inside Passage.

But I cannot even begin to share, to explain the beauty of this area I have the privilege of paddling through. Words cannot express the sights, the sounds, the smells. The whales, wolves, bears, eagles, loons, the people, the spirits permeating these ancient forests, the mountains, and, of course, the water. It's all so magical. I feel so very fortunate.

Cocoa watched my every move as I packed up the next morning, and followed me up and down the beach as I loaded my kayak. I petted him gently, looked deep into his eyes, and asked that his spirit stay with me and keep me safe. I could tell from his expression that it would and thanked him by giving him my last piece of jerky. It was hard to say goodbye to Cocoa and Puff. They ran through the forest and out onto the point as we paddled away, watching us until we disappeared on the horizon. Each time I looked back over my shoulder, they were still standing there, watching, waiting.

Together

IN LESS THAN TWO HOURS we paddled into the nautical ghost town of Namu, a defunct cannery, full of ghostly élan, like a dusty mansion with all of great-grandma's furnishings in place. Giant, dilapidated piers hung out over the water. They once served as a welcome mat to a bustling community with a booming salmon industry and large cannery operation. But in 1980, BC Packers closed their doors and walked away, leaving the community to dissolve back into the sea in its own time. First impressions were uninspiring, but if you looked long enough, I thought, you could feel the nostalgia of a lost era, the sense of history behind the dilapidated clapboard facade, the hustle and bustle of the old cannery, and the traces of the people who made their living here.

"Ahoy!" yelled Theresa, one of three caretakers, kneeling down to grab hold of my deck rigging. We tentatively paddled up to the rotten dock and I wondered if the whole thing would give way and tumble into the sea. "Welcome to Namu!"

With brief formalities out of the way, we clamored out of our boats and stretched our legs on the slippery wood. Fallen from years of neglect, the sagging roofs, rain-soaked planks, peeling paint, and rotting rope were evocative of an aging woman who has let herself go.

"Watch your step," Theresa said repeatedly. We followed her around the property, her index finger pointing out various notables, as if on a docent tour. Her reminders did not go unnoticed; hazards lurked everywhere, including loose planks, gaping holes, crumbling walls—and dog poop.

"You can pitch your tents on the dock," she explained, "or for an extra fifteen bucks, sleep on a bed in the old Namu Cafe. There's no electricity or water. No sheets either, but you gals got sleeping bags, right?" We nodded. "There's flush toilets just down the dock," she added, pointing to a shabby building not much larger than a telephone booth. Sold.

I unfurled my sleeping bag on top of a stained black and white striped mattress lying lumpily on a rusted frame. Vintage 1972 or thereabouts. Large rusty pots sat on the floor, strategically placed to catch the drips from the leaky roof. I looked out across the piers and Namu Harbor through a large picture window, surprisingly still intact.

"Whales have swum right up under those windows," Theresa said, "so keep a keen eye." She told us the story of how Namu was the namesake of the killer whale Namu, the second orca ever displayed in captivity, who was captured nearby in 1965. She explained how the whale had gotten snared in a drifting salmon net, close to shore, and how the fisherman who owned the net sold Namu to the Seattle Marine Aquarium, transporting him in a floating pen all the way to Seattle, where he would be incarcerated, star in a movie, entertain tourists—and die, probably from loneliness, within one year.

Becky hung her damp paddling top on a cracked counter stool, eyeing a similarly rusty bed frame next to a gray marbled Formica countertop with teal trim. Although a meal hadn't been served for years at the old Namu Cafe, silver napkin dispensers still held rectangular paper napkins, and half-full salt and pepper shakers sat beside them. Sugar packets filled a glass jar, and an electric cash register, still plugged in, rested under the counter where I imagined the cook shouted "ORDER UP!" on numerous occasions. Three dry erase boards showcased the menu, and a suspended chalkboard announced the specials of the day: pizza by the slice for $2, split pea soup and green salad for $4, fish and chips for $5. We craned our necks to read the slanted handwriting, salivating in unison. Confident our lair was ready for the evening, we walked back down to the lower dock to check out the cooking arrangements.

"How does crab sound for dinner?" Theresa asked.

"Yes, ma'am," we answered enthusiastically and simultaneously.

"Well, there you go," she said, pointing to a large bucket swarming with live crabs. "Fellers just dropped 'em off. Don't come any fresher than this." With her thumb and forefinger she snatched one out of the bucket, cracked it violently against the dock railing, discarded the shell and innards back to the sea, and threw the meaty legs and bodies into an empty bucket. One, two, three large crabs awaited us for dinner that night! All vestiges of gentility were thrown overboard with the crab shells. We consumed every last morsel, dipped in melted butter with shallots, garlic, rosemary, and parsley, the herbs freshly picked from Theresa's garden. We feasted for over an hour. Finally, butter dripping from our elbows, our shirts covered with crab meat and shell debris, we waved the white pig-out flag and surrendered.

Later, while Becky wandered about the property, I dug a chocolate bar out of my day hatch and ate it under the bunkhouse roof. Rain sprinkled lightly all around me. Except for the hum of Theresa's generator, all was tranquil and calm. I stuffed the crumpled wrapper into my pocket and walked through a nautical time warp; past the gutted cannery and former warehouse, past the doddering downtown, past the machine shop, past rusted propane tanks and rotted rope. I wound my way up the elevated wooden sidewalk along the hillside and above the sea, to my retrograde bed with the stained striped mattress, and a peaceful night's sleep.

THE COMMUNITIES OF SHEARWATER AND BELLA BELLA lay about thirty miles to the north of Namu. On a quickly dropping tide, Becky and I paddled past thousands of sea anemones clinging to cliffs that were plastered with starfish, purple urchins, and sea-salted barnacles. A rainbow of color splattered sheer rock faces, as if someone had tossed a bucket of tie-dye paint against the cliffs. The mushroom-like bodies of bright orange lion's mane jellyfish pulsed up, then down, beneath our hulls, and nearly transparent moon jellies, resembling white parachutes, lethargically floated with the current. A forest of long, hair-like tentacles cascaded from the underside of their jiggling somas. Forty-ton humpback whales graced us with their poise in Fitz Hugh Sound, spouting and displaying their large tail flukes for us to admire. We drifted and watched, cameras raised, waiting for the next spout, the next glimpse of a whopping tail fluke, or a stately, glistening black body as it surfaced.

Soon, a sharp dogleg to the west revealed our entrance into Lama Passage. We intended to camp at Serpent Point at the east end of the passage, but large mounds of bear scat spoke volumes that it might be best to push on. It began to rain, and we scanned our charts—and the shoreline—for other options. Other potential sites farther up the channel didn't pan out either; Westminster Point and Canal Bight both appeared dangerously close to becoming a shallow saltwater pond come high tide.

So we kept paddling, and in a light mist on the last day of May, we pulled into Shearwater, my third resupply port and the ending point for Becky's leg of the journey. It was eight p.m., twelve and a half hours and

29 nautical miles after we left Namu that same morning. Rumpled and ravenous, we tethered our kayaks to the dock and walked up to the only lodging option in town, the Shearwater Hotel. A pathetic pair, we stood dripping wet at the lobby counter, two puddles slowly forming beneath our pruned feet.

We promptly learned that each room featured one twin bed—and went for a whopping $107, plus tax. Janice, the receptionist, a plump woman in her early forties, listened intently as Becky and I discussed who would sleep on the floor. Taking pity, she reached out, took my ice-cold hands in both of hers, and sighed heavily. "You girls desperately need a hot shower and a warm meal, and I can't bear to think either of you'd sleep on the floor after what you've been through!" She fished around beside her desk for a moment, and soon a pudgy outstretched hand with pink fingernail polish held out two keys to two separate rooms that shared a bathroom. "That'll be a total of $107, plus tax," she winked. We didn't argue. And, since the kitchen was closing in forty minutes, we didn't shower either, in spite of an 11-day hiatus from proper personal hygiene.

After retrieving a few crucial dry bags from our kayaks, we changed into dirty but dry clothes and ran through the raindrops to the only pub in town. Two pints of dark beer and approximately 2,000 calories later, we retreated to our rooms and flipped a Canadian coin to see who would take the first shower. I lost. While Becky showered, I futzed with my gear more to stay awake than anything else. Before long, a thick pink plastic curtain stuck to my body as I stood under a stream of warm running water—deliciously clean, non-salty, warm running water. The hot and cold knobs squeaked as I twisted them to the off position. Standing with a towel wrapped around me, I could hear Becky snoring through the thin walls. Within minutes, I collapsed into my own deep sleep.

The next morning, after a lengthy phone call to Jim, I made plans to paddle north in two days. Solo again. The joint venture had come to an end. Sharing this leg of the journey with Becky was a delight and a privilege, an honor that heightened and deepened my experience and made me even more aware of the beauty and awe of it all. Rewinding our journey together, I visually embraced the scenery, the wildlife, the spirits that abounded out there, the people we had met, the kindness we were privy to. It was all so staggering. I thought about the inner and outer strength one acquires from doing something of this nature day after day. We'd paddled in different boats, but were united by the same sea. Although we'd traveled the same section of the Inside Passage together, our respective journeys were sometimes oceans apart. Yet, to sit next to each other on a rock at lunchtime, to marvel at the scenery together, to soak up the sun, or shiver side by side in our soggy paddling gear—two buddies anticipating the next camp, a hot meal, and our respective tents—broadened my experience. Although I thought of my journey as a solo, enjoying the camaraderie with Becky reminded me how much I cherished our friendship—and how much I missed other dear friends back home. Our time together was the perfect break for me, an intermission of sorts, which recharged me and helped refocus my intent. When I set off solo again, on my thirtieth day, I'd be paddling into the second half of my journey.

That night, I wedged myself in a corner of Shearwater's marine store, sitting in front of an old Hewlett Packard PC I'd rented for five dollars an hour. Facing a cement wall, with the ocean at my back, and a tall freezer stuffed with TV dinners three inches from my right elbow, I muddled along on the glacially slow Internet connection. As gale force winds built outside, I typed an email blast to my loyal followers, recapping the last leg of the journey and touching on upcoming hopes and expectations. I told them that tomorrow, weather permitting, I would paddle north toward my next destination—the large seaport of Prince Rupert. That Becky would take the ferry back to Port Hardy a few days later. That I anticipated a poignant departure whose only consolation was knowing that her beaming face would later greet me in Bellingham, where she would scoop me off the Alaska Ferry, the blue-hulled vessel that would transport me back to the starting gate, rewinding my entire trip in three short days. With gratitude, I thanked my followers for their encouragement and support. I wrote about the things I missed most and about how I vowed to not take these amenities for granted.

My not-to-take-for-granted list:
- running water
- warm running water
- clean hair that you can actually run your fingers through (because it was washed in warm running water)
- cream in my coffee
- clean fingernails
- napkins
- butter
- clean underwear
- shaved legs
- clean cotton socks
- a flat place to sleep
- heat
- two bars on my cellphone
- did I mention running water?

But, I continued in my email, I wouldn't trade this lack of amenities for the world because here's what I get in its place:
- whales
- wolves
- bears
- marine life galore
- amazing interactions with people who live on the sea
- dramatic scenery
- wind, waves, swell

- courage and determination
- a high fitness level
- the smallest waist I've had since 8th grade
- and soon — ICEBERGS AND GLACIERS!

Leg 4 ⛵ 250 miles ⛵ 10 days

Leg 4
Shearwater to Prince Rupert
approximately 250 miles • 10 days

Five

Bella Bella
to Prince Rupert

*The longer and more difficult the journey,
the better the rewards along the way.*

—Author unknown

Achilles Heel

EARLY IN THE MORNING, on the third day of June, I stuffed my hatches one bulging dry bag at a time, as a torrential downpour threatened to dampen my enthusiasm. Becky looked on empathetically as the pouring rain foiled my attempts to keep things dry. I quietly swore under my breath at my skirmish with the rain, the stubborn hatches, and the piles of gear. A quart of Vaseline and a long-handled shoehorn might have made filling every last fistful of space in that boat a tad easier. At least I was warm from the exertion.

With a sense of urgency, I wrestled the chart numbered 3720 into its malleable clear rectangular case that was tethered to my deck, slightly annoyed at its lack of cooperation. I slipped eight other successive charts that would eventually guide me to Prince Rupert into a separate dry bag, along with pertinent books and journals. Finally, the last item securely stowed, I snapped the hatch covers onto their rims, donned my sprayskirt and PFD, hugged Becky goodbye, and shoved off.

I was eager to fly solo again, yet it didn't seem right to be paddling away, leaving Becky standing on that beach alone. We'd just shared 150 miles together over an eleven-day span. Now, she would catch the ferry back to Port Hardy, and I would continue north in my sea kayak. To celebrate our last night of the trip together, we'd rented a beach flat in Bella Bella, a small First Nations community across the bay from Shearwater. Blinking back tears, I glanced over my left shoulder several times as my friend's waving arm, and the town of Bella Bella, disappeared behind me. Alone at sea once more.

My boat felt sluggish, loaded down with two weeks' worth of food. I paddled slowly for several hours, easing back into my solo groove. When I approached Ivory Island, I spotted a classic red and white lighthouse perched on its south end, high above the water. In my mind I munched on cookies and drank hot cocoa with the lighthouse keepers, or "wickies" as they were often called. Before many lighthouses became automated, the lighthouse keepers would climb to the top of the lantern room, where lamps that ran on oil fueled a fixed white light and a flashing red light. The wickies, who kept the lights burning, would trim the wicks on the lamps so they wouldn't smoke and create a sooty film on the glass. I'd be on my best behavior and the wickies would invite me to spend the night with them, or so my pipe dream continued. I had read accounts of other kayakers having this good fortune, and I longed for a similar encounter.

With a rising tide, I landed on the north end of the island as my chart, and Audrey's notes, indicated. I tied up Chamellia, slung my camera over my shoulder, and began a precarious twenty-minute hike toward the lighthouse on a rotten, dilapidated boardwalk through a magical, old-growth forest. As the trees began to thin, I saw more sky and heard roaring surf. Leaving the boardwalk, I climbed up a short cliff face and stood atop a helicopter pad. In large white block letters, facing Milbanke Sound, the words "IVORY ISLAND" were thickly painted on the cement pad. Weather-beaten mangled cedar and spruce trees loomed above me. A red and white wind sock blew almost horizontally in the stiff wind. The incoming swell collided with submerged rocks, forming boomers that exploded violently below me. I sauntered across a modern and inviting bridge, also red and white, to the lighthouse and main grounds. Humming generators, a brand-new John Deere lawnmower parked in the freshly mown grass, and fluorescent lights left on in several buildings gave promising signs of life.

"Helloooooo, anybody home?" I hollered. Silence. *Darn.* In spite of my loitering, lingering, and snapping photos for an inordinate amount of time, not a soul surfaced to invite me in. Unhurriedly, I retreated back to my kayak, keeping a keen ear for a delayed response—remaining hopeful for cookies and cocoa. *Double darn.*

Instead of an iconic red and white structure as my sleeping quarters, my drab olive-green nylon tent would have to suffice. A short distance away, my camp at Roar Islet would complete a sixteen-mile day. I spied the perfect flat spot, safe from the highest tides, and pitched my tent, trying not to sulk. My tiny private island had sweeping views of Blair Inlet and Seaforth Channel. The smooth pebble beach afforded easy access, a short haul, zero bugs, and a lack of fine sand to pervade my gear. Only a curmudgeon could mope for very long with these amenities.

THE NEXT TWENTY MILES brought me to a lovely campsite perched on the eastern edge of Jackson Passage, at the western side of Rescue Bay, with sweet views looking north up Mathieson Channel. I'd read that it was a popular anchorage for power boaters because of its protected waters. Sure enough, when I arrived, a beautiful wooden boat with a forest green hull was anchored in the bay. The Canadian flag attached to its stern deck flapped in the breeze. A man dressed in khaki shorts and matching collared short-sleeve shirt rowed over in a small skiff with his dog shortly after I landed. He packed two large canisters of bear spray on one hip and a pistol on the other, which reminded me that grizzlies roamed this land. Employed by the prawn industry, Robin was charged with checking for regulation compliance by all boaters in the area. He immediately put me at ease by mentioning his wife was accompanying him on his work boat.

"Don't hesitate to call us on the radio if you become spooked," Robin said as he and Coyote shoved off. "Channel 9. Always comes through in the cabin." Every night on this journey I had slept with my VHF radio within arm's reach, along with my usual arsenal: a flare gun, diver's knife, bear spray, cellphone, and SPOT. I could spray an intruder, I figured, then fire my flare gun point-blank, cut a hole in the other side of the tent with my knife to escape, call for help on either the VHF or cellphone, then depress the 911 button on SPOT so they would know where to find my body. But this night I felt safe knowing this nice couple and their dog were anchored not far away.

The next morning, leaving the protected waters of Rescue Bay, I felt rested, strong, and confident. Gear had cooperatively slid into the hatches, Chamellia had slid quietly into the water, and I had slid gracefully into Chamellia. The rough edges of gravity seemed to have melted away. I floated effortlessly, existing in a different reality, on top of the gouged-out channels that characterize the deep coastal fjords of British Columbia. The terrain was changing, and as I progressed up the ever-narrowing channel of Jackson Passage, I paddled into a dramatically different landscape, an intimate channel with high forested ridges soaring overhead. Its beauty seemed primeval. Heavily forested, gently rolling hills sensually met the water's surface. Smoke-like cloud tendrils wrapped around the tops of trees and then slowly wafted down the hillsides, enveloping all that was green.

As intimate and comforting as Jackson Passage was, it connected two huge channels of water: Mathieson and Finlayson, both of which had the potential to be discomforting. Jim had traversed this area on day 47 of his trip; I was here on day 32 of mine. He wrote in his journal:

One has a sense of being grudgingly allowed to traverse these waters. They are big, and when they are quiet, one is even then aware that safe passage can be withdrawn in the blink of an eye. It is with a bit of tension and trepidation that I paddle these waters.

Carrying a hint of Jim's trepidation with me, I worked my way through this beautiful channel flanked with stunning mountains, experiencing only dead calm waters. Eerily calm. Ghostly quiet. As I paddled, the only sounds were my breath, my blade piercing the water's surface, and the slight cavitation of my stern as it displaced the water beneath my hull, leaving a trail of spinning bubbles behind it.

Gradually the terrain became steeper and more abrupt, and I wondered how anything could take root on these sheer cliff walls, let alone grow skyward. Snow-covered mountains loomed above nearly perpendicular cliffs, which in turn plunged straight into the sea. Unlike a mountain climber, I couldn't detect the curvature of the earth from the vista of my kayak, yet my view was every bit as stunning. The clear waters beneath my hull were replete with colorful sea cucumbers, jellyfish, and anemones. Shades of green and slate-grey dominated nature's palette, frequently punctuated by the stark white tail of a bald eagle. I'd lost count of how many I'd encountered—well over a hundred that day alone.

By the time I arrived at the First Nations village of Klemtu, it had started to drizzle. I pulled up alongside the community dock, crawled out of my boat, and took stock of my surroundings. As the drizzle turned to a hard rain, I wandered around some buildings in various stages of disrepair. I saw no one until I entered what appeared to be the only restaurant in town. The owner, wearing a black-and-white checkered smock and stained white trousers, greeted me with a warm hello as I stood dripping on his cold tile floor.

"Any place in this town where a girl could buy a roof over her head?" I asked as confidently as I could. He reached out and enthusiastically shook my pruned hand.

"Wet adventure today, eh? Let me make a few phone calls."

I searched his face as he returned from his small office down the hallway. I had a roof all right—a $125 roof. And that, I was told, was deeply discounted for a lone kayaker on a wet, blustery day. The newly constructed $1.5-million Spirit Bear Lodge, owned by the Kitasoo/Xaixais First Nation, had recently begun offering guided tour packages into the Great Bear Rainforest for travelers hoping to glimpse the lodge's namesake, the white spirit bear. I didn't really have a budget; my plan was simply to be frugal. This was not frugal—but with limited and unappealing options for camping nearby, I gulped back my budgetary woes and agreed to take it.

I threw my damp, sandy gear onto a king-size bed and scanned the sparkling white kitchenette. The bathroom offered a full tub, designer soaps, plush white towels, and a hair dryer. The empty lobby provided a laptop with Internet access, and a front-loading washer and dryer occupied an adjacent room. In the Great Room, two twelve-foot solid cedar tables sat beneath cathedral ceilings, and the large windows afforded a panoramic view of Klemtu Passage. I plopped down on a large black leather couch and caught up on emails, downloaded more than four hundred images from my Nikon to my online photo storage, and made a few phone calls. A paltry three days into this leg, it all seemed hugely overindulgent.

Later, sliding under the decadently deep and soft covers of my bed, it seemed preposterous that I was here, freshly showered, with a full belly, my salty clothes dangling on velvet hangers in an oversized closet, sleeping between satin sheets in a palatial bed. I didn't want to be here. I had grown accustomed to fresh air. I now craved it and felt a deep need to be outside. The four walls seemed artificial and claustrophobic to me. I didn't want a glass window pane, no matter how spectacular the view, between me and my world.

Prying my eyes open the next morning, I felt impatient to get on the water. It was time to go. Gratefully putting Klemtu behind me, I stroked my way up Klemtu Passage, which merged into Tolmie Channel, which in turn became Graham Reach—the first of the infamous reaches, an arduous leg of beauty and grandeur that would test my grit and patience. I hugged the mainland side of Graham Reach and spied a humpback whale quietly surfacing and exhaling in the middle of the channel. A heart-shaped cloud of whale breath momentarily hung above the dark, polished body. About an hour later another welcome distraction, this time a smaller but stocky minke whale, surfaced nearby.

A cursory glance at my charts revealed dreadfully long white fingers that represented the cavernous reaches, long narrow passageways that bisected equally lengthy and largely uninhabited islands from the mainland. After Graham Reach got done reaching, it became Fraser Reach, which merged into McKay Reach and finally the 45-mile long Grenville Channel.

Nautical charts typically display most of their detail on the *water*, but it was the beige contours of *land*, with all their squiggly wiggly black lines, that concerned me. I was a paddler, not a hiker, but I knew enough to realize that these were a chart maker's efforts at noting some extremely steep-ass terrain. Mouthing some of the place names on my chart— Countess of Dufferin Range, Burnaby Range, and Bare Top Range—I snickered, thinking they sounded like scenes out of the 1960s TV series *Dark Shadows*.

The numbers scattered on top of the beige contours, indicating the height of the mountains less than one mile offshore, made me take notice as well: 2,730, 2,605, 2,765, 3,345 feet. At the point where I would enter it from the south, Grenville Channel was about a mile wide, with low-lying forested hills. Within ten miles, the channel would be contained between steep walls rising more than two thousand feet. Twenty miles further, the fjord narrowed considerably, squeezing more tightly in with vertiginous walls. Peaks over three thousand feet would tower above me, and sheer cliffs would plunge below me: my chart showed depths of nearly 1,200 feet in some areas. I was paddling through what had once been a river of ice, the obvious handiwork of the deepest Pleistocene glaciers.

Thumbing through *Kayaking the Inside Passage*, I scanned the pertinent sections and read what the author had to say about this remote area:

It is wild and steep, subject to strong currents and very isolated. ...Campsites are scarce ... shores are mostly perpendicular precepts. Landings—much less campsites—are few, tenuous, and impractical. Currents are a bit odd ...Winds freshen in the afternoon ... and can be funneled with alarming velocity.

I prayed his book was outdated.

After rising at four a.m. to catch most of the flood up Graham Reach, I finally spotted the eastern end of two-and-a-half mile-long Work Island. I'd been paddling for nearly seven hours and looked forward to overnighting at Butedale, which was just around the corner, tucked into a cove on the northeast side of the very large Princess Royal Island. Work Island separates Butedale Passage from Malcolm Passage, signifying the end of Graham Reach and the beginning of Fraser Reach, a lingering stretch of water I would contend with tomorrow. For now I was so delighted to put Graham Reach in my rear-view mirror that I burst out in song, concocting my own version of the movie Oz's *The Witch is Dead*: "Ding Dong! The reach is dead, the reach is dead, the wicked Old Graham Reach is dead. Wake up, sleepyhead, rub your eyes, get out of bed. Old Graham Reach is dead!"

Inspecting the inset on my chart for Butedale, I noticed Jim's penciled notes stating "abandoned, dangerously collapsed docks and buildings." I'd read in my guidebook that a caretaker resides in Butedale and there were some amenities. I'd read elsewhere that other kayakers had overnighted here. Surely, I thought, there had been some repairs.

My brief stay at Butedale, with its peculiar nautical ghost town feel, was reminiscent of Namu. Surveying the grounds, I wondered if I hadn't stepped back in time, or stumbled into a Twilight Zone episode. Butedale was one of about twenty large Canadian fishing operations along the Inside Passage that thrived until overfishing depleted the salmon runs.

"In its prime," wrote my guidebook's author, "Butedale Creek, plunging vertically from Butedale Lake, provided power to the flourishing community via a giant Pelton wheel turbine hooked up to a wooden penstock." By 1973, all canning had ceased, and only a caretaker remained to provide moorage and dole out heavenly treats.

"ICE CREAM," read a large wooden sign with rough, hand-painted letters. I had just entered the cove leading into Butedale, lured in by the sound and sight of the rumbling waterfall on the cove's north end, when I immediately noticed the sign perched high on a moss-draped rock. I was desperately low on chocolate, growing ever more weary of granola bars, and a sucker for direct marketing. I paddled faster toward dilapidated buildings that stood out over the water, like a house of cards, dominating the landscape. Lou, the caretaker, waited on the dock as I approached, craning his neck, obviously wondering where the other kayakers in my group were.

"You all alone?" he asked in awe.

"Yup, flying solo," I said while he steadied my kayak against the rickety dock. "Your ice cream sign certainly got my attention." I rolled out of the cockpit, trying to get my land legs after too many hours of sitting in a fixed position.

"Butedale Lou," a bespectacled man whom I estimated to be in his late sixties, was from Quebec and spoke in the charming French Canadian accent indicative of that area. He was pleasant and outwardly harmless, wore black dungarees, a tan tee shirt, and a black ball cap. He had a firm handshake, a barrel chest, and a jowly face with gray sideburns and matching gray hair—what little of it I could see under his hat. Bert, a mangy old dog, also with salt and pepper hair, was always by his side. Tiger, a tabby cat who looked like he had already lived eight of his nine lives, slept fitfully on the dock.

Jim's chart annotations from 1992 still stood true: I saw zero evidence of any type of restoration having taken place. Most buildings stood in a state of unabashed disrepair. Some structures were so far gone that they resembled a game of pick-up-sticks; you didn't dare touch one piece lest the whole kit and caboodle come tumbling down. A mere puff of wind might collapse any number of buildings perched cockeyed on the rolling hillside. Large wharves crumbled into the sea. Trees grew straight up off thickly moss-covered roofs, and dense vegetation monopolized every nook and cranny around the buildings. Rotting lumber floated around the slippery dock, which was barely intact. Piles of frayed rope, rusty metal parts, rotten wood, and other debris littered the ground. Taking all this in, I wondered exactly what Lou's job description was since he presided over the ruins of a town folding in on itself—whatever it was, he certainly didn't seem to be doing a very good job.

Yet, he was a kind man and warmheartedly took me under his wing, insisting I have a roof over my head for the evening. The condition of the roof was what concerned me. I cautiously followed Lou and his ragtag family to a gutted house on the hill, walking past several other structures that had once housed over four hundred workers living onsite, employed by the canning, fishing, logging, and mining industries.

The roof of our target house appeared to be intact, I noted with relief. Retired Christmas lights were strung in odd patterns on the front porch and scratched music CDs were intermixed with the lights—someone's attempt, I thought, to add an artistic touch. The front door, barely hanging on its hinges, creaked open, and we stepped inside. A dank, musty odor greeted my nostrils and I surveyed the peeling paint, warped linoleum, and broken panes of glass in tiny bug-encrusted windows.

"The water heater broke last winter," Lou said, turning the cold water faucet on the kitchen sink clockwise until a stream of cedar-tinged water came out. The sink was ringed with rust and lime patterns, and dead flies lay scattered inside it. A plastic Palmolive bottle stood behind the sink, a layer of green gunk congealed on its lid. "But you got all the cold water you need, and a toilet, too," he said, proudly pointing to the commode down the hallway. It was also ringed with rust and lime, and the lid had a deep crack in it. Lou hooked up a propane cooking stove that sat on the counter and then made a roaring fire inside the pot-bellied wood stove which occupied the middle of the kitchen. My living quarters suddenly seemed more agreeable. And all these amenities for only twenty dollars—

how could a girl go wrong?

"You got a flashlight?" Lou asked, observing me inspecting the cobweb-laden, frayed electrical lines that hung laughably from the ceiling.

"I'm all set, Lou. Been camping for weeks, so I'm just fine without electricity."

A water-powered generator provided electricity in the main house where Lou lived, but that was the extent of the power supply. To harness the energy from the nearby waterfall, Lou had ingeniously masterminded a system using a sizable marine battery, automotive belts and alternators, pulleys, an inverter, and salvaged wire. To my untrained eye, it was a haphazard contraption, but to Lou it was a logical, effective system to keep the lights on in his house.

"Come on down for ice cream later if you'd like," Lou said and then wandered back down the hill with Bert and Tiger at his heels.

After dinner, I stared at virgin rows of chocolate, vanilla, and strawberry ice cream that filled a five-gallon plastic bucket perched on Lou's kitchen counter. "Dig in," he said, handing me a tarnished ice cream scoop, the heavy, antique style that might live in your grandmother's kitchen gadget drawer. With Lou's blessing, I scooped out only the chocolate, leaving a frozen Neapolitan crevasse between the white and pink layers.

Below us, the gunmetal-gray waters in Butedale Passage quietly licked at the dock. Lou told me about the white spirit bears that live on Princess Royal Island and often wander into Butedale. Two days earlier, directly beneath the ice cream sign that had enticed me the day before, he'd seen one sniffing around. Now *that* would have been a Kodak moment!

My belly bloated with cream and sugar, I thanked Lou and declined his offer of a bacon and eggs breakfast, wanting nothing more than to enjoy my "suite" with an agenda-less morning. I rolled out my sleeping bag on the lumpy black and white striped mattress that lay on the floor and fell fast asleep to the sounds of the near-vertical Butedale Falls plunging not far from my window.

I had arrived on a northerly flood current and, according to my chart and guidebook, I needed to exit on an ebb—an ebb that would also flow north. The odd tidal currents in Princess Royal Channel gushed in from opposite ends, colliding in the middle; their juncture was an inlet just south of Butedale. My rendezvous with the ebb train was at eleven a.m. No need to get on the water until ten o'clock, a late start compared to my normal routine. I could sleep in. I intended to camp on the southwestern corner of Gribbell Island that night, 23 miles away, and needed to make good time once on the water.

Flipping through my guidebook the next morning for some quick pre-launch advice, I learned that for the first thirteen miles, with one small exception, I would encounter "perpendicular walls with absolutely no landings." There on my chart Jim had penciled in a similar warning: "Almost impossible to come ashore between Butedale and Angler Cove."

Lou, Tiger, and Bert greeted me as I carried a load of gear from the house on the hill down toward the rickety dock. Lou graciously helped with the next load, saving me a trip. We laughed when my bulky PFD bounced off his barrel chest when I wrapped my arms around him to hug goodbye. He stabilized my kayak, and I clambered back in, at the exact spot where he had first greeted me the day before. I pushed off, waved, and paddled away. After a few strokes I let the boat glide, swiveled my head, and waved again at Lou, who was still standing there, alongside the salt and pepper dog and the tabby cat.

I COULDN'T IMAGINE THE SCENERY in Fraser Reach improving, but it did, becoming peacefully calm and stunningly beautiful. I enjoyed the cooling spray from a series of cascading waterfalls that fell thousands of feet, piercing the stillness with their sea-pummeling pandemonium. Although I had just refilled all my dromedary bags back at Butedale, I paddled beneath the first waterfall and topped off one of the bladders by simply unscrewing its cap and sticking my arm out to let the cold, clear liquid gush in, ballooning it to capacity. It was the clearest, cleanest, coldest, sweetest-tasting water that had ever passed my lips. Nature's magnificent water fountain.

As expected, once Fraser Reach took a sharp dogleg to the west, it transformed into McKay Reach. Like the runt of the reach litter, it was a delightfully short eight miles, while Graham, Fraser, and Grenville were a whopping nineteen, thirteen, and 45, respectively. By the time I neared the end of McKay Reach, I'd been on the water for nearly nine hours. I looked down at my chart and studied the seven channels that converged in Wright Sound. From the bird's eye view of my one-dimensional chart, it resembled the nucleus of a gigantic mutant octopus, one that could swallow me up if I didn't mind my Ps and Qs. On the other side of this octopus roundabout lay the entrance to the interminable Grenville Channel, a foreboding finger of water I'd enter the next day, weather permitting, when I left my campsite on Gribbell Island.

I first had to find this campsite and, with darkness dangerously approaching, I paddled up and down Gribbell Island's coastline seeking a decent spot to call home for the night. It had been a long day, so my standards for decent waned rapidly. Desperate, I was willing to settle on just about anything where I could lay my head. And settle I did, on a wretched and practically nonexistent beach that would be completely submerged within a few hours. A jumble of large driftwood logs, tossed in from previous storms, lay scattered between the fast approaching sea and my only recourse: a pitifully small, uneven speck of earth crammed up against the cliffs.

I stared dejectedly at the driftwood-strewn obstacle course that lay before me. I lugged gear bags, paddles, and water bladders until there was nothing left to move but Chamellia herself. Grunting, I dragged her across the logs until I was confident she wouldn't float away in the night. I tied her to a log that I knew wouldn't budge in even the fiercest storms. I then sat next to my kayak and nursed my poor attitude with a dark chocolate bar, hoping it would also give me an extra boost to set up camp.

I gazed across Wright Sound as the chocolate melted in my mouth and anxiety flooded through my body. This sensation started in the pit of my stomach and then traveled up through my chest and lodged in my throat. I didn't know where this anxiety had come from; I couldn't understand it, nor could I quell it, so instead I ignored it and retreated to my tent. By eleven p.m. I was zipped inside my sleeping bag, making a journal entry by headlamp while the tide lapped within inches of my nylon rainfly. A restful night's sleep was not in the cards, and unbeknownst to me, this was the genesis of misery.

Wild Cards

AT FIVE A.M. ON DAY 36, I gaped beneath my rainfly at the whitecaps on Wright Sound and the small surf washing up on the shores of Gribbell Island. Groaning, I flopped back into the warmth of my sleeping bag. Two hours later, I awoke to an unmistakable "PWOOF" just outside my tent. Orcas! I quickly unzipped the door as eight six-foot-high dorsal fins knifed through the water directly in front of me, heading north, like I was. Within minutes, their fins were merely specs in the distance, but my heart still pounded with excitement long after they had disappeared from my view. Without the whales to focus on, I noticed the whitecaps had eased up a bit, so I listened to the weather report. Before I could change my mind, I decided to get the hell out of Dodge. Based on what I was hearing and seeing, I knew crossing the sound wouldn't be easy, but it was doable. I gleaned a few discouraging nuggets of information from my guidebook: *Douglas Channel is subject to extreme winds; Wright Sound should be approached with caution.*

I slammed the book shut, set it on a rock, and looked out across

Wright Sound. I glanced sideways at the book, its front cover flapping in the breeze, then back across the water, shifting my upper lip back and forth like I often do when I'm edgy. To further fuel my anxiety, I picked it up again and continued to read:

> *So extreme that it has its own marine weather forecast. Inflow and outflow winds gather speed over vast areas of fetch and create rising seas of 4, 6, or even 8 feet ... winds pick up, meet the Douglas Channel blows in Wright Sound, and mate like a pair of depraved badgers.*

Lovely, I thought. *Just friggin lovely.* Robert Miller's advice was to depart early; I had already breached that cardinal rule. Still, I made the commitment to push on, and pushed away, as best I could, the same feelings of anxiety that had surfaced the night before.

Because I had grown somewhat accustomed to the claustrophobic nature of the narrow channels I'd been transiting the past few days, the openness of Wright Sound intimidated me. Douglas Channel extended due north out of the sound's oblong core, like a prehistoric arm waiting to snatch up the unwary paddler. I began to grasp the concept of localized winds, imagining that each of those sea monster arms could contribute their own form of chaos, with inflow and outflow winds colliding smack dab into the middle. I wondered if I would meet Miller's "depraved badgers" in the monster's abdomen.

Promise Island would be my first landfall, four miles to the west. My inauspicious start brought prompt headwinds and a contradicting tide that slowed my progress to a crawl. My mariner's math was simple, yet dispiriting: four nautical miles at a two-knot pace equaled two hours of gut-wrenching effort.

"Promise Island doesn't look very promising," I prattled, slogging toward this chunk of land that appeared to have quietly broken off the mainland. My chart, with all its shapes and colors, resembled a jigsaw puzzle, and Promise Island, with a little nudge, could have easily popped right back into place. Finally, I landed on Promise's Cape Farewell and stood in awe as I surveyed its open beach and cushy flat spots further up in a quiet forest. It would have made a splendid campsite, an oasis compared to the previous night's difficulty.

Ravenous, I munched on energy bars, gorp, and dehydrated fruit as I studied the chart on my lap. From my vantage point on the south end of Promise Island, I gazed across the western edge of Wright Sound toward the northern tip of Gil Island, where it jutted into the sound.

I couldn't help but remember the catastrophic event that had occurred four years earlier, in March 2006: the infamous sinking of BC Ferries' *Queen of the North*, with 101 people on board. She was southbound for Port Hardy and failed to make a critical course change, running smack into Gil Island. Because she sank stern-first in about an hour, most passengers had time to escape in lifeboats. Two perished, their bodies never recovered. A controversial story ensued blaming human error, hanky-panky, and the calamitous inattentiveness of the helmsman and second and fourth officers, who were in charge of navigation that night.

However she met her demise, the 410-foot long vessel now sits at a depth just shy of 1,400 feet, upright and intact on the bottom of Wright Sound. I imagined what it was like for those 42 crew members and 59 passengers on that cold, rainy evening when the *Queen* lurched violently and then screeched to a halt in the blackness of night.

An article in *Popular Mechanics* painted a grim picture:

> *As the bow rose skyward to near vertical, a semitrailer chained to a lower deck broke free with a crash. Machinery and vehicles smashed together. Passengers in the lifeboats found themselves staring at the ferry's forward deck, where windows began to explode with the rising air pressure inside the ship. Metal shrieked and groaned. Then the Queen of the North slid into a bubbling cauldron of seawater.*

AS NICE AS PROMISE ISLAND WAS, I didn't feel the four measly miles—hard-earned or not—were enough to warrant stopping just yet. My goal that day was to break the five-hundred-mile mark, and Sainty Point, a camp several miles up Grenville Channel also known as "the Ditch," would put me just past that coveted milestone.

In the southern reaches of Grenville Channel, I watched the numbers on my GPS slowly transition from 499.9 to 500. With this milestone behind me, I began searching for Sainty Point. I remembered that Jim had camped here on his trip, and he had warned me, just like my guidebook narrator, that campsites were scarce. I didn't want to miss this one and vigilantly compared the shoreline and seascape with my chart, until I approached where I suspected it was.

If I had a machete and a lot of time, I could have carved out a more hospitable campsite amid Sainty Point's tangled, chest-high understory. I had neither, so instead I set up a marginal camp at the northwest end of the cove just below the point, high on a bluff above the water, backed up against a thicket of wilderness, a steep and impassable forest. With the minus tide, the deep basin below me had drained to a puddle, resembling a toilet bowl after a Great Dane slurped it nearly dry. I'd spent an hour schlepping my gear, then sat at the top of this basin and watched the water continue to drop. It appeared a long way off. I studied it from where I was camped, and thought surely the tide couldn't come up this far. I was wrong.

Later that night, and for two more sleepless nights I spent in equally treacherous campsites, I watched in horror as the water consumed the land and the molten blackness encroached on me inch by inch, further backing me up against that inhospitable forest, with no place to go. Like a cruel joke, the highest of the second high tide of each day fell in the wee hours of the morning, starting just past midnight back at Gribbell Island, then arriving about fifty minutes later each consecutive night I spent in the Ditch. In my defense—I'm really not a total moron—all these campsites from hell were marked on my chart or written about in guidebooks as "great beaches with good camping."

The wild card here, and what my guides didn't take into consideration, was the extreme tidal difference that could happen under certain conditions. And I was experiencing those conditions, thanks to the new moon and approaching summer solstice. Jim had lightly penciled a notation on my chart in the most minuscule handwriting: *beware of high tides*. Each night, I tried to sleep beneath the thin veneer of my nylon tent while seawater sloshed and crept and reached toward me. Not only was this maddening, it was impossible. I accepted this and even made a game of it, if only to keep my sanity. Every morning I would check the tides for that day, my eyes scanning the tabular data generated from the corresponding tide stations on my GPS screen. This information would tell me the height of the tide and, practically to the minute, when the tide would start to recede. Nineteen feet tonight. 19.8' tomorrow; 20.3' the next day. And rising. Before crawling into my tent at night, I'd triple check the bowline I'd used to tether Chamellia to a large tree so she wouldn't float away in the darkness. Everything but the tent and my sleeping bag would either get hauled high onto rocks or snags, or went inside the kayak. When the witching hour came, I'd snatch up my tent just as the water poured in and patiently wait for it to recede, standing in the briny muck or on a piece of driftwood if I was lucky. It was the bane of my reality, but I was resigned to it because I truly had no other options. As I progressed through the channel, I was grimly aware that the tide would be even higher the following night and prayed that the weather would allow me to paddle further up the Ditch the next morning.

As if this peek-a-boo game with the highest tides of the season wasn't enough to keep me entertained, at my second stop in Grenville Channel a new headache arrived: black flies! I'd outmaneuvered blood-sucking mosquitoes and dealt with ferocious bugs before, but having my eyelashes caked black with these menaces, thick and sticky, made me the epitome of a Tammy Faye Bakker mascara meltdown. Eating in my tent was a big no-no; this was bear country after all. I quickly pushed the food past my pursed lips, yet still swallowed dozens of flies with each bite. At bedtime I hastily spat out black-speckled toothpaste and retreated to the sanctity of my tent at last. In a fit of exasperation, I blindly groped for the zipper but not before a dark swarm followed me in. Feeling like bug bait, practically in tears, and desperately craving sleep, I swatted and smeared black bodies on the inside of my once-sacred home, until I had annihilated enough of them to satisfy me.

I awoke at one a.m. for my serial date with the ocean to find my left eye swollen shut and the left side of my face and neck disfigured. I gently touched my left temple with my index finger, then winced in pain. Although it was swollen and red, I was able to see out of my right eye, and I kept it on the quickly arriving tide, as a wave of nausea came over me. What concerned me the most was my rapid and irregular heartbeat. Those wretched pests had spawned a severe allergic reaction. I rummaged through my first aid kit for some Benadryl, reaming myself for not taking it earlier.

Before the sun came up, I quickly packed, swatting and cussing at the black flies mobbing me. It wasn't until I took my first strokes that I finally left the infernal bastards behind in their dreadful black cloud.

With willful attempts at composure, I made my way toward the end of the seemingly endless Grenville Channel, feeling a dire need to get out of this abyss for my own safety. It seemed to go on forever; and I began to dream about the day I would bust out of these dispiriting bowels of the IP, at its anus near Bonwick Point. Steep, deep, and narrow, the Ditch is the main route for ferries, cruise ships, freighters, barges, fishing boats, and every sort of recreational vessel. Rounded domes and craggy summits loomed overhead, but I was too tired to embrace the view and just slogged along.

Somewhere between Sainty Point and my next campsite I resisted the overwhelming urge to close my eyes. Laying my paddle across my lap, I thought, *I'll just close my eyes for a few seconds. Just a few.* I don't know if it was ten or twenty seconds later, or just how long a person can remain asleep and upright in a kayak, but whatever it was, lulled by the subtle rocking of Chamellia under my hips, I momentarily dozed off. My head collapsed abruptly forward, then forcefully jerked back, an unchecked eight-pound bowling ball waking me from my abridged slumber. Like a kid caught nodding off in math class, I was dazed, disoriented, and slightly embarrassed.

A Sense of Urgency

I WAS EXHAUSTED, yet made good time my third day on the Ditch, riding the tidal currents and enjoying the perspective of land sliding by quickly as I paddled north. An early start, combined with a northerly flood current and a dreamy tailwind, swiftly delivered me sixteen nautical miles to my intended camp at Nabannah Bay.

Munching on cheese unaccompanied by crackers, I rummaged into my lunch bag, searching for something more comforting. At my last campsite back at Mosley Point, some heartless ravens had plundered my food bags—left unguarded for all of two minutes—and devoured the handful of crackers I had been hoarding. My feathered foes punctured a hole in one of the food bags, piercing two of the foil pouches inside. I had run up the beach like a madwoman, screaming and wildly waving my arms at them. They retreated to a branch high above their messy heist and mocked me as I cleaned it up.

Now I choked down an energy bar while bent over my chart and simultaneously consulted my guidebook, as I often do, toying with the idea of pushing on. Then I took a short stroll up the beach and three observations made the decision for me: scraggly hairs wedged in the bark of a large tree, six-inch claw marks on said tree, and bear scat below the tree. I promptly flopped back into the boat and resumed paddling.

Jim had told me that if my timing was right, topography could have a pleasant card to play here. When there is a flood current, it comes in on either end of Grenville Channel and meets about halfway through at

Evening Point on the southern tip of Nabannah Bay. Likewise, when the tide is ebbing, it flows out both ends of Grenville Channel. My timing was perfect, as I had been riding the northwesterly flood current all morning through the lower portion of this saltwater gutter, and to my utter amazement I rode the ebb current out the other side. But soon I learned that there really is no such thing as a free ride.

A cold wind kicked up that afternoon, and a noticeable drop in temperature greeted my already chilled skin. Thick clouds descended into the canyon and let loose on Grenville Channel, engulfing me in a downpour for hours. Heavy raindrops pounded Chamellia's deck and poured in rivulets off the brim of my rain hat and onto my PFD. The wind funneled up the channel with increasing velocity and yanked hard at my paddle. My white-knuckled grip tightened around the shaft. The waves, generated from the wind's bad attitude, relentlessly rebounded off the sheer cliff walls I paddled beneath. Water spilled over my cockpit and engulfed my shrinking waist, filling in the spaces around my torso, and then poured back into this mixmaster sea. I felt cold water trickle in through the waist tunnel of my sprayskirt, its layers of once-waterproof fabric delaminating from rubbing against my PFD and the repeated rotation of my torso. My body temperature slowly dropped. I was hesitant to stop and put on more layers because I feared that opening my hatches would only let in more water. Perhaps this reasoning was flawed, and the initial stages of hypothermia were making me stupid. I shivered and knew that I *had* to get off the water, set up camp, and get into some dry clothes.

My chart indicated some options, but as I came around a corner— my bladder so full I thought it might burst—on the only open pocket beach stood a husky mama grizzly with two cubs. Preoccupied, she skillfully pawed at boulders and logs, and grazed on barnacles much like moviegoers would eat popcorn. I slowly floated by her, less than thirty yards offshore, until she caught my scent, stopped digging, and intently looked my way. I quickly angled away from her and increased my stroke rate, my heart nearly exploding out of my chest. After my adrenaline spike subsided, I scanned my chart, and it became clear to me that there were no haul-out options for several more miles. Those several-more-miles came and went, my bladder expanded, and another postage stamp-sized pocket beach appeared. Another mama bear stood there, unamused by my presence. I heard her snort, then watched her two cubs immediately scamper into the thick, wet understory. I was still feeling rattled from the previous bear sighting, and of course wasn't too keen on camping beside her, so I kept paddling. *Damn, trumped again*, I thought. Whatever confidence I may have started with that morning was undermined, replaced with fear that burrowed deep inside me. Crushing fatigue overwhelmed me, and soon every stump and rock began to resemble a bear. I shivered violently and knew that Grenville Channel wasn't letting me out of her grasp just yet. I also sensed that I was on the cusp of being in serious trouble.

I'd moved 35 miles up the Ditch that day, according to my GPS. Darkness wasn't too far off. The cold wind still whisked north, although the terrain broadened—along with my bladder. I gave myself permission to pee in the boat.

Next stop, Bonwick Point. You have to make this work, Susan. Roughly twelve hours and forty unintentional, self-propelled miles from where I'd slept the night before, I settled on another marginal campsite, without any visible bears, in a cove I knew would flood early in the morning and then drain to a stream at low tide, leaving me stranded until the cold water returned. But I was completely out of steam, and nearly out of daylight, with limited options to land, let alone camp, and paddling any further was a terrible idea.

It wasn't until I stood up that I realized I'd been sitting in several gallons of water. My ice-cold fingers fumbled with my hatch cover so I could retrieve my guidebook. I slipped it out of the Ziploc bag I kept it in, its pages fluttering in the brisk wind. As legions of whitecaps danced on Grenville Channel, and fat raindrops bounced off my body, I traipsed through a dripping tangle of vegetation searching for a reasonable place to pitch camp. With Robert Miller's book unfolded in my hands, I turned

360 degrees, scanning my surroundings, in a frantic attempt to discern where his alleged "suitable ground for camping" was. I determined that it simply wasn't. It really, truly wasn't. I had no choice but to make do. I slogged back to the kayak through acres of briny dung and began the laborious process of putting this day, and myself, to bed in the most miserable campsite of the entire trip.

I mindlessly clutched a few dry bags to my chest and plodded through the eel grass and muck to an area I had reluctantly chosen to call home. My mind raced to keep up with my heart, but my feet were sluggish beneath me. Suddenly I slipped on the slimy grass and then stumbled on a small boulder, my body crashing to the ground. Dry bags dropped, forming a rainbow of color around me as I lay moaning in the mud. My thud to the earth took my breath away and, like Dorothy in the poppy field, I wanted only to lie there and fall asleep until the pain went away.

"Okay, Susan, get a grip." The words barely lumbered over my lips as the classic symptoms of hypothermia took hold. My soggy clothing clung to my body and when the wind kicked up another notch, my core temperature and comfort level continued to drop. The situation was deteriorating, growing even more serious.

In slow motion, my mind played the tape of what I needed to do to survive: rig the tarp, set up the tent, change into dry clothes, eat something, collapse, wait for the high tide, retreat, collapse, sleep, repeat.

Still shivering in my soaking wet clothes, I struggled with my green nylon tarp as the wind belligerently and repeatedly whipped it out of my hands. I turned my face away from the stinging sideways sheets of rain and fought with the tangle of wet line connected to my tarp's grommets. Nervously chewing on my lower lip as if it were a piece of gum, I glanced at my VHF radio and considered calling for help. One short burst of communication, and someone monitoring nearby would come to my rescue. I'd be pulled on board, swaddled in warm blankets, fed steaming bowls of lamb stew with hearty bread slathered in butter, and sleep below deck to the soothing rocking of a big, safe, dry boat. Jolted by this image, I extracted myself from my fantasy and fumbled with the tarp until my adrenal glands kicked into overdrive. I screamed at the top of my lungs, incensed by the rapidly deteriorating conditions, belting out an alarming variety of expletives. It was a life-giving rage, a blood-warming, soul-shocking rage that transformed my feelings into action and refocused my intent. Determination conquered despair—even though I appeared like a raving lunatic.

As if scared into submission by my temper tantrum, the tarp magically cooperated. And the tent? Although wet and heavy, it went up with nary a struggle. Keeping things organized and dry in adverse conditions was an art in itself, and I now had a safe place to stash a few critical items. I peeled off my sopping wet clothes. The cold air on my cold skin swelled my goosebumps into buffalo bumps. I dressed in nearly every piece of non-paddling clothing I owned, finishing the ensemble with rain pants and a rain jacket. Even in somewhat dry clothes, I was still chilled to the bone. Having a fire in this deluge was out of the question, so I made myself keep moving.

Under my tarp, on my hands and knees in the soaking wet grass, I huddled over my stove, shielding its precious flame from the wind and sideways rain with my body. Although I'd not anticipated conditions quite this grave, I'd packed some meal-in-a-pouch options for those evenings when I was totally spanked. My reward was a saucy Indian lentil curry dish that unfortunately resembled dog vomit. Albeit a meager number of calories compared to what I had just exerted over the course of the last twelve hours, it tasted divine. I licked my spoon, put it in my pocket, swabbed out my tin cup with questionable water from a nearby brackish puddle, and retreated to my tent at last. Shivering inside my slightly damp sleeping bag, I inhaled two candy bars and relived the hell I had just been through. The tarp whipped violently, and torrential rain battered the taut rainfly just inches from my face. Lying flat on my back, I pulled my hat down over my ears, closed my eyes, and surrendered to the night, telling myself this would all be over soon.

Ten miles away, the small community of Oona River was on my radar for two reasons: the absence of bears, and the rumored presence of a bed and breakfast. "Bed and breakfast." Mouthing those two delicious words over and over, I consoled myself with thoughts of a hot, soapy shower, warm dry sheets, a pillow beneath my freshly washed hair, and eggs Benny swimming in hollandaise beside a mound of country-fried potatoes. Mind candy.

I nearly fell asleep to these visions, until I remembered my date with the high tide. It was predicted to reach 23 feet that night, the biggest tidal exchange of the trip thus far. The tidal elevator would reach its top floor at three a.m. I had become quite savvy at this game, even semi-comatose, but when the hour came, it was a tremendous energy expenditure to change out of my warm, dry clothes and put on my cold, wet rain gear to deal with such a tiresome scenario, only to strip back down thirty minutes later, vainly trying to keep the dry items dry, and slip back into my synthetic cocoon.

I awoke two hours later to discover it was still pouring and blowing outside. I gulped some water, my throat sore from my meltdown that night, and drifted back to some much-needed sleep. Four hours later the weather hadn't changed. I sifted through my shrinking food bags and wondered how many days I would be trapped here by the weather.

By noon I had to pee, so I crawled out of the tent. By the door sat a large sodden pile of bear shit that was certainly not there when I retired. I had never heard the bear over the loud whipping sounds of the tarp and tent and the pouring rain. The bear apparently wasn't interested in what was inside my strange shelter. In disbelief, but too exhausted to care, I shrugged and tended to my business. Then it dawned on me that something was different. It was *quiet*. The wind had softened and the rain had stopped. *Hey, Susan, look skyward. The clouds are lifting. Over there—a small pocket of blue sky!* My spirits soared. I packed up in record time, as more pockets of blue teased through the clouds, and pointed my bow toward Porcher Island and Oona River, out of the grip of Grenville Channel. *Goodbye and good riddance.*

Long Tall Glasses

WITH VISIONS OF EGGS BENEDICT still cemented in my head, I rounded the large stone breakwater protecting the town of Oona River from the sea's moodiness. A man and a woman conversed from their respective boats behind the breakwater, and flashed me big smiles as I came into their view. She stood half in, half out of the cockpit of a double-masted sailboat, and he stood on the stern deck of a 37-foot gillnetter; they had parked opposite each other alongside a wooden dock. About a dozen other boats crowded the small harbor.

I paddled over to them, curious about my options in this little town. My choices were limited, I soon learned, because it seemed the shindig of the century was underway in Oona River. This sleepy community of about 35 folks had ballooned to over two hundred to accommodate a wedding party. The wedding had occurred earlier that day, and the reception was expected to build momentum well into the evening, culminating with a celebratory bonfire in the forest behind me. Everything was booked solid, and some locals were putting up partygoers in their homes or on their boats.

"You're welcome to sleep on my couch if you'd like," said Bart, the man in the gillnetter, sensing my disappointment. I would have kissed his feet if I wasn't still sitting in my kayak and he wasn't standing ten feet away on the deck of the *Pacific Coast*. He'd sleep on his boat that night, since he had offered his island cabin to a handful of friends. The cabin's two bedrooms were spoken for, but the couch had my name on it. With infinite gratitude, I loaded my gear into a stainless steel wheelbarrow and shadowed this shaggy-haired man whom I had just met to his home in the woods. I didn't know anything about him, yet I harbored no fears about walking with him for ten minutes through a forest I knew nothing about, on a trail where I had never been. We soon veered left onto a narrower spur trail and twenty paces later, in a small clearing, came upon Bart's cabin. It stood there, unpretentious yet stately, welcoming and warm. Wisps of smoke spiraled out its chimney and a brook babbled through the forest behind it. The heat from a wood stove greeted me as I walked through the door, immediately on Bart's heels. I followed him down a short hallway and looked over his shoulder as he pushed opened a heavy wooden door, revealing a modest bathroom. I wondered if he could smell the horrific stench coming from my body.

"Feel free to take a bath," he said, flashing that same expansive smile I'd seen when I'd first met him. "The water's a bit brown from all the tannins, but it won't hurt nothing." My gaze turned to the coffee-colored stains on the porcelain bear claw tub and then flitted to the white pedestal sink, also slightly stained. Bart explained how the tannins from the needles of the cedar trees predominant in this area would seep into the water source. Locals had been bathing in and drinking this water, untreated, for centuries.

"Join us at the red schoolhouse for the party, if you'd like," Bart said, pointing through the window to a meandering path. "It'll go all night— come any time." Without looking back, he walked through his living room, and closed the door behind him.

I draped my wet gear near the crackling wood stove, started a load of laundry, and deliciously anticipated a long, languid bubble bath. While my clothes spun in this stranger's dryer, I soaked in his tub. My big belly laughs jostled the slightly tinged bubbly bath water. Was it only yesterday I had struggled and screamed and succumbed to all that was thrown in my path? These two days seemed poles apart, yet were so close, separated by only a few miles and a few memories. I had, overnight it seemed, gained a healthy dose of tolerance and humility. *Throwing a snit really doesn't help matters*, I realized, *because Mother Nature doesn't care if your tent is growing mold and your sleeping bag is as damp as your mood.*

Standing in front of the oval vintage bathroom mirror with a towel wrapped around my body, I studied my tanned face and slowly twisted the tiny pearl stud earrings I had worn since departing Anacortes. I braided my wet hair, cleaned the dirt from under my fingernails, and smeared some lip balm on my chapped lips. I was 39 days into my trip and my body was lean and hard. I'd anticipated some weight loss, but judging from the way my pelvic bones protruded beneath my ever-loosening wetsuit, I estimated I'd lost at least ten pounds in the Ditch alone. My body was also bruised, bug bitten, and welted; any semblance of femininity was gone, but it was replaced by strength, confidence—and really hairy armpits.

Within an hour I sauntered down another narrow dirt trail toward the bonfire by the old red schoolhouse. About thirty people stood around a roaring fire that threw sparks high into the tree canopy looming precariously above it. The bride, still in her white dress, seemed charmingly out of context in the deep, dark woods of a temperate rainforest next to this crackling fire. The bridegroom, a tall, robust young man, resembled a lumberjack, in black Carhartts and a long-sleeved red and black plaid wool shirt festooned with a bow tie. A willowy young woman wearing a flouncy dress twirled flaming rings while fireworks lit up the sky behind her. Musical instruments suddenly surfaced, and campfire songs from beautiful melodic voices wafted through the forest. The fire crackled; laughter was everywhere, and I felt welcomed by the wide smiles and open hearts.

A long-limbed, handsome man dressed in blue jeans and a green flannel shirt handed me a tall glass of white wine. "Hi, my name's Bill," he said, grinning like a Cheshire cat, revealing a slight space between his two upper, squarish teeth. "I don't recognize you from the wedding party. What brings you to Oona River?" He was younger than me, but not by much, and had dark blond hair that grazed his shoulders.

"I paddled here," I said, my finger sublimely wiping the condensation off the chilled wine glass. "Had a rough go of it in Grenville Channel, but I'm a happy camper now 'cause I'm not camping!" I laughed.

Bill listened intently as I summarized, as best I could, this journey I was on, and all the vexing life lessons I was still trying to make sense of.

He lit a Camel cigarette, and offered me one.

"Shoot, after what I've been through these last few days, it probably can't hurt if a girl has a smoke, eh?" I grasped the cigarette between my index and middle fingers. I'd long since quit my pack-a-day habit, but in certain social situations, especially where alcohol was involved, I'd covertly smoke one or two. In between exhalations, I told him about running into Bart and how grateful I was to not have to worry about the tide or bears or wind or rain or anything else that night.

"You must be hungry," he said, his eyes twinkling, and motioned to the schoolhouse beside us. It was small, and insanely cute, with a steep metal roof, red clapboard siding, and white trim. Everyone had long since eaten, but through the screen door, if I sat real tall, I could see tables full of food. "There's still plenty left. Help yourself."

Wooden floorboards creaked under my weight. Two long tables covered with checkered cloths graced the middle of the room. My eyes darted between beguiling pans of halibut, plates of venison, bowls of green salad, and scalloped cheese platters, then to the delicate baskets of crusty sourdough bread, crocks of fat-laden butter, and overflowing bowls of fruit that adorned a small side table. Thick porcelain plates sat beside a stack of crisp white napkins—so civil, I thought—and tidy rows of silver forks and knives sparkled under the fluorescent lights. Dumbfounded, I stared like I'd never seen food before.

Bill walked in and handed me another glass of wine, this time a deep red, and returned to the group outside. I took a sip, then sat the glass down in order to have both hands free to load up my plate with a colorful mountain of food. I'd burned tens of thousands of calories over the past several days, and my lengthy and gluttonous grazing session at the buffet was quickly replacing them. I went back for seconds. Finally sated, I walked down the stairs and took in the camaraderie and good will in the forest below me. I had stumbled upon this magical microcosm and realized that I'd been living in a social vacuum for the past ten days. Now Oona River, and the zenith of this serendipitous experience, touched my heart and nourished my soul. My energy and spirit felt rekindled, as did my faith in humankind.

The party continued until the wee hours of the morning—after all, Oona River doesn't often experience this type of gala. But by midnight my eyelids were drooping. I found Bart sitting deep in an old lawn chair next to the fire, drinking scotch out of a paper cup. "I've got a couple of long days ahead to get to Prince Rupert, so I better hit the sack, Bart," I said, and thanked him again for his generosity.

"You know, you can catch a ride with us in the morning," he nonchalantly offered. "We'll get you as far as Port Edward—that oughta shave off a few miles for ya."

"Really?" I asked, almost in disbelief.

"Sure, no problem. We'll just slide your boat up on the stern of mine. We'll have to time it with the tides though, so we'll pull out at noon."

THAT NIGHT I HAD POUNCED on the offer to hitch a ride with Bart into Prince Rupert, knowing it would shave off nearly thirty nautical miles of Chatham Sound's churning waters. But first thing the next morning I sheepishly called Jim and hoped he would tell me this little diversion wasn't cheating. After all, I had set out to *paddle* the Inside Passage, not bum rides hither and yon until I eventually ended up in Skagway.

"Hell yeah, go with it, Suz!" Jim immediately encouraged, typical of his undying support. He sounded cheerful enough, but I detected a weakness in his voice.

"What's wrong, Jim?" I asked suspiciously. It was then that he told me about the stent. I'd known he'd experienced minor heart issues ever since a backcountry skiing incident outside of Fernie, British Columbia, the previous winter. I wasn't on that trip, but had heard earfuls of backstory regarding that day—a mountainous harbinger of what was to come. He detested doctors, but after much insistence from friends and family, finally acceded to a thorough examination.

"Three docs have approved a heart catheterization," he confessed.

"I'm listening," I said.

"Best case outcome is a stent—one, maybe two. It's just an outpatient deal. If untreatable by stent, it's on to a bypass."

"When? What time?" I asked.

"June 24th, 7:30 a.m.," he replied. It was June 13th and I quickly calculated the time and distance in my head, and figured I'd be in the vicinity of Ketchikan on that day.

We spoke for a few more moments and just before we hung up he added, "Hey, Suz, I'm going to a ZZ Top concert in Missoula tomorrow!"

"Great, Jim," I said. "Be sure to bring your nitroglycerin."

Suddenly it felt like someone had laid an X-ray apron on my chest. I stared at the blank screen in my hand and tried to ignore the heaviness in my heart and the tightness forming in my throat, and to not picture Jim in the hospital with his chest split open. It was far more pleasant to put him at the ZZ Top concert, clapping and swaying, his generous stent-free heart pounding from the thunderous music.

After the phone call, I organized my gear, ate breakfast, put my dry bags in the wheelbarrow, and pushed it back down the trail to the dock. It was 11:30 and Captain Bart and his deckhand Dave were rigging the boat for departure. On the dock that morning I learned that the *Pacific Coast* was a gillnetter-turned-research vessel. Bart and Dave were biologists, and made regular trips back and forth between their homes near Prince Rupert and their cabins in Oona River, collecting data and analyzing water samples from the area. Their focus, they told me as they finished rigging the boat, was studying sediment loads caused by the inflow of the Skeena River, and its effect on marine life, particularly whale populations.

A massive river system—British Columbia's second largest—the Skeena is one of the world's largest undammed rivers. As it descends 360 miles to Telegraph Passage from a small trickle high in the Skeena Mountains, it metamorphoses from a series of intensely braided channels, to a broad river valley, to an even broader delta, draining more than fifteen thousand square miles of northwest British Columbia.

"YOU MIGHT WANNA HOLD ON—we've got some ferry wash comin' at us," yelled Bart from his captain's swivel chair in the wheelhouse. Crouching low on the open stern of the lurching vessel, I grasped my kayak with one hand and the railing with the other in a desperate attempt not to get washed overboard in the deluge. The Who's *Who Are You* blared from the cockpit of the *Pacific Coast* as she pitched and yawed in the large gray swells of Chatham Sound. Grinning ear to ear, I held on for dear life. Just another day at sea, battling the sullen westerly swells typical of this chunk of the Inside Passage.

Smack in the middle of my sea journey, I now found myself bucking waves between the tiny community of Oona River, where I had just spent one delicious night, and Prince Rupert, my last Canadian resupply port. For the moment, my biggest challenge was trying to pee at sea.

"Keep your feet firmly planted—like suction cups," Bart said, motioning to a bucket tied to the railing. The embarrassment of being washed into the sea with my pants down flashed through my mind. I was all about avoiding a woman-overboard situation. Bart disappeared into the cockpit to afford me a pretense of privacy. I untied the bowline, and as the *Pacific Coast* swayed in moderate seas, steadied myself over the bucket, the soles of my rubber boots firmly glued to the deck, and giggled at my predicament.

In a mere two hours, we arrived at Port Edward, covering a problematic stretch of water that would have taken me a couple days to paddle. Bart killed the engine in Porpoise Channel, swung the boat sideways to flatten out some of the swell, and off-loaded my kayak from the stern of the *Pacific Coast*. With nine miles to go, I scrambled into Chamellia's cockpit, snapped on my skirt, gave these two kind men a thumbs-up, and paddled toward Prince Rupert.

Leg 5 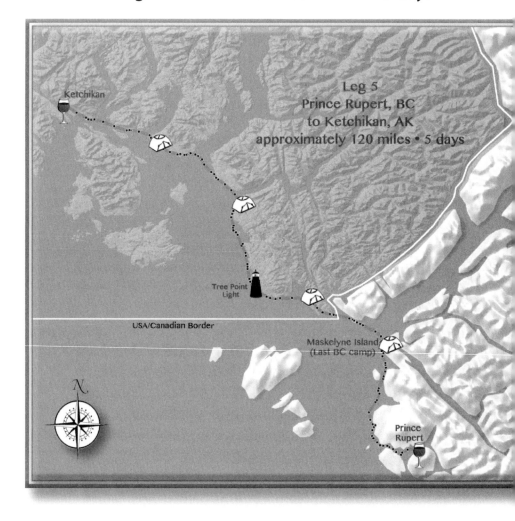 **120 miles** **5 days**

Leg 5
Prince Rupert, BC
to Ketchikan, AK
approximately 120 miles • 5 days

Ketchikan

Tree Point
Light

USA/Canadian Border

Maskelyne Island
(Last BC camp)

Prince
Rupert

N

Six

Prince Rupert to Ketchikan

Fear is more of a problem than the problem feared.

— Audrey Sutherland

Next Stop, Alaska!

THREE HARD-EARNED LAYOVER DAYS in Prince Rupert recharged me, and I was ready to put on some more miles. My last night in town I'd slept restlessly in the cubbyhole hostel room I'd rented. I awoke at 3:45 a.m. and by six o'clock I paddled away from the Prince Rupert Yacht Club on an advancing tide. It was dead calm. The rising sun was already casting muted shadows on the harbor, and the saturated colors of the flower planters, umbrella stands, and cheerful buildings grew more vivid. A fog bank loomed in the distance, but overhead, clear and sunny skies were promising. I left the crowded harbor and entered the main channel, paddling under erector-set like structures loading massive container ships with supplies probably bound for Asia.

Dixon Entrance, a foreboding body of water that loosely defines the border between Canada and Alaska, weighed heavily on my mind. Once I reached its more exposed portion, I would be back in the States. It would certainly be a milestone on my trip, and the last of four cruxes I expected to contend with.

Venn Passage, the conduit between Prince Rupert and the deeper waters of Chatham Sound, challenged my navigational skills. Its shallow channels were choked with seaweed and scads of small islands. Not entirely trusting the navigational buoys, I consulted my GPS for the second time that morning—and only the third time for the entire trip—to make sure I was indeed where I thought I should be. Not only did I enjoy the tangible pleasure of using old-fashioned chart and compass to stay found, I also believed that two words could render even the best of electronic devices null and void: dead batteries. Instead, I viewed the GPS as a confidence-inspiring electronic second opinion of sorts to soothe any fears of miscalculation.

Paddling along in the still and solitude of the morning, my thoughts turned to Alaska, less than thirty miles away. I kept looking at the chart on my deck and staring at the dashed line that represented the Alaskan border. I studied the shapes of Kanagunut and Sitklan Islands—two islands I'd be paddling between tomorrow—in Alaska! I couldn't see it through the fog, but I could feel its huge expanse before me. I brimmed with optimism and excitement knowing I would be in Alaska the next day. And if all went well, in Ketchikan, my first Alaskan port of call, in five days.

That night I awoke to the melody of a humpback whale sleeping less than twenty yards from my tent. Listening to her snore, I mused on what a nasal strip might look like for a whale and if visions of krill appeared in her dreams. Long and labored "PWOOF" sounds mixed with sonorous wheezing and whirled toward me as she hovered in her slumber at the ocean's surface. I was camped on Maskelyne Island, my last Canadian stop. The two humpbacks playing in Work Channel earlier that day had overridden the less desirable aspects of this camp, such as a resident colony of mosquitoes and a lack of sunshine on the north-facing spit of land. Not far away, a hundred-mile-long inlet, the longest fjord in North America, collided with the ocean. In the morning I would cross Portland Canal's five-mile mouth; from there the Alaskan border was practically spitting distance.

On my 45th day at sea, with seven hundred miles trailing behind my stern and approximately five hundred ahead of my bow, Chamellia and I bobbed on the imaginary border that represented the separation of Alaska from British Columbia. Estimating from my chart and nearby landmarks, I had reached a major milestone—I had arrived at the Alaskan border via sea kayak. I had paddled myself to the last frontier, and back to America. I was sitting on Alaska's doorstep! Bobbing in the chop on the north end of Chatham Sound, I wondered how many of my friends were watching SPOT's bouncing digital bread crumb trail. I was certain Jim was tuned in, but I didn't know that at that very moment, as I bobbed on that watery border, he'd pressed the send button, delivering a message to me and all my followers that said—in thirteen different languages—"Welcome to Alaska, Susan and Chamellia." I would burst into tears when I read this email five days later in Ketchikan.

With my waterproof camera clipped to my PFD, I snapped a photo of my bow pointing into Alaska, then pivoted in the cockpit to capture my stern in Canada. Tears streamed down my face; I had just freaking paddled to Alaska. *How cool is that?* I thought. Emotions washed over me as I tried to digest and distill this major accomplishment. I was proud. Euphoric. In awe.

Nine months earlier, I had stared at this point on the chart and tried to image what it would feel like. And now I was here, with Alaska's vast landscape in front of my bow. A new adventure within an adventure. Each day on this journey had promised new sights, sounds, smells, and sensations; mirror-calm seas and surging waves; sky and wind and all the elements the day could dish out; the feel of the tide pushing or pulling on my hull. But it was the connecting with gracious people who reached out to help me, in often unexpected circumstances, that had further cemented my deep bond with the Inside Passage. I realized then that my journey was becoming a portal to a new inner resiliency, a new strength and sense of courage that I actually always had, but didn't know how to fully tap into. I had then vowed to fully embrace the trip. To embrace myself in Alaska. To love Alaska. To love myself. To relax more. And to be open to all this portion of my journey could offer.

I PADDLED UP A NARROW CHANNEL speckled with several inviting beaches. Brilliant red Indian paintbrush flourished in pockets of sparkly white sand. Chards of mica-speckled obsidian rocks and veins of quartz punctuated the rocky seashore.

I arrived at Tongass Island at the crack of noon, on calm seas, merely stopping for a lunch break. I had only paddled fifteen miles so far and intended to push on to Tree Point another ten miles to the north. I remembered Jim being fixated on this landmark. But his notes—"steep, slippery ramp, dark, and haunting forest,"—didn't sit well with me. I also remembered he had had a bear encounter there. The open, south-facing beaches of Tongass Island were much more appealing, with their splendid view out to the Lord Islands and Cape Fox. They contained no bears, no flies or bugs, and no cocky high tide to be concerned with. I reminded myself about my vow to relax more. I decided to stay.

While I was putting the finishing touches on my first Alaskan camp, I noticed a skiff approaching my island from the channel I had recently paddled through. I braced myself for an intrusion, and attached my bear spray to my hip. A thickset man with a roundish face, wearing faded dungarees and black rubber boots, debarked his boat in the shallow bay facing my tent and tethered it to a large driftwood log on the beach. He carried a steel bucket and began walking the beach without looking up. Odd, I thought, that he didn't even acknowledge me. At a loss for what to do, I walked out on the point, climbed up on a rock and pretended I wasn't watching him. "PLUNK" went one mysterious item after another into his steel gray bucket. He never lifted his head. Irritated, I slowly stood up and walked nonchalantly toward my tent, where he was now stooped over, digging in the sand. *This dude has no sense of space*, I thought to myself.

"Hello," I said in the best cool-as-a-cucumber voice I could muster. I got a hello back, more like a grunt actually, but not a whole lot more. Eventually, he did tell me his name was Frank, that he lived a few miles away on a houseboat in Lincoln Channel, and that he came here almost every day to stretch his legs and beachcomb. He said he had seen me come through, but otherwise seemed disinterested as to why I was there alone, and what I was doing. This also seemed odd to me, because I'd gotten used to people barraging me with questions about my journey, but at that moment I really didn't mind not having to tell my story.

"There used to be an Indian village here," Frank said and held out his hand, which contained two brightly colored Indian beads. Fascinated, I stared down at his hand, and imagined this island bustling with activity: the sounds of dark-skinned children playing on the beach, the smell of smoke drifting through the forest, perhaps rows of fish hanging from a line stretched between the trees. Ten minutes later, he stepped back into his boat and left me alone again on Tongass Island.

Relieved, I busied myself with beachcombing and after that, hair washing. I had an abundance of time, fresh water, sunshine, stove fuel, and dirty hair, so why not? Wilderness hair washing, it turns out, is an arduous process. First, I filled my ten-liter black dromedary bag with fresh, cold water and laid it on a black rock to heat in the sun. I took a catnap and dreamt of silky clean hair, while the sun's rays brought the water to a tepid state. Then I filled both my cooking pots with fresh water from a nearby creek and brought them to a boil. I added this hot water to the warmish water in my dromedary bag and hung it from a sturdy branch above me. With towel and biodegradable all-purpose Campsuds nearby, I ducked my head and let the warm water dampen my grimy locks. Lathering up, I noticed, out of the corner of one soapy eye, that a martin was watching me, but when I made eye contact, he scurried into the underbrush. After a quick rinse I plunked myself down on a large flat rock and let its heat radiate into the backs of my legs and my butt as I vigorously towel-dried my hair. The tide was still ebbing while all the intertidal creatures patiently waited out their six-hour fast. Thin spurts of seawater pulsed skyward as long-necked clams, buried in the tidal mudflats, went about their business. Gulls and cormorants cavorted on a nearby rock ledge, and I reveled in my solitude, and my clean hair.

Tonight was extra special; a celebration was in order. I commemorated my first night in Alaska by reveling in some much-deserved gluttony: a bottle of merlot accompanied by cheese and crackers and a tin of smoked oysters, followed by an overflowing pot of pasta wheels drizzled with garlic-infused olive oil, tossed with rehydrated veggies, and sprinkled with parmesan cheese. I balanced my blackened and dented aluminum pot on my knees and poured a stiff shot of dark rum into the twist-off cap attached to my flask. Then I toasted myself, my journey, and all the beauty surrounding me. After the fourth stiff shot, my camera precariously propped on a rock, and me precariously balanced on a log, I snapped selfies to share with friends back home. I'd somehow lost the cork to the wine bottle, and not wanting to waste any of it, I continued sipping while I cleaned up the dinner mess. Savoring my beachside debauchery, I admired the crimson sunset playing out in front of me, biding my time before settling in for the night, even though darkness was still a ways off.

Alaska has its own time zone, an hour ahead of Pacific Standard Time. The sun, still hovering on the horizon at nearly eleven p.m., continued to offer a glimmer of light for another hour, and even then it only halfheartedly set, as if it couldn't make up its mind. I then understood why southeast Alaska is described as the land of the midnight sun. And this midnight sun would begin its ascent by four a.m., stymieing my much-needed beauty sleep.

That night I dreamt of a spider. A twisted, hairy tarantula whose legs, as long as my kayak, spun me in its rope-sized web. This, of course, made no sense at all because tarantulas do not spin webs and prefer hot, dry climes, but it was *my* dream after all. In this dream, Chamellia and I were caught in a tumultuous wave, fighting frantically to stay upright, although most of the time we were *inside* the wave, with the spider. Terror enveloped me as I stared into its massive abdomen. I could taste the saltwater, feel the cottony web against my face, all the while screaming underwater, wondering why I wasn't drowning. I gasped out loud, then lay motionless, except for my eyes darting from one corner of the tent ceiling to the other. Relief flooded my body. It was only a dream. This would make a heyday for a dream interpreter, or a shrink. But I'd feared spiders ever since my brother and cousin thought it would be riotously funny to introduce me to the black widow who lived under our family sawmill. They carried me, like a human stretcher, Billy at my arms and Robby at my legs, while I kicked and shrieked, and then swung my six-year-old writhing body horizontally, back and forth, with each undulation bringing my little face closer to the spider's abdomen, which hung patiently from its web under a creosote-soaked log.

A couple years later, on a late spring afternoon, I would suffer another spider incident. While seated at an old organ on my family's back porch, I was screeching through a bout of *Greensleeves* when a large nest of daddy long legs fell splat on the keyboard, sending a flurry of spindly legs up my arms and neck. Fortunately, Mom was plucking a chicken at the kitchen window and witnessed the whole thing. She came to my rescue, dishcloth in hand, and calmly swooshed them all away. Then she took my sobbing little body in her arms and brought me into the house, where she immediately changed me into a fresh pair of plaid culottes—those hideous knee-length one-piece outfits of the sixties that were part short, part skirt—and nearly as dreadful as spiders. She then artfully diffused the drama with a bag of M&Ms. I was duly distracted and successfully soothed, yet still traumatized for life. This was a rare occurrence in my childhood where I remember my mom as a soothing and compassionate parent.

A THIRTY-MILE PADDLE WORKED OFF the hangover on my 46th day at sea. I dragged myself out of the tent at five a.m., broke camp, wolfed down a modest breakfast, and was paddling by seven o'clock. A thick band of sea fog rolled in quickly and collided with the land fog that was working its way offshore. Thankfully, the rising sun burned off the fog, and I paddled under sunny and clear skies, atop slightly swollen seas, along Alaska's shoreline toward my final crux—Dixon Entrance.

Fear Stuck Still

The ocean—the open stuff—is alive, moving, bounding, rebounding, crashing, rolling, breaking, sucking back, roaring, hissing, thundering, and ominously quiet.

—Jim Chester's Sea Diary, 1992,
describing Dixon Entrance, Alaska

MY KAYAK SLID OVER the robust swells of Dixon Entrance, and my surroundings, I thought, were beginning to take on a different look and feel. The sea exploded against the cliffs and I pulled harder on my right blade to move further out. Chamellia and I skidded around the next point, and there it was: an alive, wide-awake ocean. The landscape seemed more open. The mountains loomed bigger. Rocks seemed shinier. The water, more blue. I noticed more hemlocks and various species of deciduous trees. It all beckoned me, as if I were paddling into another dimension. The ocean was breathing and I rested on her diaphragm.

Dixon Entrance was behaving moderately well, so mostly out of curiosity and with some significant second-guessing, I stopped to check out Jim's Tree Point campsite. I landed at the small, semi-protected cove south of Tree Point Light, which was the only lighthouse to be built on the mainland and the first Alaskan lighthouse I would lay eyes on.

Concrete pillars and a large hoisting boom hung over the water, and the front end of the elevated and gutted boathouse it was once connected to stood gaping above me. One door hung crazily askew, only partly hinged. On the ocean side, rusted steel tramway tracks dead-ended, truncated in mid-air, a good thirty yards shy of the hoisting boom. The boathouse, perhaps forty feet in length, was open at both ends, with tracks entering and exiting the rickety building. Jim had told me that an inhospitable shoreline directly below the lighthouse necessitated a narrow tramway and wooden boardwalk that snaked high above the forest floor for nearly a mile, all the way to the lighthouse. Supplies were offloaded via the hoisting boom and shuttled to the lighthouse on this tram.

On August 8, 1992, Jim took refuge at Tree Point, 88 years after the first beacon of light emanated from this structure. He penned these words on the 73rd day of his trip:

> *I'm hunched over a cup of coffee in an eerie boathouse at an abandoned lighthouse on the Alaska coast. This place is straight out of a Hardy Boys or Nancy Drew mystery with vacant staring windows, long silent staircases, tumble down structures and smothering green vegetation reclaiming all. Ghost, my kayak and I arrived here last evening just ahead of a dark storm on the sea. It was with relief that I stepped onto land and discovered the shelter here. I will stay a couple of days—to explore, to rest, to linger in a mysterious yet magical place.*

STRONG SOUTHWESTERLIES WOULD HAVE RENDERED my already sketchy landing dangerous, and I was concerned the westerly wind would veer south while I was scoping things out. So I hurriedly explored, finding Tree Point almost surreal, mysterious, and somewhat of a haunting landfall. The old boathouse and carriage tracks were much more dilapidated than when Jim had been there eighteen years earlier. I started to walk the rotten boardwalk that sliced neatly through the thick vegetation toward the lighthouse, then realized this was not the smartest thing to be doing—tiptoeing on a dilapidated promenade thirty feet above the forest floor, in the middle of nowhere. One slip or one errant plank could result in a nasty fall and any number of broken bones. I wouldn't be found for days, or possibly even weeks. I wasn't really keen on heights anyway. I grumbled out loud that I should just remain at sea level. I had attached SPOT to my belt loop so at least my searchers would have a last-seen-point to recover my body in a more efficient manner. With alarm, I noticed that blueberries were everywhere. *Bears like berries!* I turned on my heels, mindful of Jim's face-to-bear rump encounter when he was there. Stepping only on the stouter cross beams, I cursed him all the way back to solid ground.

As I slipped back into my kayak, I noticed the beach was strewn with beautiful white speckled rocks. I hadn't noticed them when I first arrived because I was a little weirded-out about being there in the first place. Now that I was leaving, and Ma Ocean seemed to be holding her modest mood, I relaxed a bit and nosed around. With my butt in the cockpit, both feet out on either side, I playfully leaned over and plucked a perfectly round granite rock off the beach. I held it in my palm and let its warmth spread through my hand, while I admired the brilliant specks of black mica scattered throughout it, like a reverse Milky Way. I cupped it tight and tried to curl my fingers around it but they wouldn't quite reach. Rocks are heavy so I had to be selective about what I gathered to mail back home, but this one spoke to me for some reason. My thoughts turned to Jim and how much he loved this place and how this would be the perfect souvenir for him. I could already see it in his home office, as his favorite paperweight. I folded my legs back into the cockpit, tucked the rock behind my seat, snapped on my sprayskirt, and shoved off.

MY EYES HAD GROWN ACCUSTOMED to deciphering Canadian charts for over seven hundred miles and I struggled to discern the much smaller scale and lack of detail on the American chart that now graced my deck. Furthermore, I felt the NOAA weather reports played second-fiddle to Environment Canada's, which were issued four times daily and chock full of helpful information. NOAA's twice-daily broadcasts sounded generic, as if they were telling their listeners which coat to wear to the county park, versus a marine forecast. Based on these sketchy reports, I wasn't entirely certain that heading back into Dixon Entrance was the best thing to do. My anxiety resurfaced.

> *The conditions of the mind must interact with the conditions of the*
> *sea; the result is a good paddle versus a terror stricken one.*

I'd first read these words in Jim's journal and was so taken by his wisdom that I copied and laminated them on a small strip of paper and tucked it beneath the bungee cord on my foredeck. I did this so I could repeat these words aloud to give me courage, inspiration, and strength when I needed them, and I'd call upon them on numerous occasions. I did this because I felt perhaps the biggest challenge for all humans, on a day-to-day basis, is becoming comfortable with the conditions of the mind in the face of unfolding reality. On the sea, this could be the difference between life and death.

I didn't want failure to creep into my vocabulary, and I didn't want to be blinded by the goal of completing the trip. I knew there would be unforeseen circumstances that might wear me down as the trip progressed. Since this was my first big expedition, I couldn't accurately predict them, but I could adequately prepare for them. In other words, I had no control over the weather, the sea state, marine events, shipping traffic, and many other things, but perhaps I could focus on my confidence in my skill level, the gear I had chosen, and the clarity of my goal. And, most importantly, on what I should control: my fear.

Fear is a wily enemy, and as a woman paddling alone on the Inside, I entertained many fears. I feared big seas and swirling currents and whirlpools and boomers; I feared cantankerous waves that go "HISS" as they break beneath my hull; I feared bears; I feared capsizing, hypothermia, and drowning; I feared getting run over by big ships; I feared getting run over by small ships; I feared getting lost; I feared men with ill intentions; I feared what was at the other end of that snapping twig deep in the forest as I lay alone in my tent at night; I feared poor choices that could render me uncomfortable—or dead. I soon realized that my body could *do* this trip, but that my mind controlled it—a mind that was scared shitless at times.

The ocean, and the journey I was on, were a like a hand-held mirror that compelled me to look deeper into and reflect upon all that was thrown in my path. It was a journey inside. For now the ocean was my coach, my confidante, my competitor. Hopefully the only thing I'd be drowning in would be my own determination. When the ocean was in a good mood, we collaborated to funnel my energies into moving north. If she was in a vile mood, I would wildly toggle back and forth from fear to courage, courage to fear. Sometimes humor worked, and I'd pseudo-confidently yell out "INTERACTING" as if trying to persuade the ocean that I could maintain a semblance of composure, even in terrifying moments. "One stroke at a time, one fear at a time," I often whispered to myself.

Years ago my therapist had handed me a pad of paper and a pencil and asked me to draw fear. I looked at her quizzically. She nodded at the blank paper and asked me to sketch what might represent fear on paper. Before this could sift through my consciousness, I took the pencil and stiffly drew a rigid, serrated line. At the end of this line my pencil stopped, stabbed into the paper. I applied more pressure but I couldn't move the pencil. It was frozen—like fear. It was fear stuck still. Paralyzing, binding, freezing fear.

There's a difference between fear—that unpleasant emotion associated with the belief that someone or something is a threat—and being scared. Being scared is an in-the-moment feeling caused by an actual threat; when that bear is actually in your campsite, or when the ship is really bearing down on you, or the hideous man's hands are groping your boobs. Each of these warrant being scared—and demand action. Fear, on the other hand, is subjective, just like risk. I wanted to acknowledge my fears, never dismiss them. Respect them. I was certainly flirting with danger at times, and perhaps inviting adversity. But my fears on the Inside Passage were often counter-balanced by curiosity, wonder, and the possibility of magic. Sometimes my fear and I would engage in a robust tug-of-war; me courageously pulling away from the fear, then the fear yanking me back off balance. My anxiety levels shifted with the moods of the sea. When the winds kicked up, my apprehension meter swung into the red zone. Calm seas swung it back, as did sunshine. Anything is more easily tackled in the sun than in the fog or rain. But there are exceptions. Occasionally, when my fears were cloaked behind the guise of a gray curtain of thick fog or clouds I felt less vulnerable. With limitless visibility across open expanses of ocean, with ominous mountains looming in the distance, sometimes my diminutiveness seemed exaggerated. I felt small. Inconsequential. Vulnerable.

And as to my fear of men with ill intentions: how often do you read that a woman accosted a male out in the wilderness? Right. But the reality was that I mostly felt respected. People, often men, seemed in awe over what I had accomplished thus far, and many a salty sailor knew what I was up against. They saw that I wasn't naive or reckless in my quest, that I possessed boundless determination, that I would probably survive. They respected that. I saw it in their eyes and read it in their body language. They understood the moxie it had taken me to make it this far. It felt good to be respected and even held in awe. Although I wavered sometimes, it was my decision to stay strong and brave just as it had been my decision to paddle the Inside alone.

Paddling through the large swells and whitecaps of Dixon Entrance, I thought about that moment in my therapist's office, and knew that I simply could not allow fear to linger in this equation. Fear would not—could not—be the arbiter on this journey. Instead I relaxed, let my hips swivel beneath me, and allowed the universe—the sky, the trees, the whales, the sea, the birds—to be behind me, with me, all around me. Fear would only freeze me in space and time. Loosening my corset of fear created more breathing room between my ribs and freed my diaphragm so I could focus and stay balanced. Many times fear prattled behind me. But I wouldn't allow it to get ahead of me, for if I did allow it in my field of view, I would reinforce its power and weaken mine. And so I paddled wildly with fear at my back.

NEARING CIVILIZATION CAN BE A MIXED BLESSING. With it comes the promise of another resupply box; a hot shower; cellphone service; a warm, dry bed—and food. Copious amounts of sustenance that I didn't have to squat down to rustle up. The flip side of the civilization coin is that campsites within a twenty-mile radius of town tend to smack of vagrancy. The wilderness feel has dissipated and in its place at times are abandoned tarps still slung carelessly in trees, blackened fire pits, trash, and dog shit, even human shit with scads of strewn toilet paper. An uneasy feeling would come over me when sleeping alone in the woods under these circumstances. Camping closer to town made it more likely for some weirdo to emerge out of the forest, stumble on my tent, and think, "Lookie, lookie what we've got here." Perhaps my fears were unfounded but, nonetheless, I'd make doubly sure that my pitiful arsenal of self-defense items were within arm's reach; maybe I'd even load a flare into the chamber of my flare gun. Ready, fire, aim. Constructed of fluorescent orange plastic, it resembled a toy gun, but if fired at point-blank range it could seriously injure an intruder.

My men-with-ill-intentions fear gave me great pause just outside Ketchikan. Two disheveled men in a small fishing boat, while feigning friendliness, radiated vibes of insincerity. Their tone was creepy, they were creepy, their boat, I thought, was creepy, and the way they repeatedly suggested the campsite I was considering was a dandy, was creepy. My confidence deflated like a flat tire on the interstate. With misgivings, I landed at the so-called dandy spot and dug out my lunch bag—and my cellphone and bear spray—keeping an eye on the creepy boat. "No service," the miniature screen told me. I sat on a Volkswagen-size piece of driftwood and ate my lunch as the two men coasted back and forth three times, indubitably watching me. Trusting my gut feeling, and my woman's intuition, I packed up, mindfully inhaled two lungfuls of dense, moisture-laden Pacific Ocean air, and moved on.

Dampened Enthusiasm

FIVE DAYS AFTER LEAVING PRINCE RUPERT, I paddled into Ketchikan with a slight tailwind and a light drizzle. The smell of chemical-laden dryer sheets wafted down from a vent on the hillside and intermingled with the organic scent of salt and sea. To my right, a car sped along a paved road, spewing out black clouds of exhaust. This peculiar combination of aromas reminded me that I was back in civilization. I had arrived at my first Alaskan resupply town on the summer solstice. This stretch had been kind to me: good weather, pleasant tail winds, magnificent scenery, accessible beaches, manageable tide levels, and a scarcity of bears. All these things helped shape a relatively uneventful leg of my journey, a welcome reprieve compared to the drama and trauma of getting myself to Prince Rupert.

Ketchikan struck me as a western Venice with a San Francisco feel. Essentially built into a cliff, most of the city's precipitous streets ended abruptly at the sea. I imagined many of the fourteen thousand locals maintained solid relationships with their brake mechanics, lest they go careening into the depths of Tongass Narrows.

Ketchikan is the first port of call for northbound boaters and a mandatory stop to check in with customs. I parked Chamellia at the public dock in Thomas Basin, just behind the mammoth luxury cruise liners. With passport in hand, I marched into the Pepto-Bismol-pink federal building to check in. The agent asked me the prescribed questions, stamped a few documents, and handed me back my passport.

After going through customs, I paddled the 45-second route over to the yacht club, where John, the manager, agreed to store my kayak for five dollars a day. Chamellia would proudly sit on the dock directly in front of John's office, and my two carbon-fiber paddles would be under lock and key beside his desk. My next task was to find a room for a night or two. I retrieved my cellphone while John dug out a rumpled phonebook and made a few recommendations.

The cheery voice on the phone at the historic Gilmore Hotel informed me they had one room left, to the whopping tune of $157 a night. All the other accommodations already had their no-vacancy signs up. Sensing my disappointment, she asked if this was a business trip. "Well, sorta," I fibbed.

"Come on up, honey. I'll give you the discounted rate of $109, plus tax." I dug deep down into my dry bags to fetch the American currency I had stashed what felt like so long ago, grabbed a few other essentials, secured the hatches, and fastened the cockpit cover.

"Thanks, John," I said on my way up the dock. "I'll be in town for at least two days, maybe three. I'll be back tomorrow to check on things and visit."

"I'll look forward to it, young lady," he said. I beamed as I walked away. It must have been all the fresh mountain air and exercise, because I hadn't been referred to as a young lady in—well, a long, long time.

Helen's smiling face at the front desk of the Gilmore Hotel matched the cheery disposition she had exuded on the phone. "Helen is my Mom's name," I told her. "Should be easy for me to remember."

"It's a good name," she replied, cradling a black phone handset in the crook of her neck while handing me my room key and retrieving her cigarettes and lighter from her faux leather purse.

I ascended the stairs to the second level, admiring the authentic oak banisters, paisley carpets, stained glass windows, and golden chandeliers. Holding my camera strap in my teeth, I juggled three dry bags and a water bottle while I nudged the key into the slot and turned the knob. I pushed the heavy oak door open with my right kneecap. A queen bed with a beautiful green comforter and six matching pillows filled nearly half the room. A mahogany desk, small nightstand, floor lamp, and a tall dresser adequately rounded out the decor. An old-fashioned metal radiator sat beneath a large window. What struck me most, however, was the view—or lack thereof. The gleaming white superstructure of the *Holland America* loomed five stories above me, eclipsing my view of Tongass Narrows. Three other cruise ships were berthed behind her. I marveled at the juxtaposition of this huge ship dwarfing the Tongass Trading Company, a large tourist trinket shop that sat just below it. Below that, a green Mack truck drove by, resembling a child's Matchbox toy.

I wondered if the gargantuan cruise ship that slid by me earlier that day, its nose pointed in the direction I was going, was among these. I had pictured its occupants being pampered with massages, steam baths, and fine dining. Its massive size had overshadowed a large freighter chugging up the passage in the opposite direction.

These metal monsters towered like floating skyscrapers above the waterfront, deploying tourists by the thousands. For the next two days I witnessed the ebb and flow of throngs of people flocking off these ships, much like I had in Prince Rupert. Once docked, tourists would spill out, storm the sidewalks, and infiltrate the bars, restaurants, and trinket shops. "Ka-ching, ka-ching," went the cash registers, their drawers opening and closing as shopkeepers smiled and stuffed crisp bills in the appropriate slots. Within hours, the sightseers, summoned by the clock, would make their way back to their soon-departing ships, and recede like the tide, leaving a human wrack line in their wake. The streets were nearly empty and the town quiet, until the next flood of travelers would descend upon Ketchikan. With a wary eye, I strolled Creek Street at proverbial "slack tide."

Creek Street isn't really a street at all, but rather a narrow suspended boardwalk built over salmon-choked Ketchikan Creek. It threads through the city's historic red-light district, charmingly lined with stilted buildings housing saloons, curio shops, art galleries, and some private dwellings.

Ketchikan receives an average of about 150 inches of rain a year. That's over *twelve feet*. It's one of the wettest places in the US, so no wonder it's nicknamed the rain capital of Alaska. Seattle, in comparison, a damp and drizzly seaside city that I occasionally enjoyed exploring, was a dehydrated dustbowl with its paltry average about 35 inches of yearly rain. In 1949, the wettest year on record, 202 inches of rain fell on Ketchikan. Fittingly, it poured nearly the entire time I was there.

The rain manifested in a medley of forms. It drizzled. It poured. It teased and threatened. The sky wept and moaned and sent the tourists all askitter. It pittered and pattered, lulling me into another blissful nap. It came in torrents, pelting sideways, then vertical sheets. Incessantly, it soused the temperate rainforest that without it would not grow two-hundred-foot trees with bases as big around as a trampoline. Sometimes intermittent, often nonstop, always soaking, nearly maddening.

Drowning gutters overflowed onto sidewalks, sidewalks morphed into shallow rivers. Sheets of featureless clouds drifted in haunting heaps and discursive layers above splashes of Ketchikan color: yellow-hooded slickers, pink goulashes, and rainbow umbrellas.

"Life isn't about waiting for the storm to pass … It's learning to dance in the rain." This anonymous quote not only ping-ponged in my head, it also occupied a shoebox, along with other refrigerator art, in my Montana storage unit. Rain seemed to symbolize my lifelong challenge to live differently from what I learned from my family, and to accept

myself fully, the dark and the light. Challenge is my rain, and sometimes I allow the storms to rock my world, while other times I weather through them—brief cloudbursts to torrential downpours—and still other times, when I am truly in control, I dance with them.

IN NO HURRY TO PADDLE in the rain, I lazed about Ketchikan for another day, and languidly tended to my resupply chores: laundry, food shopping, calling friends and family, mailing a few things back to Jim (including his Tree Point souvenir rock), showering, sleeping, and seeking out high-calorie comfort food. Once again, I had the pleasure of seemingly eating my way through town. Back in Prince Rupert, I had stepped on the scale in the hostel's public bathroom and weighed myself. The needle hovered between 125 and 126. For years I had maintained a somewhat muscular build on my 5'7" frame, and my weight fluctuated between 145 to 150 pounds. When I set off on this journey I weighed 140 pounds. Anticipating some weight loss, I wanted to bulk up for the trip, but I was so doggedly determined to whip myself into the best shape possible, that I ended up being leaner than I'd originally hoped. I had calculated that I would need to consume a minimum of four thousand calories a day just to maintain my body weight. I had assumed that as the trip progressed I would become leaner and fitter, which would further boost my metabolism and require even more calories.

In addition to stuffing my face and busying myself with resupply chores, I sometimes, though rarely, primped. While camping it seemed pointless to spend time on anything more than the basics of personal hygiene. I'd brush and floss (my dentist would be proud), run a comb through my chronically damp hair, then braid it, and apply lip balm. That was the extent of my beauty regime.

Now, with a large and ornate mirror in front of me and seductive trial-size designer soaps, lotions, and potions sitting on a plastic tray, I went wild. I scrubbed my face with a deliciously soft washcloth steeped in warm, soapy water. My face, leathery and tan after living outdoors for weeks, absorbed a palmful of creamy white facial moisturizer like a weathered sponge. "Satiny smooth and yummy for your skin," read a tiny bottle of complimentary body lotion. I unscrewed the cap, sniffed the bottle, and squeezed a large dollop of the lavender-scented emollient into my calloused hands, then smeared it all over my arms and elbows. *More*, I thought. I wanted more. I pounded, and squeezed, and coaxed the upside-down bottle until the "yummy-for-your-skin" elixir finally oozed onto my hands, then onto my legs. My five minutes of decadence concluded with a manicure with the world's tiniest pair of silver nail clippers, which I had tucked inside my toiletry kit.

All glammed up and smelling pretty, I decided to check on Chamellia. During this expedition, she'd always been in my sight and leaving her unattended was a bit nerve-wracking. I wandered down toward the yacht club and found her right where I had left her, as if patiently waiting for me. Other than a small skiff and sailing dinghy pulled up on the dock next to her, she was surrounded and overshadowed by hundreds of boats many times her size—charter boats, private yachts, pleasure skiffs, water taxis, and sailboats whose masts towered over her. Beyond this menagerie, the cruise ships bottle-necked the top end of the marina. A stately yacht, trimmed in teak and brass, quietly steered out of the harbor, dwarfed under the prow of *The Golden Princess*. Chamellia held her own, in spite of her diminutive size, and in the right hands was every bit as seaworthy as these larger vessels.

Confident that Chamellia was safe in port, I slipped onto a barstool at the Totem Bar, two doors down from my hotel. A frosty mug of cold, dark beer slid down the shellacked counter top. To my right, a fellow wearing tattered Levis and a dark blue hoodie with "Glacier National Park" imprinted in white struck up a conversation. Turned out he lived in Montana for a spell. Quickly, we realized that we both knew some of the same folks. Small world. We talked about mom and pop radio stations, Glacier Park, and the eclectic ski resort town of Whitefish. Landlocked

Montana and maritime Alaska share some similarities: mountains, beauty, big skies, and hearty, adventuresome souls. I told him about Jim, and all the caving, kayaking, and exploring he'd done in those landlocked mountains.

Later that night, as I drifted off to sleep in my warm, dry bed, my thoughts turned to Jim. He would undergo the knife first thing in the morning. If the stent insertion was successful, we could all take a deep breath. It was the alternative that worried me. Linda and Dave, our friends visiting from Great Britain, would take Jim to the surgery center in Kalispell. They promised to phone as soon as they knew more. I resolved to not paddle away from the dock until I received that all-important call.

Early the next morning, under a steady rain, I packed my kayak on the yacht club's dock where I had paddled in just two short days before. My cellphone sat face up in its waterproof case in my cockpit, with the ringer set loud. A small crowd of onlookers began to gather, asking the same questions I had fielded over and over at these ports of call. I was tense today, not my jovial self. As my mood deteriorated on the dock that morning, so too did the weather. A stiff wind had picked up, and the rain, which had been nearly round the clock since I arrived in Ketchikan, kicked up a notch. *Fuck the metaphors*, I thought. I was restless to get going, worried about crossing Clarence Strait and camping in some serious bear country, rebellious about the rain, and agitated that my stuff was already getting wet. Most of all, I was anxious about the phone call from Linda.

A well-meaning elderly man asked the quintessential question, "Where do you sleep at night?" I bit my tongue in order to not sneer out *I sleep in a fucking Motel 6 every night. Where the hell do you think I sleep? I sleep in a ridiculously thin nylon tent in the middle of this godforsaken, sodden country running amok with bears that would snarf me down like an appetizer. I sleep on the cold, hard ground, piss in the bushes, and dig a hole to shit. I squat to cook my meals, I lug this freaking heavy boat around all by myself. I have another 450 miles to paddle until I run out of ocean at Skagway. And YES, I'm doing this for fun. Any other questions?* There, I felt better entertaining myself with a barrage of words that would never, God willing, leave my lips. I was entitled to my snarky fits.

Startled, I looked over at my cellphone, ringing loudly. I recognized England's country code on the caller ID—it was Linda, calling about the surgery.

"The stent won't work," she stated matter-of-factly. My heart sank. "Jim's got too much blockage, and his bloody kidney issues aren't helping matters." Jim's only option—quadruple bypass surgery—was scheduled for the 30th of June, less than a week away.

John overhead the conversation, and although he could see that I was visibly upset, he lacked bedside manners. He mentioned a friend of his who had bypass surgery and that all it did was "buy him a couple of years." Within seconds, a cloudburst opened above us, releasing, with all its fury, a torrent of raindrops that bounced on the wooden planks where we stood, as if emphasizing John's ignorant remark. I packed faster and politely asked John for my paddles. As he handed them to me he warned me again about the brown bears. "A fella was gobbled up by a griz a couple weeks ago—right where you'll be paddling by!"

Knowing that Cleveland Peninsula and this stretch of the Tongass National Forest had the heaviest concentration of grizzly bears on this entire stretch of Alaskan coastline didn't help matters any. Fighting back my tears, I took my paddles, wheelbarrowed my kayak off the dock until her bow plunged into the cold, dark water, and paddled off into Tongass Narrows. A hard rain drummed on Chamellia's deck. I sobbed for miles.

Leg 6   **150 miles**   **7 days**

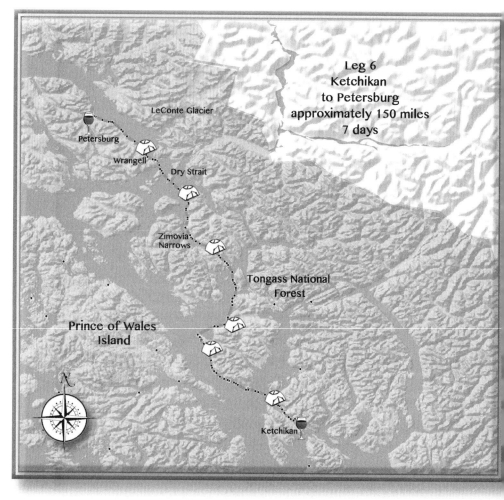

Seven

Ketchikan to Petersburg

Life is an ever shifting kaleidoscope:
A slight change and all patterns alter.

—Sharon Salzberg

There Bear

LEAVING KETCHIKAN, I paddled beneath the hulking bows of berthed cruise ships, dodged float planes and various pleasure boats, and followed my own bow north past the industrial complex lining the shore, then past the city airport, until after what seemed like an eternity, the city finally disappeared behind me. Roughly 150 water miles zigzagged between my bow and my next resupply port of Petersburg. I slowly settled back into the rhythm of the paddle and desperately tried to put thoughts of Jim out of my mind.

In spite of my meltdown at the dock, it felt good to be back in the boat. Such a lovely fit, Chamellia and I. I appreciated her gracefulness, how I wore her, how I was one with her, how we glided together on this journey, and how this journey was more than just me and this fire-engine-red kayak moving north. It was about the ocean, the moods of the sea, leaning into the elements, and the possibilities of adventure. The *womyak*, half-woman, half-kayak, was on a life-changing journey, still absorbing the magic of it all. *Stay in the moment, stay focused*, I kept repeating to myself.

IN THE WILDERNESS OF SOUTHEAST ALASKA, an American flag flapped in the breeze on its pole above a welcoming, manicured lawn. I'd left Ketchikan two days earlier and had covered approximately 33 miles. Curious, I paddled up to the property, wondering if this was the small community noted on my chart as Meyers Chuck. This puzzled me; I didn't think I had paddled that far yet. A small boat was backing out of the cove, its five exuberant occupants waving to a couple left standing on shore. The laughter from the small boat quickly scattered in the breeze and the man and woman warmly waved me in.

"Helllllloooo," I said. The man's outstretched hands reached for my bow, which was scraping up on shore. He reminded me of my grandfather with his red suspenders, broad smile, and hard-working hands liberally speckled with age spots. "I'm just passing through, on my way to Petersburg. Looking for a place to pitch my tent."

"You can pitch your tent right here," the woman said, pointing to their inviting, grassy lawn. Her rosy cheeks glowed under black-rimmed glasses and a black ball cap. "No, wait—come to think of it, our daughter is gone for a spell. You can stay in her cabin." Her dangly hoop earrings jostled with her enthusiasm. Her husband nodded in agreement. My gaze traveled past the lawn and up to a pale green shack. Three small, paned glass windows sat beneath dark green shingles and a sleepy smokestack. Four plastic lawn chairs, also green, were propped against the ocean-facing wall.

Fibrous gray clouds hovered over a patchwork of green forest and green mountains, hugging them like a woman's shrug. At last the rain had stopped, which felt like a magical touch to a day that started off rather crummy. The weather had been churlish, the sea had grown boisterous, high tide issues had returned, bears roamed the beaches, and Jim was scheduled for open heart surgery. After my hasty and sodden departure from Ketchikan, I was feeling a little down. Earlier that day, as the pounding rain rinsed the salty tears off my face, I had gently rocked Chamellia back and forth underneath me, trying to soothe myself, then slowly paddled forward into the somber weather. Pain radiated deep down my right shoulder as I carried out the cyclical motion of paddling. I had tweaked it the previous day while performing multiple reverse sweep strokes to maintain course in strong afternoon winds.

My gracious hosts' names were Dan and Karen. "Dan, sweetie, why don't you fire up the propane water tank?" I fixated on the nearby outdoor shower that Dan started walking toward, and Karen motioned for me to follow her to the cabin. "Feel free to fill your water bags from our rain tanks," Karen said as we walked, pointing to two large galvanized metal cisterns alongside their house. Behind Karen's delicate hand, the door of her daughter's cabin creaked open, and she immediately apologized for the musty smell.

"Karen, this is like the Waldorf Astoria to me!" I said, throwing my head back and laughing. We chatted for a bit, standing just inside the cabin's doorway. She told me about how they'd bought this property years ago and enjoyed it as a family getaway. Now that she and Dan were retired, they lived here full-time, reveling in the solitude and beauty, but also delighting in its close proximity to Ketchikan. The group of people leaving when I had paddled in were her relatives, on an impromptu visit from town.

"There's a partial lunar eclipse tonight," she said as she walked down the stairs to leave me to my chores and thoughts. "If you stick your head out at about two-ish, you might catch a glimpse of it."

Small pieces of kindling were stacked neatly next to the cast iron wood stove, a pile of newspapers lay bundled on a wooden chair, and a box of large stick matches sat on top of the papers. Cushy toilet paper accompanied a spotless vault toilet less than twenty paces away from the door. *Wow,* I thought. I had stumbled into a patch of paradise: a roof over my head, a hot shower, a soft bed, a refuge from bears, and a crackling fire to dry my things and warm my heart. Before I could finish that thought, two humpback whales appeared in the distance, exhaling with the rhythm of the strait they were traveling through, intuitively navigating the sea. Later that night, I settled under the flannel covers, a book propped on my chest, happily reading in the beam of my headlamp, while the full moon pushed the tide high on Karen and Dan's property.

Hours later, with my book still on my chest and my headlamp still glowing, I awoke as the full moon shone brilliantly through the little cabin's window—the last full moon I would experience on this trip. I groped for my eye drops, moistened my contacts, and stepped outside. The moonlight bathed Dan and Karen's lawn in a dazzling display of muted shadows and caricatures reminiscent of a Doctor Seuss fable. My eyes followed its beam across the weathered driftwood, down the smooth pebble beach, and out onto the coal-black water of Clarence Strait. With heavy eyelids, I glanced at my watch, took a gulp of the thick ocean air and retreated to my warm cabin, sliding back under the covers. The moon would have to partially eclipse without me.

Early the following morning, a bird soloed outside my window, a song worthy of an encore, yet one which stopped suddenly. Still in bed, I listened to the stillness around me. It was all that I could hear—a palpable quiet where the soft hum of the universe hovered above the cabin.

A few hours later, Dan helped me haul my gear down to the low tide line with his four-wheeler. A 21-foot tidal difference was slated for that day, and the beach was slick and mucky. It was hard to leave the ease and comfort of their cabin; I pondered what it might be like to live with this wilderness at your doorstep every day.

A slight tailwind ushered me through the last bit of Clarence Strait, but when I hung a right into Ernest Sound, a headwind rudely greeted me. The sky collapsed into torrents of wind-driven rain. *Aargh!* Any remaining energy from my restful cabin reprieve quickly waned, and I fought to sustain a lousy two-knot speed.

Paddling through bear country again, I planned to camp on small islands whenever possible. Bears swim, though, so before settling on any campsite I gave it a thorough inspection. That night, after performing my ritual of scouting the islands, I found a suitable campsite on Sunshine Island, tucked into Vixen Inlet, where it was fairly dry under the heavily wooded interior. I was packed up and ready to depart at 6:30 the next day, just as the morning sun began to shine on Sunshine Island. Behind me, a prominent dome-shaped mountain burst through a swirl of clouds, its peak ablaze in crimson and gold, a tequila sunrise tumbling down its slopes.

I crossed over toward the mainland and hugged the shoreline, paddling in a trance-like state. A mama grizzly bear with one fluffy cub stood grazing on a blind corner, startling me as I floated practically right under her nose. Eyeball to eyeball we met, hers big, brown, and foreboding, set deep in her furry dished face. I quickly averted my icy-blue eyes, but this mental imagery would resurface for many nights thereafter while I lay hushed in my tent.

YEARS AGO, JIM WORE THE BADGE of a National Park Service ranger and so he was experienced at analyzing bear scat. He once said that if I took my index finger and inserted it fully into a pile of bear dung and if that entire finger went in without resistance and was warm, then I should get my finger—and the rest of my body—out of there pronto. If the pile was light and had a thin crust on top (think Bisquick biscuit) then Jim suggested that I might have time to stop panicking and contemplate the evidence in front of me. In other words, I could unhurriedly assess the risks of staying or moving on. Good advice from someone who had spent two summers sticking his fingers in piles of bear shit.

I spent nearly twenty years living and camping in northwest Montana, where many grizzlies of Glacier National Park consider humans part of the food chain, much more so than their coastal cousins. This didn't make me any less edgy when camping in bear country in the Pacific Northwest. The coastal grizzly bears, a subspecies of the brown bear, generally are bigger than their inland compatriots—sometimes twice the height—due to the rich salmon diet they favor. The coastal grizzlies tend to prefer the mainland and larger islands like Alaska's Admiralty Island, where density is estimated to be one bear per square mile. Eventually, I'd be paddling in the vicinity of Admiralty Island, but—thankfully—the broadness of Stephens Passage would separate me from the land of the one-bear-square.

I'd already passed through the only area on earth where the Kermode bears roamed. I knew that the more familiar black bears were found throughout the Inside Passage, including on the smaller islands, which they had a penchant to swim between. Grizzlies, rumor had it, tended to stay put.

In dealing with bears, I took all the preemptive steps to dissuade encounters, except hanging my food. It was a huge hassle, although I suppose nursing wounds from a grizzly mauling would be more of a nuisance. But on the IP, it's not always possible to string up food. In places it's a jungle habitat, where I couldn't even see my feet, let alone move through the mess to find a suitable hanging tree. Plus, if the food was not properly hung, it merely ended up being a bear piñata.

Distance was the only other solution, so I would stash my kayak as far away as possible from my camp, and stow my food bags and garbage inside the hatches at night, along with a triple-bagged handful of mothballs. A fellow kayak-adventurer had shared the tip of using the strong odor of mothballs to mask the odor of food, emphasizing they not touch the food, to avoid contamination. I figured he was still alive to write about it, so I dutifully shoved them in the hatch each night, hoping he knew what he was talking about. Either I was extremely lucky or this technique was effective for me; not one scratch on Chamellia's deck or hull resulted from the paws of a nosy bear.

I chose to travel alone in bear country, and I fully understood what the risks were, and that by virtue of traveling solo I was at an enhanced risk of bear confrontations. Groups tended to naturally cause more disruption in the wilderness, thereby giving the bear plenty of advance warning to gather cubs, if applicable, and disappear before the humans showed up. A single person walking on a soft trail in the deep, dark forest with wetsuit booties doesn't make much of a racket. Bears certainly understand the path of least resistance; they like trails too and can be fairly reluctant to surrender them, so my interest in walking on deep, dark trails in bear country was zilch. Instead, I opted to stay put on the open beaches.

I didn't carry a gun. If one is going to pack a gun in the backcountry, one really should know how to use it. I'd timidly *touched* a gun twice in my life, not counting a few painful, hematoma-forming rounds of paintball. I had no desire to learn how to properly handle a gun and had even less desire to piss a bear off with nonexistent marksmanship skills. I had to rely on other precautionary measures.

I needed to be a lot of things to be bear safe. I needed to be noisy, tidy, smart, and observant. I had a protocol when choosing a campsite in bear country. First: Is there a bear standing in the proposed campsite? I wasn't about to get in a property dispute with some bruin, so my first rule was if there was a bear on the beach I wouldn't camp there. Pretty basic rule. If bears were not visibly loafing in my intended campsite, I would land and have a look around. Rule number two: If there were *signs* of bear, such as a steaming pile of bear dung (I didn't need to stick my finger in it), tree bark gouged by two-inch claws, or long, coarse strands of bear hair snagged in the tree bark, then I would move on.

When on land, I kept my super-sized canister of bear spray always within reach, if not attached to my hip. I also carried an obnoxiously loud whistle, a foghorn, and bear bangers. A bear banger, impressively loud, would scatter anything in my vicinity and gave me a transitory peace of mind. No bigger than a pen, it deployed much like a handheld flare. The device had a spring and a firing pin attached to a sliding trigger mechanism that, when pulled, struck a cartridge, propelling it about thirty yards, at which point it exploded, ear-splittingly loud. I'd practiced unscrewing the barrel and pulling the chain many times, knowing full well my knees would be mush and I'd be shaking like a leaf if I had to deploy it in a combat situation.

Just as you may prefer that guests not eat chocolate pie on your white davenport, I needed to keep my rehydrated soups, granola bars, and cans of tuna off my tent, sleeping bag, hatch cover, clothes, fingers, hair, and even the moss or logs in camp. I didn't want to extend any invitations to unwanted visitors, but even so, my campsite locations near the tidal line put me right next to a veritable supermarket. Mussels, clams, crabs, and other sea critters, fish, and sea plants were numerous and in various stages of being alive or dead and were a big draw for bears, raccoons, birds, and a myriad of other wildlife. Ample wild berry patches and the occasional abandoned fruit orchard also caused a bit of discord between me and the bears. And just when I thought I had it under control, I found a half-eaten salmon on my tent stoop, probably dropped by some butter-taloned eagle.

The kindest of human intentions can also be a problem in bear country. Fishermen, spotting a kayak on the water, tend to develop a mothering instinct. They want to give you seafood, and the catch of the day is fresh and unimaginably scrumptious. It is also messy, smelly, and hard to cook. An entire regimen of odor control can go out the window with a big slab of cod. Once, I graciously accepted a slippery donation from a well-intentioned fisherman. Later, as garlic and fish oil dripped down my elbows, I realized the grievous error of my choice. Without a hot shower to hop into afterward, I was essentially walking bear bait.

Nonetheless, I reasoned I was much more likely to die from any of my other fears than from a nasty bear encounter. The fifty-degree water I was paddling on, for starters, could zap my body of precious heat 25 times faster than the cold air. Playing chicken on the nautical superhighway with a big ship was also a more plausible method to meet my demise.

Making a stupid decision was even more probable than getting eaten by a bear. Still, I would be vigilant and hedge my bets in bear country, and I would keep my imagination in check.

To avoid being on any bear's dinner menu, I cautiously played my bear cards. I didn't smear my body with salmon oil, and I didn't camp in berry patches. I didn't walk on deep, dark trails and I never, ever ate or kept any food in my tent. I fully intended that any too-close-for-comfort bear encounter would go something like this: I see the bear; the bear sees me. We both panic. I reach for my bear spray; the bear turns and runs into the woods, never to be seen again.

Measure Twice, Paddle Once

DURING THE EIGHT WEEKS I'd been paddling, my hands, pickled in salt brine and continually irritated by the friction of salt and sand between my skin and the carbon shaft of my paddle, had become quite horrid. I'd tried wearing both full and fingerless gloves, but they only seemed to trap the irritants and were ineffective at deterring the blisters that appeared in new spots, it seemed, nearly every day. Some days, I would bandage my hands, but the bandages never stayed. Eventually calluses formed, yet my hands were swollen and tender, pruned, pale, and seemingly bloodless, my cuticles white and cracked, my nails paper thin and caked with dirt. The saltwater stung like lemon juice on a fresh cut, and almost as a consolation, the occasional wicked hangnail gave me something to chew on to take my mind off the discomfort.

Fatigued, I allowed the tranquility of Zimovia Strait to lull me into complacency, and floated deeper into its potent silence and luminous solitude. But I wasn't alone. A pair of loons drifted beside me, aware of my presence, yet atypically unafraid. I stopped paddling, simply listened to the quiet, and studied their beauty. A droplet of saltwater clung to the bottom of one's broad black beak, which led skullward to a tear-shaped eye turned sideways, a blood-red ruby, inset hauntingly into its coal-black face. A triangular band of black and white vertical lines adorned its neck and joined an emerald green choker that encircled the thickest part. Self-assured, the birds floated low in the water, like I did, the top of their checkerboard backs barely above the surface. They called briefly to each other, keeping in touch. I waited patiently to hear their distinctive cry, often a quintessential wail or tremolo that eerily pierced the silence. Now less than ten yards away, both loons simultaneously dipped their necks and knifed their bills underwater. Their broad bodies followed and they slipped out of my sight. I was alone again, breathing in the wholesome, sweet wildness of the Inside.

Meanwhile, back in Montana, Jim pecked at his keyboard. Nothing, it seemed, would escape his literary clutches, not even his own health crisis. I was able to access Jim's brief group email on my cellphone a few miles south of Wrangell:

To undisclosed recipients

June 25, 2010
SUBJECT: A Medical Cape Caution

Hi everyone,

Just a quick update. My heart catheterization found significant heart disease. While on the marginal edge of being addressed with cardiac stents, reduced kidney function is indicating that a multiple bypass is the safer option. Things are moving quickly. The surgery is scheduled for June 30th.

Susan is aware of this development. I will keep in touch with her trip, as I can. She is now north of Ketchikan 'n kayakin' — propelled through the earth's winds and over her restless waters by the force of your support and well wishes! Thank you for being such good friends to Susan.

It has been a great pleasure for me to be part of her adventure and to renew contact and friendships with some of you, and to cyber-meet others. Let's stay in touch, everyone!

Thank you for the encouragement in my attempt to "armchair kayak" the Inside Passage and for your well wishes.

Jim

I *was* aware of this development, yet reading his words made me fully understand that Jim's love affair with my adventure had just collided with his medical reality. I felt leaden, glum, and helpless and couldn't shake the image of him lying on a cold, sterile table, with his heart exposed to the mercy of a surgeon's hands. I'd had an in-depth phone conversation with him the night before. He had sounded positive and strong, but his optimism didn't squelch my concerns. His voice smacked of confidence in his surgeon—one of the best, hailing from Alamo Cardiothoracic Surgical Associates in San Antonio, Texas. *Cardiothoracic*: I repeated the word several times to myself, my tongue tripping over the syllables, my mind refusing to grasp what it really meant.

A medical Cape Caution did indeed loom on Jim's horizon, just as he had implied in his email. The doctors would intentionally keep him anemic to minimize the blood needed. His post-op instructions strictly forbade driving or lifting for six weeks. Jim had already cancelled all his plans for the summer, including a caving expedition into the Bob Marshall Wilderness in Montana and a Bowron Lakes kayak jaunt in British Columbia. Now he also hung up his correspondent hat, sending one last group email, wishing everyone a good summer, and me congratulations in advance. "Well done, kid," was the last prose he typed relating to my journey.

After a thirty-mile day I took a short time-out from my wilderness paddling and camping routine, and landed at a public campground just outside Wrangell. A civilized reprieve, it featured a covered picnic table; a broad, flat area to pitch my tent; and a vault toilet a fair distance away. The community of Wrangell, with all its niceties, sat a mile north of the campground. I headed into town to grab a shower at the laundromat and a bite to eat at a local inn.

A magenta sunset lingered in front of me, a sweet accompaniment for my walk back to camp. Once there, it was time to do homework again. I spread out my chart and current tables and fired up my GPS. The next day, I'd be going through an eerie, problematic chunk of water that I had been forewarned about—Dry Strait—where the largest navigable undammed watershed in North America meets the sea. The mighty two-hundred-mile-long Stikine River dumps into this ticklish patch of water, creating a shallow deltaic flat spanning nearly twenty miles. Dealing with its extensive mudflats would require precise timing and a bit of strategy; successfully negotiating the seventeen-foot tidal difference that can occur in a span of six hours would take balls. I measured and remeasured the distance, while pushing away persistent feelings of self-doubt. *Time to be logical, not emotional.* I systematically checked the speed of the tidal currents in Sumner Strait and read, then reread the tabular tidal data on my GPS. *Self-doubt, go away!* I needed to be 100% certain that I was extrapolating my data from the correct date and tidal station.

It wasn't rocket science to know that I needed to paddle through here on a rising tide. There would be absolutely no dillydallying. Dry Strait would reach its peak flood at four p.m. I calculated it would take me four hours to get through the thick of it, with a reserve of water under my hull until I entered the deeper waters of Frederick Sound. A noon departure seemed like a good strategy, yet I seesawed from being resolute in my decision to sweating a miscalculation that would leave me stranded and vulnerable to hypothermia. Being off by just an hour could mean being grounded for up to six miserable ones. I was also forewarned that if I did screw up to STAY IN THE BOAT, unless I enjoyed quicksand. *Got it. Better yet, get it right the first time. Measure twice, paddle once. Calculate twenty times, paddle right on through, and pray for a tailwind.*

I would leave my campsite on that Tuesday morning, on day 56, knowing that Jim would be undergoing quadruple bypass surgery Wednesday at seven a.m. The surgery would last about six hours, the same amount of time it would take for a full flood cycle to chug up Dry Strait, and he would remain in the hospital for six or seven days, with at least two of those days in the intensive care unit.

I TOOK MY FIRST STROKE out of Wrangell just before noon on a rising tide. Skies were overcast, and the sea barely rippled, but the weather forecast looked grim. Awake and restless since four a.m., I was tired and moody and worried about getting through Dry Strait. Jim's surgery continued to weigh heavily on my mind. The water was murky from glacial silt and churned-up mudflats. Twice my paddle blade hit mud, and I held my breath, thankful I couldn't see how close the ocean's bottom came to kissing my hull. Back in camp, I had taken my grease pencil and drawn in a squiggly black line on my chart that I wanted to follow. I was lined up for the south end of Kadin Island as Wrangell grew smaller behind me. From there I headed west to Rynda Island, aiming for Blaquire Point, and I scooted right on through anxiety-producing Dry Strait.

Relieved, and proud of myself for negotiating a drama-free passage, I obediently hugged Mitkof Island. A brooding green forest fringed the waterway, lined up to watch the parade of a solitary kayak. A great blue heron stood at the water's edge, with a quiet dignity, unlike the raucous Heckle and Jeckle ravens that frequently pillaged my camps, then soothed me with their cryptic caterwauling. I paddled beneath a gray curtain of clouds until I was confident that Chamellia and I would continue to float. Finally, my shoulders dropped about two inches and my eyes began to take in the dramatic Alaskan coastline, commanding my attention. And I discovered that in spite of my anal-retentive, obsessive-compulsive calculating and extrapolating of data the night before, I still managed to get something wrong. I had figured my next campsite was 24 miles away—but it was really only seventeen miles away. I had erred in my favor! I only had to paddle to the top of Mitkof

Island, hang a left, and I could accurately welcome myself to Petersburg.

A Decision Made

I PEERED OUT FROM BENEATH my sagging tarp and marveled at the scenery of the Tongass National Forest. I was camped in a small cove on Mitkof Island, just south of Petersburg, enjoying a splash of spiced rum and nibbling on dried nectarines and squares of dark chocolate while admiring the view. The huge expanse of Frederick Sound loomed in the foreground. Hundreds of icebergs, having escaped from LeConte Bay, rode the northerly current toward Petersburg along the opposite shore. Many were bigger than suburbans.

Holy cow, I thought, *my first icebergs*! One of the holy grails I had sought on this trip. Suddenly, spouts appeared between the icebergs: humpback whales! The icebergs borne from North America's southernmost tidewater glacier now had the company of these large, acrobatic mammals. I stood up and retrieved a pair of small waterproof binoculars from my deck bag. I pressed the barrels against my eye sockets and rotated the focus rings until the ethereal blue and white shapes filled the lenses, fully losing myself as I gazed peaceably at the parade of icebergs.

Then, my attention was diverted when I caught a whiff of what was simmering on my camp stove. After a long day on the water, I was ready to chow down. I dined on a delicious stir-fry, with rehydrated tomatoes, peppers, mushrooms, broccoli, snap peas, pineapple, and tofu. My meal was seasoned with coconut milk, red curry and a pinch of tarragon, and served over a bed of whole-grain rice that I had cooked and dehydrated that previous winter. I washed down the feast with a glass of merlot and reveled in my good fortune and my full belly. Although I ate fairly well on this trip, thanks to an entire winter of food preparation, meals like this were extra special.

The next morning, I descended the boulder-strewn beach, slipped into Chamellia's cockpit, and speared the water's mirror-like surface with my blade. I knew Jim was deep in the throes of open-heart surgery while I paddled fifteen chilly miles on my way to Petersburg.

I thought about this as I paddled into my 57th day at sea, alongside floating icebergs, undulating dolphins, and beaches littered with brilliant fuchsia fireweed. I worried about him when I paddled beneath craggy mountains, atop a super-sized aquarium over dazzling intertidal life clinging to seaside cliffs, past loons, cormorants, and guillemots indignant about my presence. I longed to be off the contemplative water and immersed into my resupply chores, where I would be distracted. I also knew that Linda and Dave would be checking in with me later to tell me how things went during the surgery. I quickened my cadence.

Leaving Frederick Sound temporarily behind me, I swung around Hungry Point and headed south into Wrangell Narrows, past the county park, past several canneries, past red and green channel markers that pitched and rolled with the fast current coasting me into the harbor. Men in bright orange fishing bibs pulled in seemingly unmanageable fishing nets, while the din and clang of the canneries hovered above them. Larger than Wrangell but smaller than Ketchikan, Petersburg harbors one of Alaska's most prosperous fishing fleets, with hundreds of fishing boats coming and going from its busy harbor every day. The big cruise ships don't dare enter Wrangell Narrows, so Petersburg is not touristy or overpriced like some of the other ports of call I'd encountered. Most of the seaside folks here were friendly, genuine, down to earth. Men and women who wore mostly rubbery yellow oilskins and stout knee-high boots, and made their living off the sea; real people living out real lives in what was called Alaska's little Norway.

"I'M NOT A TOURIST," I said, annoyed. "I'm a traveler." I set the empty beer glass down on the maple-top bar and gestured to the bartender for another. "I'm paddling the Inside Passage." The jack-ass drunk was seated beside me, and I hoped he'd take his pool cue and go back to his game.

But instead he egged me on. "Oh, I thought you were a surfer chick," he said in a smarmy tone, swilling his whiskey. He had dark, greasy hair that lightly framed his pock-marked face.

"Why, because I'm blond and tan?" I asked with a not-so-subtle hint of disdain.

"Pretty much," he said, arrogantly twisting the end of his pool cue into a small block of blue chalk. A waitress wearing black slacks and a red checkered shirt plunked down a plastic, paper-lined basket of fish and chips and tartar sauce, thankfully disrupting the scene. As much as I wanted to antagonize him, I picked up the basket and carried it with me to a table in an adjacent room. Many communities full of friendly, genuine people have schlubs like him, I reminded myself, and I certainly didn't need this situation to escalate. I was hungry and tired, yet fully aware that I was a woman alone in a bar full of rednecks.

After dinner, I walked back to my room at the Tide's Inn and sorted through a few charts and seashells and other odds and ends I had picked up along the way. I still hadn't heard anything about Jim, but I would mail these items back to him for safekeeping: all the way to Eureka, Montana, to his home perched above the Koocanusa Reservoir. A small home with an old piano, a Venus flytrap, a compendium of books, a quartet of cats, and an astounding view of the Canadian Rockies. I didn't know how long he'd be in the hospital, but envisioned him opening this box when he returned home, looking at all these things, and picturing me, following in his paddle strokes, blazing a path up the Inside Passage. I knew, if all went well, Jim's recovery was predicted to encompass the rest of the summer and into the fall. Suddenly, I felt a deep need to see him as soon as I could. From my motel room overlooking the harbor and the narrows, I made the decision to end my trip in Juneau instead of Skagway, ninety miles nearer to where I presently stood.

It was as if a voice of reason took over to help me reflect on the course I'd just taken and offered up a way to help me judge the course ahead. Ending the trip in Juneau now made sense and seemed the prudent choice on logistical, emotional, psychological, and practical levels. I felt good about my decision. It was the right thing to do. Even though I was having the time of my life, my heart and soul ached to be reunited with friends and loved ones back in Montana. I was a bit homesick, and worried sick. Plus the nagging pain deep in my right shoulder concerned me because it was not going away like it used to when the muscles warmed up.

Lynn Canal, and the miles of water between Juneau and Skagway would just have to wait until another time. I made my ferry reservations for an early morning departure out of Juneau on July 13, and I arranged for Becky to meet me at the ferry terminal in Bellingham, Washington.

Thinking of Bellingham made my mind wander to a few coveted items left behind in a duffel bag in Becky's possession: my hair dryer, dangly earrings, a silver ring, skinny jeans, a white cotton T-shirt, some frilly underwear, a non-sports-bra bra, a pair of pink cotton pajamas, an oversized towel, and a pair of fluorescent orange running shoes. I smiled, imagining how deliciously self-indulgent it would feel to be wearing cotton again. For over two months I had worn the same two synthetic tops, nylon pants, sports bra and "technical underwear," and I was ready to slip into something *not* made of nylon, fleece, or rubber, and that didn't have a permanent stench to it.

I decided to take a short stroll through Petersburg to clear my head, grabbing my cellphone on the way out, in case Linda called. Just a few minutes into my walk, the phone vibrated in my pocket. Shielding it from the rain with my open hand, I answered Linda's call.

"Jim is out of surgery. It's gone well, and he's in intensive care now," her endearing British voice said on the other end. I breathed a sigh of relief. "We've spoken with his surgeon, who seems quite positive." She paused, waiting for my reaction, but at that moment only tears would come. "Jim insisted the rock you sent from Tree Point go with him to the hospital. It's on his nightstand," Linda added, as if to break the silence and soothe my spirits.

We talked at length about Jim's ongoing care and how my returning to Montana a bit early would dovetail nicely with their plans; how I could step in as caregiver while he continued his healing process. By the time I returned, Jim would be back at his home in Eureka, and Linda and Dave could head out on their big caving expedition in the Bob Marshall Wilderness, the same trip that Jim had been planning for over a year but had been forced to back out of. Linda had already scheduled twice-weekly visits with home-health nurses. Things were falling into place, and we all remained hopeful. When the cavers returned, we would have one big party to celebrate my safe journey and Jim's recovery.

Unbeknownst to me at the time, less than 24 hours after Jim's surgery, complications set in. Internal bleeding, clotting, and renal failure necessitated a brisk second operation. Surgeons opened his chest once more, then released him back to his recovery room in the ICU. I was already back on the water, and Linda, not wanting to upset the ballast of my trip, didn't tell me when Jim's world went awry. There was nothing I could have done on my end, anyway. Juneau was in my crosshairs. I was near the finish line. My summit hovered less than a week's paddle away, if Mother Nature cooperated.

Leg 7   155 miles   7 days

Eight

Petersburg to Juneau

In the end only three things matter:
how much you loved, how gently you lived,
and how gracefully you let go of things not meant for you.

—Buddha

Out There on the Inside

U NAWARE OF JIM'S COMPLICATIONS, I left Petersburg on a cool,
somber morning and paddled north toward Juneau, reveling in
a more leisurely pace. My muscles slowly warmed from the repetitive
motion of paddling, and my mind focused on the beauty of Alaska for
this final chapter of my adventure.

A boisterous colony of nesting cormorants populated a rocky island,
and the putrid ammonia smell of guano hung thickly in the air. I cupped
my neoprene-covered hand over my nose and mouth, trying to keep the
odor from leaching into my lungs. All but two flew away, neither fearing
nor showing interest in my presence. Looking back over my shoulder at
the two holdouts, I wondered why they didn't flee with the others. What

kept them steadfast? How did they know I wouldn't harm them?

Further up the strait, a small triangular iceberg rolled over in front of me. I studied its icy blue depths and wondered how long this chunk of thousand-year-old glacial ice would continue to melt and roll and flow with the current. Like me, it was always seeking equilibrium, shifting its weight, bobbing, metamorphosing, simply being. I paddled closer and lingered for half an hour, lost in the lens of my camera, so utterly happy. Other icebergs drifted nearby, and I flitted from one to another, like a bee buzzing from one flower to the next, deliriously snapping photos of these fickle entities rising vertically from the flat, level plane of the sea, bursting skyward, reaching, towering over me. This was part of the beauty of the journey. It was days like this where a sense of peace stayed with me hours after I was off the water. I had found my bliss in Alaska and I held tight to the euphoric feeling deep in my heart.

That euphoric feeling was transient. I soon was reminded how briskly things can change in the wilderness. I hadn't noticed the menacing clouds lurking on the horizon. I was penalized for my inattentiveness when I stopped for a lunch break, and those clouds dumped their punishment on me in a soggy outburst. In a feverish attempt to retrieve my storm jacket, I managed to scrape most of the skin off the knuckles of my right hand on the sharp edge of the hatch. As I watched my blood drip onto the deck, my ears picked up a peculiar, and unsettling, sound. Swooshing, gurgling water. This was odd to me because the sea had been calm up to that point. Horrified, I looked up to see that an impromptu rip—an isolated stretch of turbulent water caused by colliding currents— had propagated itself less then ten yards offshore. The rip malevolently stirred up the water like a witch's brew. Irregular waves rolled toward the foreshore and began slapping my boat back and forth, its bow wedged in the sand but the stern floating free in the once-calm water, now transformed into seemingly spontaneous mayhem.

I threw my half-eaten lunch into the hatch, snapped the lid shut, scrambled into my gear, and gave the boat a frustrated shove. With my paddle in one hand, I plunked myself down into the boat, bringing more sand and seawater into the cockpit with me, in a slap-dash effort to launch before the rip intensified. I was not successful. A rogue wave spun my heavy boat sideways and promptly filled the cockpit with a slurry of sand and water, soaking me up to my waist.

"God dammit!" I bawled, shaking my clenched fists at the ocean. Tears rolled down my cheeks and I shook with exasperation. I knew that I'd be wet on this trip: it is a water sport after all, and I was paddling through a rainforest. But that day I had been desperate to stay dry, and oh-so-tired of being cold and wet. I had wanted nothing more than to have a leisurely lunch where I didn't have to wolf down my food, shivering, counting the miles still to go before I could settle in for the night. Unglued, sitting in a pool of water, I paddled for about ten minutes until I was out of range of the disturbed area, and then bilged the cockpit.

Breathing heavily, I snapped my sprayskirt around my now-dry cockpit and pressed my mental rewind button to review the little pity party I had just thrown for myself. What a sad sack I was. I was furious with myself, embarrassed about my over-reactive outburst, and thankful no one was around to observe my juvenile behavior. This was just a stupid little inconvenience, not a major catastrophe. What had happened to the highs I had experienced just a few moments earlier? And what had happened to the sea-will-teach-me-patience thing? Why didn't I simply wait for the confused water to dissipate? Why was my knee-jerk reaction to plunge head-first into this scene, creating drama out of thin air? I refused to write it off as my simply being exhausted. Yes, my shoulder throbbed. Yes, I was frazzled. But I wanted to finish strong, in good spirits. Screwing up now would be like skiing flawlessly down a double-black-diamond run and then wiping out at the bottom of the chair lift, in everyone's view. It was time to change my perspective, again. I vowed to not act so reflexively, to govern my emotions and act maturely. I would not play victim. I would take this little calamity as a lesson—the iceberg had been a gift.

I reminded myself that in spite of being wet, cold, sore, exhausted, bug bitten, and miserable some of the time, I actually *liked* paddling. I enjoyed the cyclical pattern of the paddle stroke; with my top hand at eye level, my hands revolved in an elliptical sphere in front of my face. My cadence was about forty strokes per minute, my breathing rhythmic. I enjoyed bringing my entire body into it, engaging my core, involving my hips and legs, loading my body weight onto the paddle, applying force down the shaft. I liked the paddler's high and how it is similar, on many levels, to a runner's high. The paddler's zone—a state of being immersed, if not intricately absorbed, in my own reality, a feeling of my body and mind being sublimely connected and life's intensity further amplified— was like a drug. Recovering from my hissy fit, I returned to my paddling trance, resolved to stay grounded in the final stages of this adventure.

Later that same day, I stopped for a pee break, lowering my wetsuit behind a large weathered log hurled far up on shore by an earlier, southeasterly storm. Why I decided to take on this modicum of modesty so late in the trip escaped me, as there was not a soul around, and I had become accustomed to dropping my drawers most anywhere I pleased. Zipping up the front of my wetsuit with one hand, I grabbed my camera bag off the top of the log and sauntered down the beach toward my kayak. Chamellia looked like a tiny speck way down there, with the vastness of Stephens Passage spilling out meaty and blue behind her.

Leaning over my hatch to slip the camera bag back in, I noticed, out of the corner of my eye, some movement up on the beach. The tall coastal grass that fringed the forest was swaying. Out of it emerged a lumbering, copper-colored grizzly bear. My gaze fixated on its dished face, and my pulse quickened. One swift glance at its unmistakable hump took my breath away. This bruin was a walking bulletin board; its message was clearly "NO TRESPASSING." It was moving toward me, lumbering right past the very spot I had peed less than two minutes earlier. This griz was fat and fluffy, its hair billowing around its legs like pantaloons. Driven with purpose—and fear—I hurriedly snapped on the rubber hatch cover, snatched up my paddle, and wheelbarrowed the kayak backward into the water. As I straddled the boat and plopped my backside into the cockpit I heard the bear snort and then watched it rise up onto its hind legs—all seven feet of it—to get a better whiff of the intruder. I backed away from that beach much like you would back out of a repulsive situation in a public toilet stall. Still paddling backward, I kept a vigilant eye on the bear, who had now gone back to standing on all fours. I watched it lower its head and then paw at a weathered log, repeatedly turning it over, probably looking for grubs. Thankful for its sudden disinterest, I cranked out a couple of arcing sweep strokes to turn my bow north and paddled out of its sight.

TWO DAYS LATER, the ethereal blue ice of Sumdum Glacier hung over my camp, frozen in time, etched in jaw-dropping beauty. It was the most pristine and seductive campsite of the trip so far, in spite of its amusing name. I knew from my pre-trip research that Mount Sumdum, Sumdum Bay, Sumdum Creek, and Sumdum Island shared the same whimsy. John Muir, I discovered, wrote extensively about this area in *Travels in Alaska*, and not once did he indicate a tongue-in-cheek attitude when he wrote about the Sumdum ice, the Sumdum seal hunters, or the Sumdum Indians. I, on the other hand, couldn't stop smirking. The *Dictionary of Alaskan Place Names* reports that the Tlingit Indians who lived nearby named it Sumdum to embody the booming sound of icebergs as they broke off the glacier. Another account states that from 1897 to 1942 the area was the site of an active mining camp, named Sumdum, complete with a tram, brewery, and post office.

Holkham Bay (as Sumdum Bay is now named), where Sumdum Glacier meets the sea, showed no signs of past activity. Camped deep inside the bay I watched icebergs flaunt their allure in front of me, suspended timelessly in the peaceful cove. Some resembled ice sculptures: swans, Volkswagens, and crocodiles. Loons, the symbol of wilderness and solitude, floated amongst them on the glassy smooth water. Around the corner of a small rock outcropping, out of my line of sight, something snorted loudly in the water. A sea lion, perhaps?

Earlier in the day I quietly negotiated around a slumbering humpback whale, floating motionless at the water's surface. This aquatic creature is known to take thirty-minute catnaps by resting one half of her brain at a time. The other half stays awake to make sure she breathes and alerts her to any possible dangers lurking in her environment. There was only the sound of her breathing and the delicate piercing of water from my blade. I tiptoed around this beautiful sleeping giant, wondering what a startled whale would do. Could she wake up on the wrong side of the bay? Would she be disgruntled with me? Or would all forty tons of her roll over and give me a cold, blubbery shoulder?

Further north, at the mouth of Port Houghton Bay, I encountered several humpback whales, all of them wide awake and competing for attention, giant cetaceans swimming circles around me. The largest one slapped the water with its white pectoral fin, then dove deep, its tail fluke spanning nearly fifteen feet, momentarily suspended between sky and sea. Three other humpbacks intermittently stayed on the surface and sang melodious and mysterious songs to each other, repeating patterns of chirrups, sighs, moans, and growls. I listened to this hauntingly beautiful outdoor symphony, watching long, curving backs the length of a logging truck oscillate through the water for a few more magical moments before they silently slipped beneath the surface, momentarily leaving gentle boils of disturbed water.

Two bays north, I floated in tranquil solitude—until a super-pod of orcas burst into Windham Bay in full-on frolic mode. Girthy, thirty-foot-long black and white polished bodies cannonballed on the water's surface. Thunderous claps filled the air as the whales breached and spiraled, then smacked the water with massive force. Their communications resonated across the water as dorsal fins, tail flukes, and a cacophony of sounds surrounded me. My gaze swept in an arc across the bay; I was afraid I would miss any number of sideshows. The big daddies, showing off their triangular six-foot-high dorsal fins, paraded in front of me. I had read in my guidebook that orcas could swim much faster than I could paddle, with top speeds clocked at over thirty miles per hour. In that same book, I read that forty sharp, brilliant white teeth crowded their mouths—teeth that are over two inches long and could masticate up to a hundred pounds of fish daily. Some orcas, generally the transients, the book explained, hunted seals, porpoises, sea lions, and even other whales.

These highly intelligent creatures are at the top of the food chain in the Inside Passage; I was somewhere near the bottom. It was simultaneously awe-inspiring and shocking to witness these large creatures emerge from the sea so close to me, sometimes heading straight at me like ten-thousand-pound torpedoes—with sharp, pearly whites. Swimming powerfully and gracefully, they undulated and then dove, cutting through the water in a trajectory that had one red kayak in its epicenter. I held my breath as one swam beneath me. Looking down in a combination of amazement and fright, it seemed as if a submarine might surface directly below me.

IT WAS DIFFICULT TO PADDLE AWAY from Holkham Bay. I'd only spent one night at the base of the glacier, yet felt a pull to further explore the beauty all around me. I was immersed in the art of lingering and utterly spellbound by my surroundings: a deep azure sky, glassy water mirroring snow-covered peaks, glaciers, icebergs, and a boisterous waterfall cascading off Sumdum Glacier all flirted with my eyes. Only three days shy of Juneau, it was no longer necessary to lug around forty pounds of water. I filled only one of my water bladders with the icy cold glacial liquid plunging behind my campsite, along with my 32-ounce Nalgene bottle. I chugged a third of it as I stood there, water pummeling around my feet. I carried the water back to my loaded kayak, an "ice cream" headache slowly subsiding. Repeatedly looking back at the waterfall, I paddled away from one paradise into another.

To the north, Tracy Arm bore deep into southeast Alaska's landmass; to the south, Endicott Arm did the same, with Ford's Terror, a shorter, narrower fjord, jutting off from Endicott. Massive glaciers sat at both ends of these fjords, and cruise ships plied the gin-clear waters, laden with tourists armed with cameras, hoping to capture calving glaciers and the countless waterfalls by pointing and shooting. Two bald eagles perched on a small iceberg that floated on a hydrous plane. Wafting tendrils of clouds hovered above the ice-covered mountains on the far side of this bay. I slid my feet off the foot braces and, with my paddle laid across my lap, I tucked forward as if kissing my spraydeck, my arms hugging the hull beneath me, and felt the stretch in my lower back. Chamellia and I gently drifted in the current, lulled by the lusciousness of it all. I sat back upright and let the sun warm my face and neck. Soaking in the warmth and beauty of this day, I felt an inner bliss that I knew would carry me through the rest of the journey.

I continued to glide through paradise on this radiant afternoon, with its glorious, eye-piercing sunshine, and contemplated the end of my journey. I would pitch my tent one last time that night. Eighty percent of this adventure had been enchanting—the other twenty percent, not so much. I had experienced many mind-blowing, altogether intoxicating moments along with the challenges that were, at times, more than I had bargained for. I had wanted to stretch myself to the outer limits of my abilities. I did. Even on this second-to-last day, I endured nearly seven hours of paddling against a mostly ebbing tide into a northwest wind to arrive at my last camp. It took a ridiculous amount of effort to sustain two knots, and another emotional outburst tried to niggle into my psyche. But I stayed true to my inner resolve to govern my emotions and simply paddled harder.

Failure was not an option; I had tried to purge it from my vocabulary long before I took my first strokes leaving Anacortes. I never lost faith that I would get here. In fact, I'd often pre-visualized my successful outcome. Even along the way, I'd sit leaning forward, squeezing my eyelids down in deep concentration, trying to imagine what it would feel like when my bow scrubbed up on the rocks in Skagway. I could feel the paddle in my hands and hear the breeze in the trees. I would turn into myself, into my aloneness and solitude, and feel, see, hear, smell, and taste what my goal would be like.

I'd made peace with my decision to end my journey at Juneau, and now, only a few thousand paddle strokes from my final destination, I felt I was making peace with myself. I was finding some answers. I felt I had approached many of my challenges analytically and my victories emotionally. I was finding strength in my softness, and softness in my strength, accepting and loving both. Patience had become a moderately toned muscle, and I felt confident that Jim was recovering nicely without me.

For my last campsite I chose a small pebble crescent beach nestled into a slim indentation just north of Slocum Inlet. Its amenities included profuse amounts of brilliant pink fireweed, a babbling brook, and sweeping views of Stephens Passage. Gastineau Channel, my final approach to Juneau, loomed in the distance. Icebergs floated by; whales serenaded me. As the night opened before me and the pulse of the day slowed, as nature fell into order and my journey drew to its end, I retrieved my journal and pencil from the tent and recorded one last entry.

Sea Diary

July 8, 2010, Day 65, Slocum Inlet

I don't want to let this special feeling go. I am deliriously tired but I don't want to go to bed. I am like the exhausted child who insists to her mother that she is not tired at all. But the pragmatic me surfaces and acknowledges that I am weary. I have a big day tomorrow. Fifteen very short nautical miles and I will be taking my last strokes into Juneau, and the end of this journey.

The sun is still casting muted, soft, delightful colors. Stephens Passage is calm. It's very still. Whales are growling, sighing, communicating to each other in the bay. I have my own private symphony again right outside my tent door. What wonderful background "noise" to fall asleep to! I can't wait to tell Jim.

A fish skipped across the water as if a child was skimming a skipping stone, and quite good at it. The brook will continue to babble and I will always remember this night. I'll remember setting up camp stark naked, airing out my body. Feels so damn good. Must go naked more. Another lesson learned.

Be free. Naked is ok. Nobody will hurt you. Relax, Susan. Be patient. Try not to force things. Live. Love. Laugh. Breathe. Paddle. Enjoy life. It's the only one you've got. Be free. Accept yourself. Love yourself. Be ready.

Joie de vivre

I GLANCED UP FROM MY JOURNAL, cradled my coffee cup, and set the pencil down. It was a Friday morning in the Inside Passage, and the last morning of my expedition. Burrowing my feet deeper into the smooth beach pebbles of Slocum Inlet, I sank lower in my now threadbare camp chair and lay my journal on the ground next to the pencil. I did this to wholly devote my attention to the spectacular display of athleticism, grace, and power that played out in front of me.

I was an audience of one, and the stage, fifty yards offshore, was illuminated by the rising sun. The cast—two humpback whales—took turns breaching and sliding back into the sea. The plot thickened: the lustrous bodies exploded vertically out of the water, gyrated sideways, then horizontally slammed the briny surface, creating a thunderous sound. Occasionally this scene was punctuated by the ear-splitting smack of a flipper. The story line was repetitive, but never boring.

Slack-jawed, I looked sideways at my tent where the camera lay. Would I have time to retrieve it and still enjoy the show? I wasn't taking any chances and would have to trust that these moments would be forever etched in my mind's eye. The camera would have to wait. The show's running time was about twenty minutes. I sat mesmerized, holding my breath, hoping for an encore, but they bowed out gracefully and left the scene silent. Finally I stood up, folded my chair, and turned my thoughts toward packing up my last camp and heading into Juneau. This sea journey was coming to an end, and it seemed appropriate that the most magnificent morning of the trip should happen on the very last day. I had only this day before my bow would touch shore at the harbor master's office in Juneau; I would have the rest of my life to consider what these past 1,100 miles meant and how they had changed me.

I dressed lightly in clothes I'd saved for warmer, calmer days like this one. My paddling pants were a rubber-like polyurethane material sandwiched with a soft fleece inner layer. It felt like gossamer compared to the thicker one-piece wetsuit I'd grown accustomed to, that was often gamey and putrid. I completed the ensemble with the same thin black fleece shirt I'd worn for most of 66 days, a paddling jacket, and a pair of rank socks so stiff with dirt that they practically stood on their own.

For once, I was stalling. It felt divine to take my sweet-ass time. I only had fifteen miles to go. The good weather was holding and, after all the bad weather I'd endured, I appreciated it that much more. *What's the hurry, Suz?* It seemed like I mostly rushed through this journey, and now, even though I was a bit worn down, I didn't want it to end. I had slowed enough to truly become present in my life, at least for the moment. This was a feeling I wanted to hold onto, and to re-create over and over again. A few extra sun salutations, one last look around, one last seashell tucked behind my seat, and I shoved off, stern first at 7:15 a.m. My heart filled with gratitude, and my eyes filled with tears. Afloat, I scanned my last campsite one final time for forgotten items. Nothing remained except the bent grass where my tent had been, and the shallow depression in the sand where I sat a few hours earlier. Soon it would be filled with the next high tide.

A gentle sweep stroke on the right aimed my bow toward Point Salisbury and the beginning of Gastineau Channel. Within striking distance of the finish line, my GPS began acting like a child's Etch-A-Sketch on crack. Stubbornly, I tinkered with the thing for about five minutes, remaining optimistic that I could resurrect it. I turned it off, then back on, then whacked it against the gunwale, but this didn't make the flickering, schizoid horizontal lines disappear, so I turned the unit off for good and stuffed it inside my deck bag. Just as well, I brooded. This electronic gadget was enabling my obsessive-compulsive behavior and self-imposed competitiveness. Speed, distance, time; go faster, go further, go longer. No matter how hard I tried to not look at my GPS, I'd give in, and if the numbers weren't to my liking, I'd push harder. Now the thing was dead, and I was free to go at any pace I damn well pleased. Maybe *now* I could master the art of relaxation. Maybe I was letting go just a bit. It only took 66 days to finally learn to go with the flow. *Well done. There,* I thought, *mindful paddling at last.*

A noisy skiff belching coal-black fumes broke into my mindful paddling trance. The aluminum boat, working in tandem with a purse seiner, was attempting to set a skein of tangled fishing net, hanging vertically in the water, a deep curtain of netting suspended by a quarter mile of bobbing red and white floats. The man in the purse seiner made dramatic gestures and yelled at the man in the skiff, but his voice was muffled by the clamor of their operation. I hugged the shoreline, skirting the debacle, continuing north.

Around the next corner, I heard the sputter of a crabbing boat floating along the base of the cliff on the right side of the channel. I watched the fisherman jam his engine into neutral, then pull his buoy, line, and finally the steel cage over the gunwale. He re-baited his trap and lowered it back to the bottom of the sea. A shrill whistle caught my attention behind him: the long orange beaks and black heads of two oystercatchers came into view as I sloshed forward in the slight chop. Nearby, a seagull harassed a starfish it had plucked from the rocks and a seal popped up alongside me, but then quickly dove the second we made eye contact. Just moments from my final destination, I paddled on an alive ocean, and embraced an alive me.

Everything I had read about paddling in to Juneau via kayak warned me to do so prudently, but my arrival was unhurried and uneventful. Alaska's capital city, with a population of about thirty thousand, was a sleepy village on July 9, 2010. Gastineau Channel ends at Juneau, forcing all larger vessels to crank out a U-turn to exit. Cruise ships, yachts, Coast Guard vessels, commercial shipping, and sea planes coming and going were all obstacles to avoid, I'd been told. I kept a wary eye on one floatplane taking off on my right, but otherwise there was nothing to dodge. I wasn't disappointed, figuring I'd had enough adrenaline surges on this trip to sustain me for a while.

Juneau is subject to the ebb and flow of cruise ships much like Ketchikan and Prince Rupert, but only two were berthed at the dock. Uncannily quiet.

As I slowly paddled under the bridge connecting Juneau to Douglas Island, my mind cinematically rewound all that I had just accomplished. I felt a sudden surge of something unfamiliar: a sense of pride that was all-encompassing. I realized that thousand-plus-mile solo kayak trips had become commonplace. People had been navigating the Inside Passage for millennia. Countless men and women before me had explored these waters, had done without the luxuries of indoor life, had pushed their bodies to untold limits. I'd read hardscrabble accounts of plucky women who had rowed across whole oceans, kayaked around entire continents— even around the world. Audrey Sutherland had paddled over *twelve thousand nautical miles*, the equivalent of half the circumference of the earth. All those accomplishments, all those great ocean voyages via sea kayak, were superlative. Mine blanched in comparison and was truly not out of the ordinary—yet what I felt was extraordinary. My adventure, although not void of chronic hardship, was more of a magic carpet ride. It wasn't so much about achieving the goal of paddling the IP, it was about the *process* of paddling that coastline, of being truly connected and open to all of life as it unfolded moment to moment. It was about letting go of things that no longer served me and trusting the ebb and flow of life, of living this dream that delivered the benefits, and unleashed the passion that transformed me. A metamorphosis had occurred within me and I could sense that I was letting go, adapting, manifesting patience. When I began this journey, I expected many lessons would be presented along the way. Every day, my objectives had been clear: to head north and successfully paddle the Inside Passage, while embracing these lessons. Through the weeks and months that I moved along the coast I began to know not only the IP as a sum of my own experience, but I began to know myself. I learned that I couldn't fully heal until I fully acknowledged the areas that needed healing.

I had finished successfully. A heightened sense of adventure, accomplishment, and confidence surged through me. I felt impassioned and humbled and balanced in a world that sometimes could spin off-kilter. This was about my own experience, my own natural high, my own thumbprint on the Inside Passage. I was living a very extraordinary, ordinary life!

ON A SUNNY FRIDAY AFTERNOON, at approximately 12:30, I took my final paddle stroke of this journey. Sixty-six days, 1,148 miles, 102 dark chocolate bars, 28 ibuprofen gel caps, seven temper tantrums, five anxiety attacks, two pairs of underwear, one foul wetsuit, and a million magical moments later, I finally laid my paddle down in Juneau, Alaska. My landing in the riprap below the harbor master's office at the Aurora Boat Harbor was anticlimactic—and a tad rushed. I had little time to feel smug or get choked up. The quickly rising tide commanded my attention, and reminded me what dictated my schedule right up until the very end. I hurriedly and unceremoniously shuffled my boat and gear up a steep, slippery embankment, and checked in with the crabby harbormaster, who was all business. Although I'd not expected any sort of fanfare, this was not exactly how I had visualized the end of the trip.

I had imagined the faces of my close friends illuminated by the glow of their computer screens as they witnessed my arrival, but Jim was still in the hospital. I wanted to call him and tell him I had made it. I rifled through a yellow gear bag, found my cellphone and nervously pressed the on button. I dialed the hospital. Jim had a direct line in his room, and he answered with a groggy, yet surprisingly strong voice. Strong for somebody who recently had his chest split open. Twice. His last day in the hospital coincided with my last day on the voyage. Go figure.

"Good job, kid. I'm proud of you, Suz," he said in a decidedly enthusiastic but wavering voice. "I can't wait to see you. How do you feel?"

"Tired," I answered. "But strong. Accomplished. More importantly, how do *you* feel?"

He was excited to move on with his life. Linda and Dave had just left on their caving expedition, feeling optimistic that when they returned he would be well on his way to the old feisty Jim Chester.

He filled me in on his hospital stay, his voice weakening and trailing off with each successive sentence. I wanted to talk longer, but I noticed, out of the corner of my eye, the harbor master waving his hand. He needed my boat and all my crap out of the way and wanted to settle the bill for storing everything until the ferry could take me home.

"Hey, Suz, I got the rock. It's right here. From Tree Point. Super special," Jim said feebly.

"That makes me smile in a big way," I said. "We've both left our thumbprint on the Inside Passage, haven't we?" The harbormaster began walking toward me. "Sorry, Jim, but I gotta go." I promised I'd call him later and apologetically hung up.

I shelled out some cash and organized my gear. Dirty laundry, electronics, wallet, passport, water bottle, and journal went into a mesh duffel bag and over my shoulder. Everything else would remain with the boat. I unzipped my PFD, like so many times before, and tossed it into the cockpit. I wriggled the spray skirt down over my waist, let it drop to the ground, stepped out of it, then placed it alongside the PFD. I secured the hatches, stowed the two-piece paddles inside the boat, and attached the vinyl cockpit cover. As an added measure of security, I placed my foul-smelling wetsuit and even fouler neoprene booties on top of my expensive carbon fiber paddles, hoping nobody in their right mind would sift through that stench to abscond with my gear. Lastly, and for only the second time that summer, I changed into shorts, sandals, and a short-sleeve shirt.

In the two minutes it took me to make my motel reservation, I watched more cars speed by above the marina than I had seen since leaving my own car in Anacortes over two months earlier. I patted Chamellia on the bow, crossed the busy four-lane highway, and collapsed on a rickety motel bed.

Sea Diary

July 9, 2010, Day 66, Juneau, Alaska

I'm done. Now I find myself in a stale-smelling motel room in Alaska's capital city. Exhausted, I just peered into the full-length mirror and surveyed my sunburned, bruised, welted, scarred, bug-bitten body ... I've challenged myself to physical, emotional, and mental extremes I didn't know were possible. But I wouldn't trade it for the world! This ocean journey has become a lens through which I must now examine and take a closer look at my own life.

This trip ended up being sort of an "internal compass" for me as it presented me with some valuable lessons and a glimpse into more of the personal inner journey versus the obvious physical outer experience.

I learned many things from this adventure of mine:

I am never alone.

I can do anything I set my mind to.

I can do patience!

I learned to live in the moment.

I learned about my fears, courage, and independence.

I found out just how truly stubborn I can be.

That I can let go.

That I truly can dance in the rain!

I was awestruck by the beauty and the power of the places I visited. I developed a relationship with the Inside Passage and learned to respect its power, and in doing so, while discovering my own hidden powers, I learned to better respect myself. For that I am forever grateful. This journey wasn't so much about miles as it was about memories—and learning to dance in the rain.

I was indeed done. I had arrived. I'd finally relaxed a bit and let it all sink in. In Powell River, Port Hardy, Shearwater, Prince Rupert, Ketchikan, and Petersburg, I felt I could never completely let my guard down because the next leg of the trip loomed ahead, and I needed to stay on my toes. Much like a pilot would run through a pre-flight checklist, I would check off my resupply chores, ceaselessly preparing logistically, mentally, and physically for the next stretch. Now, other than getting my butt, boat, and gear on the Alaska Ferry in three days, I had no agenda. And it felt absolutely sublime.

Yes, I had learned that I could do anything I set my mind to. But I had also learned that I couldn't do it all. That it's okay to need and to accept help from others. It's a beautiful dance, a glorious sharing where I can trust in myself and have faith in others. I can listen and I can declare. I can receive and I can give. I can be an expert in one area and soak up another's expertise, willingly, with no ego. It is another way that our existence balances itself out, each of us helping the other. I also came to understand that those same lessons were presented to me multiple times throughout my journey, manifesting in different forms. Fears, both real and imagined, were interwoven into the fabric of this adventure. At times I felt as if I were trying to out-paddle my fears, that fear was always at my back, but in essence, I had paddled forward *through* my fears, my hopes, my doubts, my pain, even my cathartic temper tantrums, and the healing simply happened. This opportunity was not only a passage to adventure, but a journey deep inside myself, a journey that revealed many lessons, and answered questions that were never asked. I realized I was exactly where I needed to be each and every day on this adventure, this coastline, this ocean, this life, this body. I had paddled along into the answer, and I hadn't even known it.

Going Home

MY BRAIN LEAPT INTO OVERDRIVE when the alarm on my wristwatch went off at five a.m. the next day. The world's least mechanical person, I could never figure out how to silence the damn thing. Knee-jerk reaction: time to pack up camp Susan, get on the water. *Oh no—wait—I don't have to. Go back to sleep. Can't. Toss. Turn.* I felt at a loss and a bit sad. Numb, actually. Post-Inside Passage syndrome? Is there such a thing? Monkey mind is back. Had all my epiphanies from the previous day sloughed off already? *Dammit, have I gained any enlightenment on this trip?*

Curled into a fetal position under the bedcovers, I listened to the rain pelting against the window. As predicted, the winds had shifted, and a northwesterly was blowing down Gastineau Channel. I should have been glad to be hunkered down in a warm, dry bed. But I wasn't. The sheets felt overly starched, and the mattress was god-awful uncomfortable, like sleeping on a chunk of thick cardboard. I briefly entertained the idea of blowing up my air mattress and climbing into my soft, familiar sleeping bag, but both of them were packed away in Chamellia. Instead, I grabbed the TV remote and flipped through a few channels. Disengaged and uninterested, I turned it off, quickly dressed, and walked down to the dock to check on Chamellia. She'd been my lifeline for so long, and I felt like a mother leaving her child unattended.

Oh, what the hell, I thought, *why not sort some gear and get a jumpstart on preparing for the journey home?* So I sorted and packed and repacked and futzed. I brought my charts back to the room and spread them out on the bed, floor, and dresser to dry. With my finger, I traced the route from Petersburg to Juneau. My spirits hovered a little bit higher. More coffee, more phone calls, more reconnecting, more resting and collecting my feelings and thoughts. I prepared to re-acclimate to "ordinary life"— whatever that might be.

I doubled-checked my ferry reservation on my cellphone, where a cheery confirmation sat flagged in my inbox. Four hundred and six dollars bought me a ticket closer to home on the *MV Columbia*, the flagship vessel for the Alaska Marine Highway. From my tiny screen, I learned that she was a beamy ship, 85 feet across with a draft of 24 feet. It also told me her 418 feet of length could accommodate five hundred passengers plus crew, as well as 134 automobiles, and that her average cruising speed was eighteen knots. She only sailed south once a week, so I made damn sure I wouldn't miss her that Tuesday morning.

Unfortunately, the ferry terminal was inconveniently located fourteen miles farther north, in Auke Bay. Logistics would beleaguer me until the very end, it appeared. Even if I had the gumption to pack my boat one last time and paddle the fourteen miles in the three a.m. darkness to catch the early sailing, the tides were all wrong, as inconvenient as the ferry terminal. The plan: Alaska Kayak and Transport would pick up Chamellia on Monday evening at 5:30. For $78, they would deliver her and all my gear to the Alaska Ferry Terminal and leave her on a pre-arranged rack nearby, assuring me that she would be safe. Another $35 booked me a cab to reunite me with her on Tuesday morning.

ALL WENT AS PLANNED, although I could barely make out the hulk of the ferry as my cab pulled into the terminal at 4:30 a.m. Relieved to see Chamellia lying on a rack a short distance away, I dug my boarding pass out of my pack. While a procession of motorcycles, cars, and RVs slowly boarded the ferry, another foot passenger offered to help me carry Chamellia on board. Crew members in neon-green vests directed us to her resting place in the corner of the ship's belly.

I headed up a flight of stairs to roam the ship and scope out my new surroundings. Bathroom, showers and laundromat: check. Movie theatre: check. Cafe, full-service restaurant, dimly lit cocktail lounge: check. Observation lounge: check. Four laps and eight flights of stairs later, I staked my claim in true Alaska Ferry style, pitching my tent on the ship's deck, wedging it next to several others. For added measure, I duct-taped the four corners of my rainfly to the steel deck and tied two of the guidelines to the railing. As the ship backed out of port, I plunked myself down in an oversized lawn chair in the partially covered, overly heated solarium.

From a vastly different point of view, I watched the twelve-mile-long Mendenhall Glacier—and the town it flowed into—disappear out of sight as the ferry pulled away from the dock just north of Juneau. On the ship's deck, moms in fuzzy slippers tended to their families, kids shared bowls of Cheerios, young adults read paperback books, and a small group of people played Monopoly. The scenery slid by, rewinding the countryside I had taken 66 days to paddle through, in three days, two hours, and fifteen minutes.

That first night on the ship, I spent happy hour with two backpackers from Switzerland, a kayaker from Sikta, and two bikers from Boston. Strangers became friends, snapshots were taken, phone numbers and email addresses exchanged.

As the soothing thrum of the engines churned the ferry south, my thoughts cycled north, sifting through memories of my journey up the Inside. I replayed scenes from the trip, the images still fresh in my mind. I had traveled within this massive body of water for more than two months, and within that time I was given immeasurable gifts and lessons, truths and wonder.

The second night, sleeping in my tent on the ship's deck, I awoke disoriented, feeling the world I was lying on bob up and down with the ocean's rise and fall beneath me and a thousand tons of steel. We were traversing the more open waters of British Columbia, and the distance between me and the end of this journey was shrinking.

The southern terminus of the Alaska Ferry is in Bellingham, Washington, a cheery, bustling seaside town, twenty miles south of the Canadian border. If not delayed in any of its seven ports of call, the ferry arrives in Bellingham at eight a.m. every Friday morning. On Friday, July 16, 2010, it was right on time. By 7:30, the blue-and-white-hulled MV Columbia was backing into the Bellingham terminal.

Packed and ready to disembark, I stood on the ship's tallest deck and watched the now-familiar brick building come into view. Within minutes, I could pick Becky out of the crowd, her arms waving high and wildly back and forth to greet me. My welcoming committee of one was enthusiastically hooting and hollering, celebrating this phase of my journey. My heartbeat quickened as my feet approached terra firma, and the tangible end of this adventure.

A crew member handed me a set of kayak wheels. Becky, her attention to detail never ceasing to amaze me, had had the foresight to bring them along. I set Chamellia's heavy stern in the foam cradle, cinched the strap over the rear deck, grabbed the bow carry toggle, and effortlessly wheeled my kayak down the ramp, coming ashore in the state of Washington.

"Hi, stranger!" Becky said with an enormous smile. We'd hugged goodbye 44 days earlier on the beach in Bella Bella. Now, rocking back and forth while holding each other tight, our reunion was nothing short of jubilant.

We loaded my kayak on top of Becky's green Toyota pickup—the same truck she had picked me up in at Alder Bay—and took the scenic, hour-plus seaside route via Chuckanut Drive back to Anacortes to retrieve my Subaru, where it was parked at a friend's house. I relaxed as Becky negotiated the curvy, narrow road with its sweeping views of the San Juan Islands and Samish Bay. Further south, the road widened and flattened as it ran through the fertile farmlands of the Skagit River Valley. In lieu of gas money, I insisted we stop at a popular rural bakery and stock up on practically world-renowned cocoa nib shortbread cookies. Pure decadence.

After I picked up my Subaru, we convoyed to Washington State Park, to the same beach where I had begun my trip 73 days earlier. Standing in the very spot where I had launched, I tuned in to the memories and emotions of that inaugural day: the champagne, the toast, the poetry, the hugs, the silliness, the seriousness, the verbal commitments, the first strokes. I noticed Becky had casually walked away, giving me a few moments to myself. Feeling gratitude for being safely delivered back to these shores, I put my hands in prayer position at my heart and flowed into three sun salutations, thanking the water gods for where I'd been, for where I was now, and for where I was going. I turned SPOT on one last time and waited ten minutes for the final waypoint to register.

The circle was complete.

Inside Out

WHEN I FIRST HEARD THE NEWS, I felt the blood run out of my face. I went cold and numb, falling to the bottom of an icy blue ocean, frozen in time. We'd all fully expected Jim to survive, but he didn't. He died exactly two weeks after I'd returned to Montana, on the 30th of July. He had confidently and proudly confronted his health issues, even downplaying them at times, as if he were merely suffering from a toothache. He'd hidden his medical ordeal from most, not wanting to take the spotlight and moral support off my journey, his heart so big and generous. Yet it couldn't fight the complications from a quadruple bypass.

After the surgery, Jim often slept in his office chair. It was big and comfortable and easier to rise out of than his bed. He had spent umpteen hours working in that chair when he was healthy. His desk, strewn with papers, stacks of books, old Mac computers, and stained coffee cups stood testimony to his labor. He reveled in his tasks, akin to a mad scientist, hair disheveled, fingers tap-dancing on the keyboard, music emanating from his Bose radio. He enjoyed composing clever letters to friends and irate letters to editors, scribing chapters of the Explorers Log, or sketching a pen-and-ink drawing.

Jim always stacked his to-do piles deliberately and tidily on the corner of his desk. When he died, his to-do pile fell to the floor with him. That's how he was found: lying in a pile of papers documenting his undone tasks. Beside him lay the white speckled granite rock I'd picked up at Tree Point. He had brought it home from the hospital and, just as I had hoped, used it as a paperweight.

It was a shocking end to his life, a shattering end to my trip, and I couldn't, wouldn't accept it. It didn't matter that I had just paddled the Inside Passage. It didn't matter that I was in the best shape of my life and that my skinny jeans hung loosely from my hips. It didn't matter that I'd had all these life-changing experiences and that I had over four thousand photos and hundreds of handwritten journal pages to prove it. None of it mattered. None of it. I had marshaled all my energies into this one goal, and then was catapulted into an emotional tailspin, my journey suddenly eviscerated. I had risen to the highest of highs, then plummeted to the lowest of lows, cemented to the trough of a bottomless wave with no clue how to climb out. I had morphed from a spirited, intrepid woman to an insipid lost soul, my dark side suddenly a deep shade of shit. I was caught on an eddy line where two opposing currents had collided in a maelstrom: half of me wanted to go one direction, the other half the opposite way. I knew it was my action that would dictate the outcome, yet I couldn't turn around and face upstream, face my fears, or ferry across this immense expanse of troubled water any more than I could get out of bed. I needed nurturing, love, and lots of hugs and felt there wasn't a soul in the world who could do that for me.

Nearly everything about my trip was connected with Jim. His far-reaching influence permeated my soul. He inspired me to consider the trip in the first place, was my rock and my counterbalance while en route, and my back azimuth to help me return safely. I couldn't deal with these reminders at the time, so instead I numbed out, and tuned the world out. "Fuckyoufuckyoufuckyou," I sobbed, slamming my laptop shut, resisting the nearly overpowering urge to hurl it across the room. A couple months after he died, I was sorting through the thousands of images I'd taken on the IP, yet couldn't come to grips with the fact that Jim was no longer there to share in my world. I wanted nothing more than for him to look over my shoulder and point to any one of the pictures and say, "That's a good one, Suz." I wanted him to reminisce with me, to share the memories of the white sand beaches, the magical cabin, the wave-battered shorelines, the spirit of the Great Bear Rainforest, and the whales and wolves and bears that live there. I wanted him to remember the caw of the raven, the haunted cry of the loon, the howl of the wolf, and the song of the humpback. But he wouldn't.

Jim's passing, and the ensuing grief, wrapped my life in a dark and tangled thicket of grief, and an emotional fog, thicker than any fog I'd experienced on the IP. I couldn't see through the pain and blundered through the sudden variety of ever-changing challenges. My life seemed out of control, as if I were bobbing aimlessly on a large, undulating sea, with no paddle in my hand to maintain my balance. I struggled not to build barriers against those who loved me the most. I fought hard to shake the depression, but it found me and latched onto me, along with a don't-touch-me-with-a-ten-foot-pole persona. The yin and yang of my life had spun off-kilter again. The contrast between a once strong, courageous woman who had just paddled the Inside Passage, and a despondent person who could barely climb the stairs without needing a nap flung me deeper into despair.

But slowly, the numbness was replaced with a tingling sensation. A hint of vibrancy gradually returned and I realized that there is no timetable nor quick fix for grief, that the process is complex, difficult, and energy-zapping—and it will take its sweet-ass time. I couldn't circumvent it, avoid it, or deny it. I realized for the first time that the courage and strength it took for me to paddle to Alaska was still there and was the driving force I needed to weather this grieving process. I had to allow the grief to surge through me, like a billowing ocean wave. Let it cleanse me, heal me. Bathe me. Release me. Release him. Let go. Flow. Brava for the resiliency of the human spirit.

It took six months before I could acknowledge my accomplishment of paddling the Inside Passage. Around that time, I came across the laminated strip of paper that had lived on my kayak deck:

The conditions of the mind must interact with the conditions of the sea; the result is a good paddle versus a terror-stricken one.

Then I was reminded that Jim's quote—that plastic strip of precious words that gave me strength and courage each day on the water—also applied to everyday life. And I realized that my journey to Alaska was a paradigm of my life's journey. Now I needed to focus on getting comfortable with the conditions of the mind in the face of unfolding reality, to simultaneously accept what life had thrown at me and make the best of it.

Carrying on without Jim's physical presence, and knowing that all who loved him also faced this challenge, gently reminded me that I was not alone. It helped me remember that challenge is my rain, and this storm was rocking my world. It was time to dance in the deluge again.

THREE YEARS LATER, on an early spring-morning, I sat in the same Subaru that I had driven to Anacortes in May 2010, with the same red kayak strapped on my roof. I was parked outside the Community Boating Center in Bellingham, Washington, where I often shared my passion with the paddling community. Exactly one year after Jim's death, lured by the promise of saltwater in my view most every day, I had moved to Bellingham after twenty years of living in Northwest Montana. In the palm of my hand I held the smooth granite rock I'd picked up for Jim at Tree Point. I'd rescued it from his house while sifting through his personal effects, along with a few of his books, charts, and photographs. Through my bug-splattered windshield, Lummi Island, barely visible through the fog, stood sentinel to the archipelago of the San Juan Islands scattered behind it. Immediately to the west was the Alaska Ferry Terminal. It was Friday and the ferry was docked less than fifty yards away from me. Its classic navy blue hull and white deck dwarfed the US Coast Guard ship moored between us. I could hear and feel the reverberations of its idling engine. I'd seen it berthed there many times since I'd returned, and every time my heart would skip a beat, the ferry's presence evoking a profound sense of accomplishment, taking me back to the Inside.

For grins and giggles, I tapped my smart phone and requested directions to Juneau. It told me that leaving the historic Fairhaven district of Bellingham, via land, I'd arrive in 37 hours and 25 minutes. 1,630 land miles. Smiling, with my index finger I scrolled west until the blue shading of water filled the screen. Pinching the screen bigger I followed my kayak route north, still astonished at the ground I had covered, and studied the familiar shapes of the islands and passages.

Now, having lived this dream, my walls covered with charts and pictures, my kitchen window strewn with beach trinkets, my bookshelves filled with tomes of other Inside Passage journeys and various watery adventures, the IP continued to have an immutable presence in my life.

It lived on inside me, as did the memories of Jim.

I looked out at the expanse of the Salish Sea and thought about how the waters of the Inside Passage, much as any body of saltwater, are dynamic, always in a flux—seesawing, yo-yoing, oscillating. Fluid by nature, water takes the path of least resistance, gracefully moving around obstacles rather than directly opposing them. Water is always changing, ebbing and flowing, like our lives and our bodies. I understood these forces now more than ever, and how working with these relationships can help manage the tumultuous waves and challenges in our everyday lives.

I had arrived. I'd moved forward to new challenges and lessons, grappling with new waves of truth as they tumbled my way—the continual becoming—still trying to find myself in the sustained frenzy of life. Paddling from Anacortes to Juneau was a significant achievement, a benchmark that I would continually draw from, knowing that if I could paddle all the way to Alaska by myself, I could do anything—but I didn't need to do it alone. I could stop running; because I finally understood there will always be another "there" that is better than my "here." That what I was seeking outside myself would be a chase and that the only way to find what I wanted was be in an honest, healthy relationship with myself. To go inside. I had unleashed my passion on this journey, and in doing so, transformed my life, not only in the space of time I was on the IP, but in my off-water life as well. This journey taught me to dance between life's most fundamental polarities: life inside me and life outside in my environment. That no matter what challenges cross my path, I can call on that same moxie and weather any storm, or, rather, dance in any rain.

Afterword

In 2008, my wife Karen McAllister and I co-founded Pacific Wild, a wildlife conservation group based in the Great Bear Rainforest. The location of our home and office in the central part of the GBR has positioned us uniquely to interact with the many paddlers, yachters and others that come to explore the B.C. north coast. It is through this work and location that I had the good fortune to meet Susan and come to contribute these closing thoughts.

As you will have learned from reading about Susan's remarkable paddling adventure, we are blessed with a coastal wilderness of awe-inspiring beauty and global importance. A landscape dominated and influenced by the Pacific that still offers the flora and fauna intact, as it would have been when first encountered by the European mariners upon arrival some three hundred years ago.

Though the abundance of many species has declined, most noticeably in the marine environment, the fact that we still have all the working parts in place is what gives us the most hope for the future. In many other parts of our small and increasingly beleaguered planet, conservation efforts are focused on rebuilding ecosystems, reintroducing endangered species. Meanwhile, on this fog-shrouded coastline, we don't have to focus on these costly, often futile efforts, we simply need to stop doing harm, protect what we have, and the abundance of life that once characterised this coast will return and thrive when it does.

The other source of inspiration and hope for this coast comes from many of the small coastal communities found along the Inside Passage. It is here that first nations and other residents fight alongside one another to keep oil tankers out of the Great Bear Rainforest; to stop the ethically and scientifically indefensible trophy hunt of bears and wolves; to establish marine protected areas and sustainable fisheries; and compel the forest industry to recognize the ecological wealth of intact ancient temperate rainforests and protect it.

Few people will get the opportunity to witness so much of this remarkable coast as Susan has, especially from the intimate seat of a kayak, but that shouldn't stop people from caring. Though I have never been to the Amazon or Serengeti, I want to know that those magnificent wilderness areas are being protected. Before, during, and after your visit, I encourage you to help us keep the rainforest safe and sustainable for all its occupants, a clearing-house for the world's carbon, and an oasis for people like you to visit.

To learn more about the Great Bear Rainforest and how you can help us push to protect it, please visit *www.pacificwild.org.*

—Ian McAllister
Award-winning photographer and conservationist
Co-founder of Pacific Wild
Author of six books including *Great Bear Wild: Dispatches from a Northern Rainforest* and
The Last Wild Wolves: Ghosts of the Great Bear Rainforest

Acknowledgments

To paraphrase Maya Angelou, there is no greater sadness than a story left untold. I refused to be that story. But my refusal didn't come easy while navigating the birth of this book. For starters, I'd often lose my bearings; cast adrift for weeks, even months at a time, in what felt like a sea of impossibility. I'd get lost in the chapters, in the research materials, in the books strewn on my floor, in my to-do lists, and in my scatterbrainedness. For it's much easier for me to sit in a wobbling kayak on the ocean, than in a steady office chair in front of a computer. I discovered that paddling the Inside Passage was the easy part. Stringing words together that properly conveyed my feelings, and the facts centered around those feelings, was much more daunting. At times, nothing felt as exasperatingly impossible, not even arduous forty-mile days, fierce head winds, or mountainous swell—as writing did.

But much like something carried me through on the physical adventure, something also carried me through on the journey of writing this book. For the longest time I couldn't put my finger on it, but now I know it was all the kindred souls who helped me along the way.

Jim Chester stands out front and center. If it weren't for Jim I doubt I would have ever tried to tackle the Inside Passage in the first place. Although you cannot read these words Jim, I will thank you anyway. Thank you for your unconditional love and support. Thank you for being my inspiration—and my exasperation. Thank you for the umpteen hours you spent with me poring over charts, sharing your very personal trip journal, the phone calls while en route, the weather checks, the consolations, your advice, your expertise, the thousands of dollars worth of worn charts you lent me, which I will now forever cherish in my permanent possession. Thank you for taking full responsibility for my logistical and resupply needs. You handled it all flawlessly. And lastly, a sea of gratitude for sharing the salty fairy dust of the Magical Cabin that leaves me spellbound and stirs something in my soul each time I visit.

Pacific Northwest hugs all around to my six dear friends who choreographed my special launching on Cinco de Mayo 2010: Becky Hardey, Peggy Woods, Linda Wysocki, Julianna Slomka, Ron Zuber, and Jim Chester. An additional chest-crushing bear hug to Becky Hardey for not only seeing me off, but for accompanying me around "The Cape," and scooping me off the Alaska Ferry for some much needed pampering and fattening up! We shared ocean swells, wind, waves, sunsets, strong dark coffee, and dark strong rum. Even the ferocious bugs will forever be treasured memories. Thank you for joining me on this incredible journey, having faith in me and the sea, and knowing it would change both of us.

Extra credit goes to Linda Wysocki for being the best childhood and lifelong friend a girl could ask for! From those first adventures shared in the back of your Dad's pickup truck, belting out the lyrics to *Jeremiah Was a Bullfrog*, our hair, part streaming in the wind, part stuck in our bubblegum, our innocence and naiveté always along for the ride. Thank you for your unfailing support through thick and thin. Your common sense, contagious smile and happy-go-lucky spirit will always inspire me. I am reminded of you every day when I look at the delightful chart you commissioned Alan Robinson to create that commemorates my journey. It adorns my wall and the front matter of this book.

A ginormous shout-out to the word-smithing ladies who helped corral my sea of metaphors, along with myriad misplaced commas and verb tenses that were often as haphazard as the tidal rapids I white-knuckled my way through on the Inside Passage. Patia Stephens, who worked through the early drafts and helped me shape my story, slowly dovetailing one section into the next with her incredibly helpful insight and expertise. Roby James, a kick-ass editor whose efficiency and cut-to-the-chase work ethic whipped this book into shape faster than a hurtling tidal bore. Her mad editing skills swooped in and slayed my mistakes like Xena the Warrior Princess. And to all the fabulous folks behind the scenes at Epicenter Press, especially Janet Kimball and Aubrey Anderson, who both oversaw the final spit polish of this book until its pages finally saw the light of day.

Undoubtedly, my trip and this book benefited greatly from the accumulated wisdom and published work of many adventurous authors: Denis Dwyer, John Kimantis, Robert Miller, Jennifer Hahn, and Audrey Sutherland to name a few, whose invaluable books are listed in the resource section of this book. Special thanks to Jennifer Hahn, my "sister of the Inside" whose book *Spirited Waters* opened my mind—and new doors—to paddling this astonishing network of waterways. "Puddle stomps," as you would endearingly say, to you and yours. Oceans of gratitude to the late Audrey Sutherland, a wilderness sage, and much more. Thank you for being the wild restless spirit that you were, for befriending and mentoring Jim, and for annotating his charts that would eventually accompany me north to Alaska. Whether you knew it or not, you too were a part of this journey. Other adventurous wordsmiths I am forever indebted to include Chris Duff, Ian McAllister, and Milbry Polk.

A sea of gratefulness to all the people who befriended me on the Inside Passage, soothed my spirit, and rekindled my energy as well as my faith in humankind. And thank you to all my friends, family and loved ones who religiously followed me on this trip, and all you sly dogs who liberally tucked those chocolate bars into my resupply boxes. You know who you are. You were my remote cheering squad, rooting me on and inspiring me to keep going—and going and going. Special thanks to Paul Rana, my "B.A.", for your warm-heartedness and wisdom, and your ability to strategize and tell me when to come home. Thanks to Debbie Arnold, Tanya Island, Cathie (Scout) Crawford, Trish Smith, Diane Potratz, Kim and Jan Richards, Jim Pederson, and Erin Tamberella for believing in me. Thanks a million to all my friends who tolerated my growing reclusiveness, turning down invitations to hike, ski, paddle, or just hang out during my writing-the-book phase.

I benefitted greatly from the quality equipment I used on my expedition and wish to acknowledge Exped and Boréal Design for manufacturing gear that's built for the long haul, and for supporting me on so many levels of this journey. And finally, Ben Wells, my second-half-of-my-life partner, and traveling troubadour who gave me the time and space to create this book, who supported me and continually encouraged me to "let my freak flag fly." He edited my drafts, clarified my ideas, brought me chocolate and believed in me more than I believed in myself. He kept telling me I could do this, I could write a book. That the world was at my feet and if I didn't take advantage of it then he would kick my butt all the way back to Alaska. Thank you for all those kicks in the butt! He suffered through all my hissy fits and temper tantrums and made me laugh by saying, "You never paddled to Alaska!" every time I complained about some minor little irritation.

In some instances I've changed people's names or descriptions, sometimes to protect their privacy, other times because I simply could not remember. And to anyone who I may have forgotten, bona fide apologies in advance; it wasn't intentional—it's a memory thing.

Inside Passage Expedition Gear List

Quality equipment is one of many components to a successful expedition. My advice is to not skimp—your life could depend on it. While planning for my journey, I often agonized over exactly what gear to bring, but in the end, my painstaking choices paid off. My most important pieces of equipment were my seamanship skills, my brain, my sense of humor, and a good dose of common sense. I tested all of these to their limits a time or two on this endeavor and occasionally misplaced my sense of humor!

Safety Gear

In addition to my SPOT satellite tracker, I packed a GPS, a VHF radio, and a cellphone. I had cellphone service regularly on the first third of the trip. After that, it was intermittent, with my longest stretch out of communication lasting for about ten days. I was able to recharge most of these devices with a compact, battery-operated charger made by a company called Tekkeon. It worked wonderfully. I carried a spare paddle and all the normal self-rescue equipment. I always wore my PFD (life jacket) while on the water. Attached to my PFD was an emergency bail out kit. In the event I became separated from my boat, I had the necessary survival equipment. In my kayak I carried, among many other items, a comprehensive first aid/trauma kit and a boat repair kit, which included copious amounts of duct tape. I had a mini arsenal of flares and various other signaling devices in the event I needed to be seen, heard, or found in an emergency situation. I wore a wetsuit nearly every day. This was a good choice as I believe I would have shredded a drysuit. I wore my dry top on stormy or colder days. Although they are not safety gear, both a deck-mounted and handheld compass were important pieces of my kit. My 32 charts were divvied up by sections, and mailed to me as needed.

The Other Stuff

Kayak and Camping Gear

- Boréal Design Labrador sea kayak, Chamellia, 18'4" x 21', skeg, day hatch,
- Kokatat MsFit PFD (personal flotation device)
- In PFD pockets: three pencil flares, chap stick, sunscreen stick, nose plugs, water dye marker, signal mirror, hand-held compass, VHF radio
- Attached to PFD: storm whistle, knife, strobe, Brunton Sherpa device, NRS hydration holster with bail out items, waterproof Pentax camera
- Bail out items: fire starter, flint lighter, regular lighter, space blanket, emergency stove with pellets, small metal cup, chia seeds, iodine tabs, energy bar
- Werner Ikelos paddle, bent shaft, 215 cm, carbon fiber
- Werner Cyprus, spare paddle, bent shaft, 215 cm, carbon fiber
- SnapDragon neo/nylon sprayskirt
- Cockpit cover
- Bilge pump
- Paddle rescue float
- Rescue sling
- Paddle tether
- NorthWater towbelt, 55'
- Helmet
- Sponge
- Chart case (charts, Nav Aid, plastic courser, pencil, sharpie, grease pencil)
- Deck compass
- Gaia waterproof deck bag, with various carabineers
- Fog horn
- Flare gun
- Exped Venus two-person, four season tent
- Exped Synmat 7 sleeping mat
- Tarp, with parachute cord and extra stakes
- Noah collapsible tarp/tent pole
- Mountain Hardwear Ultra Lamina women's sleeping bag, 15°
- Bear spray & bear bangers
- Mesh backpack (for town days)
- Mesh duffel bag for carrying small items to and from camp (a must!)
- Crazy Creek chair
- Large Rite in the Rain waterproof journals – three total for trip, mailed in resupply boxes as needed
- Small Rite in the Rain waterproof notebook (for deckbag)
- West Marine binoculars, waterproof
- Headlamp, waterproof
- Ipod, with waterproof case and earbuds
- Sunglasses and spares, neoprene chums
- First aid kit/emergency kit/repair kit
- Space blanket (to function as an extra tarp or ground cloth)
- Toiletry kit (toothbrush, floss, hair brush, make up — kidding!)
- Vitamins & meds
- Towel (microfiber)
- Bandana
- Sunscreen
- Bug dope
- Thumb/wrist brace
- Potty bag (trowel, tp, wag bag)
- Lady Jane/Whiz pee bottle
- Folding saw
- Extra batteries
- Small canvas wallet: Canadian and American cash, debit card, two credit cards, driver's license, health insurance card, phone cards, spare car key, two checks
- Passport
- Talisman good luck pouch

Books & Related Resources

- *The Inside Passage,* Robert Miller
- *The Wild Coast,* Volumes #2 & #3, John Kimantas
- *BC Atlas Volume 1*
- *2010 Current Tables*
- *2010 Tide Tables*
- Various copies, notes, GPS coordinates for certain campsites, etc.
- Ferry schedule

Electronics

- GPS (Garmin Etrex) (2 lithium AA batteries), waterproof
- VHF Garmin Radio (6 lithium AA batteries), waterproof
- Olympus digital voice recorder (2 AAA batteries)
- SPOT satellite tracker (2 lithium AA batteries), waterproof
- Cellphone in waterproof case, with earbuds (USB charger)
- iPod, with waterproof hard case and waterproof earbuds, USB charger cable
- Nikon CoolPix 10 MP camera in drybag (4 AA lithium batteries)
- Pentax Optio waterproof camera, five extra batteries, extra memory card
- Brunton Sherpa device (anemometer, wind gauge, barometer, temp, time, etc.)
- Tekkeon charger for all USB devices
- Wristwatch, waterproof

Clothing

... While paddling

- NRS 3-mil Farmer Jane wetsuit with relief zipper
- Boréal Exofleece bottoms (for warmer, calmer days)
- Thin, long-sleeve fleece shirt, and/or thin capilene long sleeve shirt and/or NRS micro tee
- BARE neoprene booties with seal skin waterproof socks or neoprene socks
- Extrasport dry top
- Extrasport lightweight paddling top
- Kokatat storm cag
- Kokatat rain hat
- Gloves: Chota Thin Skins, NRS Mystery Skin, NRS fingerless
- Mystery Skin skull cap with chin strap
- Nylon baseball cap, with cap retainer

... On land

- Extrasport rain/paddling pants
- Salomon lightweight rain jacket
- Fleece lined running tights
- Sporthill fitness tights
- Patagonia heavy weight fleece top
- NRS micro tee
- Patagonia puff fleece jacket
- Fleece vest
- 1 cotton tee shirt
- 1 pair of Kokatat nylon zip off pants
- Bathing suit
- Jog bra
- 3 pairs nylon underwear
- 1 pair wool socks

- 1 pair fleece socks
- 2 pairs sock liners
- 1 pair capilene glove liners, lightweight
- Fleece hat & fleece ear band
- PJs — thin cotton jammies and lightweight

fleece top
- Keen sandals with heel strap
- NRS woman's Descent Shoe/trail runner/ town shoe

Kitchen Gear

- Coleman anodized aluminum nesting pots
  - 24-oz pot for boiling water/cooking
  - 16-oz cup/mug for hot drinks
  - Small frying pan, doubles as lid— Inside this pot set fits:
    - Alcohol stoves (2)
    - Flint lighter
    - BIC lighter
    - Hurricane lighter
    - 5-oz plastic fuel bottle
    - Wind screen
    - Chammy dish cloth
    - Plastic scraper
    - Scrungie
    - Spork
    - Plastic lip protector for rim of cup
- Denatured alcohol (fuel for alcohol stove)
- Square 1-pint Rubbermaid® Nalgene bottle for quick oat breakfast
- Square 1-quart Rubbermaid Nalgene water bottle

- 10 oz plastic booze flask
- plastic, take-apart wine glass
- Cutting board, thin, plastic, pliable
- Knife
- Thermos
- Iodine tablets (in first aid/emergency kit)
- Heavy-duty paper shop towels
- Various bags, ziplocks, tinfoil, etc
- Garbage bag (stuff sack, with plastic grocery bag liners)
- Clothespins
- Camp Suds
- Spices:
- Salt and pepper (non-humid)
- Garlic powder and curry (double-sided spice container)
- Tabasco
- Olive oil in small dark jar
- Mrs. Dash
- Cinnamon
- 10-Liter Dromedary water bag
- 6-Liter Dromedary water bag

References

Books

Scholars and authors whose words and wisdom have given insight or knowledge to portions of my journey and the writing of this book.

Dictionary of Alaska Place Names, USGS, 1971.

Broze, Matt; Gronseth, George. *Sea Kayaker Deep Trouble: True Stories and Their Lessons,* Camden, ME: Ragged Mountain Press, 1997.

Burch, David. *Fundamentals of Kayak Navigation,*

Guilford, CT: The Globe Pequot Press, 1993.

Dowd, John. *Sea Kayaking, A Manual for Long-Distance Touring, 5th ed.* Vancouver, BC, Canada: Greystone Books, 2004.

Dwyer, Denis. *Alone in the Passage: An Explorer's*

Guide to Sea Kayaking the Inside Passage, self-published - CreateSpace, 2013.

Dwyer, Denis. *Point to Point: Exploring the Inside Passage by Kayak, CreateSpace, 2011.*

Fredston, Jill. *Rowing to Latitude.* New York: North Point Press: 2001

Hahn, Jennifer. *Spirited Waters.* Seattle, WA: The Mountaineers, 2001.

Herrero, Stephen. *Bear Attacks: Their Causes and Avoidance.* Guilford, CT: The Lyons Press, 2002.

Hutchinson, Derek C. *The Complete Book of Sea Kayaking.* Guilford, CT: The Globe Pequot Press, 1994.

Kimantas, John. *The Wild Coast 1: A Kayaking, Hiking and Recreation Guide for North and West Vancouver Island.* Vancouver, BC, Canada: Whitecap Books Ltd., 2005.

Kimantas, John. *The Wild Coast 2: A Kayaking and Recreation Guide for the North and Central BC Coast.* Vancouver, BC, Canada: Whitecap Books Ltd., 2006.

Kimantas, John. *The Wild Coast 3: A Kayaking, Hiking and Recreation Guide for B.C.'s South Coast and East Vancouver Island.* Vancouver, BC, Canada: Whitecap Books Ltd., 2007.

Kimantas, John. *B.C. Coastal Recreation Kayaking and Small Boat Atlas, Volume 1: British Columbia's South Coast and East Vancouver Island.* Vancouver, BC, Canada: Whitecap Books Ltd., 2007.

Kimantas, John. *B.C. Coastal Recreation Kayaking and Small Boat Atlas, Volume 2: British Columbia's West Vancouver Island.* Vancouver, BC, Canada: Whitecap Books Ltd., 2007.

Kopecky, Arno. *The Oil Man and the Sea.* Madeira Park, BC: Douglas and McIntyre, 2013.

Lydon, Tim. *Passage to Alaska.* Blaine, WA: Hancock House Publishers, 2003.

McAllister, Ian and Read, Nicholas, *The Salmon Bears: Giants of the Great Bear Rainforest,* Victoria, BC: Orca Book Publishers, 2010.

McGee, Peter, editor. *Kayak Routes of the Pacific Northwest Coast.* Vancouver, BC, Canada: Greystone Books, 2004.

Miller, Robert. *Kayaking the Inside Passage.* Woodstock, VT: The Countryman Press, 2005.

Millman, Dan. *The Warrior Athlete: Body, Mind and Spirit.* Walpole, NH: Stillpoint Publishing, 1979. From the book Body Mind Mastery. Revised Edition Copyright 1999 by Dan Millman. Reprinted with permission of New World Library, Novato, CA. *www.newworldlibrary.com*

Moyer, Lee. *Sea Kayak Navigation Simplified.* Seattle, WA: Alpen Books Press, 2001.

Muir, John. *Travels in Alaska.* Boston: Houghton Mifflin Company, 1979.

Raban, Jonathan. *Passage to Juneau.* New York: Pantheon Books, 1999.

Rasmussen, Greg. *Kayaking in Paradise: Journey from Alaska Through the Inside Passage,* Vancouver, BC, Canada: Whitecap Books, 1997

Ricks, Byron. *Homelands: Kayaking the Inside Passage.* New York: Avon Books, 1999.

Rogers, Joel W. *Watertrail.* Seattle, WA: Sasquatch Books, 1998.

Thoreau, Henry David. *Walden and Other Writings.* New York, Bantam Books, 1854.

Vancouver, George. *A Voyage of Discovery to the North Pacific Ocean and Round the World: In which the Coast of North-West America has Been Carefully Examined and Surveyed.* London, UK: J. Stockdale, 1802.

Washburne, Randel. *Kayaking Puget Sound, the San Juans, and Gulf Islands.* Seattle, WA: The Mountaineers, 1990

Washington Water Trails Association. *The Cascadia Marine Trail Guidebook.* Seattle, WA: Washington Water Trails Association, 2003.

Wise, Ken C. *Cruise of the Blue Flujin.* Fowlerville, MI: Wilderness Adventure Books, 1987.

NOAA. *2010 Current Tables: Pacific Coast of North America and Asia.* Tidal Current Tables for the Pacific Coast of North America, information provided by NOAA since 1890, and now printed by private companies. Tidal Current Tables provide daily predicted times of slack water and predicted times and velocities of maximum ebb and flood currents. Northwind Publishing, 2009.

Websites

http://weather.gc.ca/canada_e.html—Environment Canada: excellent source for updated weather info along the British Columbia coast.

http://www.noaa.gov/—National Oceanic and Atmospheric Administration: updated weather from the National Weather Service, including marine weather forecasts.

http://www.bcmarinetrails.org/ Excellent website and useful planning tool for the marine network of campsites and access points along the coastline of British Columbia.

http://wwta.org/water-trails/cascadia-marine-trail/—This water trail on Puget Sound is a National Recreation Trail and designated one of only sixteen National Millennium Trails by the White House.* Suitable for day or multi-day trip s, the Cascadia Marine Trail (CMT) has grown to 66 campsites and 160 day-use sites.

https://sites.google.com/site/insidepassageregistry/—A plethora of knowledge about "all-things-Inside-Passage!" Created and maintained by Joel McNamara, it is a registry of trips made through the Inside Passage by kayaks, canoes, rowboats and other vessels that rely on human power as primary propulsion. The site is divided into four different sections: registry and trip reports, books, free information sources, gear.

http://www.bcferries.com/ VBC Ferries' schedule, reservations, and other useful information.

http://www.dot.state.ak.us/amhs/—Alaska Marine Highway System. Information on fares, schedules, reservations, and anything you may need to know about the Alaska ferry system.

http://www.env.gov.bc.ca/bcparks/—Ministry of Environment, Lands and Parks, BC Provincial Parks Division offers information on BC Parks' reservations, camping fees, safety considerations, and much more.

http://denisdwyer.blogspot.com/—This website, created by Denis Dwyer was an invaluable resource for me while planning my expedition up the Inside Passage.

https://sites.google.com/site/seakayakingtheinsidepassage/—Another of Denis Dwyer's remarkably detailed sites.

http://www.popularmechanics.com/science/a12051/4263605/—*Tracking the Queen of the North Sea Disaster: What Went Wrong.* For half a century British Columbia ferries had safely navigated the provinces ragged coast. All it took to sink a ship with 101 souls onboard was one 14-minute distraction. Engaging article that appeared in the June 2008 issue of Popular Mechanics, (volume 185, no. 6) written by Margo Pfeiff.

http://www.coastandkayak.com—A most enjoyable site for paddlers. Warning though—you may get lost and spend an inordinate amount of time perusing all the beautiful photos, helpful links of where to go and how to do it safely, plus back issues of *Coast and Kayak Magazine* and the sparkling brand new *Wild Coast Magazine*, and much more.

http://www.marinetraffic.com/ais/home— Alleviate that dooming feeling of getting run over by a big ship with this slick resource! It uses AIS (Automatic Identification System) to display real time positions of vessels all over the world, including speed, vessel name, and size. Zoom in and out to an area you're interested in and see what vessels are on the water.

http://pacificwild.org/—British Columbia's Great Bear Rainforest is the world's largest remaining tract of intact temperate rainforest—and it's threatened everyday. Pacific Wild is a leading voice for wildlife protection in this area. Visit this sight to see live streaming cameras, campaigns, field dispatches, stunning images, documentaries, and more.

http://blog.pacificwild.org/—Stay up to date with these informative dispatches from the heart of the Great Bear Rainforest.

About the Author

Susan Marie Conrad is an adventurer, writer, educator, and speaker. She's also an accomplished paddler. Her tenacious exploration by sea kayak has fueled her stories and images of the natural world for decades.

Susan grew up on a small farm in upstate New York, where she scaled stone walls and trees and roamed and romped through five hundred acres of fields and woods. By dint of exploring the mountains of Colorado, Oregon, and Montana, she eventually discovered the dynamic and addictive environment of coastal British Columbia and Washington State, where she still thrives as an adventure-seeker. She has worked as a graphic designer, photographer, journalist, kayak guide, and instructor. She lives with her second-half-of-life partner, along with a ridiculously large dog, and two normal-sized cats in Oso, Washington.

Learn more at *www.SusanMarieConrad.com*